Series on the Iraq War and its Consequences – Vol. 2

Iraq Beyond the Headlines
History, Archaeology, and War

Series on the Iraq War and its Consequences
(ISSN: 1793-1711)

Published

Vol. 1
The Iraq War and its Consequences: Thoughts of Nobel Peace Laureates and Eminent Scholars
edited by Irwin Abrams & Wang Gungwu

An extraordinary collection of essays on the recently concluded Iraq War by Nobel Peace laureates and leading scholars. The Iraq War and its Consequences is the first and only book that brings together more than 30 Nobel Peace laureates and eminent scholars to offer opinions, analyses and insights on the war that has drawn both widespread opposition and strong support.

Vol. 2
Iraq Beyond the Headlines: History, Archaeology, and War
by Benjamin R Foster, Karen Polinger Foster & Patty Gerstenblith

Series on the Iraq War and its Consequences – Vol. 2

Iraq Beyond the Headlines

History, Archaeology, and War

Benjamin R. Foster
Yale University

Karen Polinger Foster
Yale University

Patty Gerstenblith
DePaul University

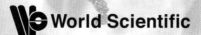
World Scientific

NEW JERSEY • LONDON • SINGAPORE • BEIJING • SHANGHAI • HONG KONG • TAIPEI • CHENNAI

Published by

World Scientific Publishing Co. Pte. Ltd.

5 Toh Tuck Link, Singapore 596224

USA office: 27 Warren Street, Suite 401-402, Hackensack, NJ 07601

UK office: 57 Shelton Street, Covent Garden, London WC2H 9HE

British Library Cataloguing-in-Publication Data
A catalogue record for this book is available from the British Library.

ISBN 981-256-476-4
ISBN 981-256-379-2 (pbk)

Printed in Singapore by World Scientific Printers (S) Pte Ltd

Contents

List of Illustrations   vii

Preface   xi

Chapter 1   Beginnings, Modern and Ancient   1

Chapter 2   Early City States and Empires   21

Chapter 3   The Age of Hammurabi   43

Chapter 4   A Babylonian Nation-State   55

Chapter 5   The Assyrian Achievement   69

Chapter 6   Babylon and Her Empire   85

Chapter 7   Mesopotamia between Two Worlds   101

Chapter 8   Iraq between Iran and Arabia   119

Chapter 9   The Muslim Conquest of Iraq   131

Chapter 10   The Age of Baghdad and Samarra   149

Chapter 11   Iraq in the Ottoman Empire   165

Chapter 12   Colonization and Monarchy   181

Chapter 13   The Republic of Iraq   199

Chapter 14   Archaeology Past and Present in Iraq   213

Chapter 15   The Iraq Museum and the Future of the Past   225

Chapter 16   International and National Legal Regimes for the
              Protection of Archaeological Heritage   245

Appendix   Iraqi Libraries, Research Centers, and Centers
              for the Arts   275

List of Illustrations

Map showing major sites and excavators (underlay map after Seton
Lloyd, *The Archaeology of Mesopotamia* [London: Thames and Hudson,
1978], fig. 2).   ix

Alabaster vase from Uruk (after Eva Strommenger, *Fünf Jahrtausende
Mesopotamien* [Munich: Hirmer, 1962], pl. 19).   230

Overturned exhibit case with the Uruk vase base in the Iraq Museum,
October 2003 (photo Catherine Sease).   230

Uruk vase fragments back in the Iraq Museum, October 2003
(photo Catherine Sease).   230

Alabaster head from Uruk (after Eva Strommenger, *Fünf Jahrtausende
Mesopotamien* [Munich: Hirmer, 1962], pl. 31).   232

Uruk head returned to the Iraq Museum, October 2003
(photo Catherine Sease).   232

Diorite statue of Enmetena from Ur (after Anton Moortgat,
The Art of Ancient Mesopotamia [London: Phaidon, 1969], pl. 87).   234

Inlaid harp from Ur (after C. Leonard Woolley, *Ur Excavations:
The Royal Cemetery* [Oxford: Oxford University Press, 1934], pl. 114).   236

Harp and other damaged pieces in the Iraq Museum, October 2003
(photo Catherine Sease).   236

Copper-alloy statue made for Naram-Sin (after Joan Oates, *Babylon* [London: Thames and Hudson, 1979], 35).   238

Gouged stairs in the Iraq Museum, October 2003 (photo Catherine Sease).   238

Ivory furniture panel from Nimrud (after Paolo Matthiae, *La storia dell'arte dell'Oriente Antico: I primi imperi e i principati del ferro* [Milan: Electa, 1997], 181, Photoservice Electa, Milan).   240

Damaged ivories in the Iraq Museum, October 2003 (photo Catherine Sease).   240

Cylinder seals from Kish and Girsu (after Eva Strommenger, *Der Garten in Eden* [Berlin: Museum für Vor- und Frühgeschichte der Staatlichen Museen Preussischer Kulturbesitz, 1978], 103).   242

Storage cabinets in the Iraq Museum, October 2003 (photo Catherine Sease).   242

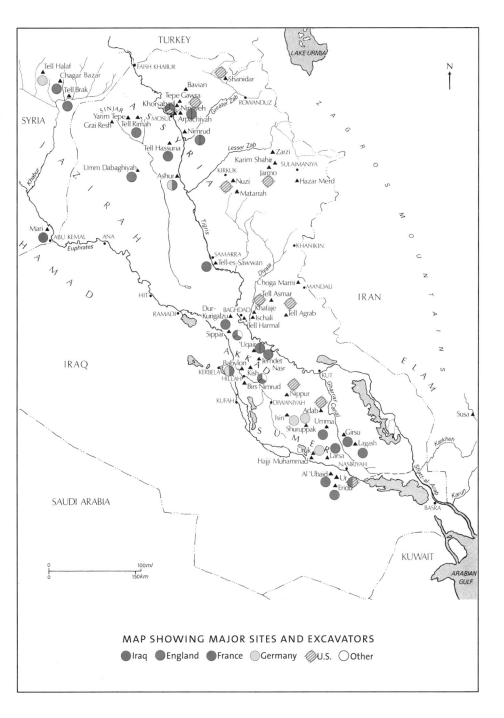

MAP SHOWING MAJOR SITES AND EXCAVATORS

● Iraq ● England ● France ○ Germany ◨ U.S. ○ Other

Preface

This book offers a brief historical and cultural survey of the land of Iraq culminating with the American-led invasion and occupation of that country in 2003. Its focus is on the discovery, management, preservation, and destruction of cultural heritage of all periods, especially pre-Islamic antiquity. To this end, it gives a brief account of the political and social history of the region, with special reference to archaeological discoveries and their interpretation, and discusses modern law governing the exploitation of cultural heritage. It is intended for readers with no prior knowledge of these subjects. Studies of warfare generally overlook its cultural consequences, preferring to focus on victory and defeat, strategy and tactics, and redefinitions of government, economy, and society in the aftermath. Yet often the cultural impact of war, in the long term, far outweighs other considerations. Military victories and defeats are replaced by other victories and defeats, but cultural destruction is permanent and irremediable.

Modern technology and weaponry, and their easy availability to anyone, mean that cultural achievements are increasingly at the mercy of people who wish to force their own vision on a landscape, regardless of consequences. The Gulf and Iraq wars highlight this, as they have taken an as yet unknown toll of the human past of all periods, from the dawn of society to the last century, opening the way to a frenzy of looting of ancient sites and museums in Iraq on a scale the world has never seen. This is far more than scavenging surreptitiously for pots in ancient mounds. Rather, thieves use heavy equipment, large, armed teams of men, satellite telephones, containerized airfreight, and the Internet. Their highly lucrative trade is sustained and paid for by collectors and museums in the Middle East, Europe, the United States and Canada, and Japan for whom the vanity of ownership prevails over all other considerations.

The book is a team effort by an Assyriologist, Benjamin R. Foster (Chapters 1–13), an art historian/archaeologist, Karen Polinger Foster (Chapters 14, 15), and an attorney/archaeologist, Patty Gerstenblith (Chapter 16), to shed light on the cultural and legal consequences of these wars in Iraq. It takes no position on the wars themselves but seeks to answer the questions often asked of us: "So what's the importance of this looting? What real difference does it make?" Our thesis is that the recent, on-going cultural destruction wrought on Iraq is as important as any strategic, political, economic, or environmental outcomes of these two wars. The loss of cultural memory and achievement is permanent, and much of it could have been avoided even in wartime conditions. The United States military in the Second World War amassed a brilliant record in protecting cultural property and restoring it to its owners, against a background of systematic looting of cultural property by other powers, especially the German and Russian military and governments.

This record stands now in stark contrast to the ignorance, lack of planning, and unwillingness to act in cultural matters, which characterized the American leadership, especially in the Iraq War and during the subsequent American occupation of the country. Unlike many armies, the American forces themselves did little looting in these wars, but they did almost nothing to stop it either. The looting has been done mainly by Iraqis to make much-needed money from the international trade in antiquities and other cultural property. In a few years, as we will show, Iraq went from having one of the best-protected ancient heritages anywhere in the world to one of the worst. No understanding of the American military involvement in the Middle East can be sound or complete without an appreciation of its long-term cultural impact.

Parts of this book originated in the McKee-May Academic Lectures, delivered by Benjamin R. Foster in Greenwich, CT, in the winter of 2004. Our thanks go to Jennifer Vietor Evans of Greenwich for the invitation that made possible this undertaking. Bassam Frangieh of Yale University was characteristically generous with his time and knowledge in discussing and checking the translations from Arabic poetry given here, and for advising on suitable selections. Poetry is widely appreciated in the Arabic-speaking world as a form of cultural and social expression, so the purpose here has been to offer some hint of its enormous richness and variety. Beatrice Gruendler drew attention to the lament of al-Rumi and allowed use of her unpublished translation. Sasha Treiger kindly checked a translation from Russian.

The book has greatly benefited from discussions with colleagues during several conferences and panels on the issues, among them "A Future for Our Past: An International Symposium for Redefining the Concept of Cultural Heritage and its Protection," held in Istanbul in June 2004; and three programs, "Iraq Beyond the Headlines," held at Yale University in April 2003, October 2003, and October 2004. Joanne Farchakh read critically Chapters 14 and 15. Catherine Sease, Dominique Collon, Zainab al Bahrani, Eva Strommenger, and Roger Atwood assisted generously with photographs. Peter W. Johnson digitized the map and designed the cover. The authors are grateful to Kimberly Chua and the staff of World Scientific for suggesting this project and for seeing it through.

January 2005

Chapter 1

Beginnings, Modern and Ancient

1. What is Iraq?

The modern state of Iraq is located in western Asia in the region now called the Near or Middle East, bordered on the north by Turkey, the east by Iran, the south by Kuwait and Saudi Arabia, and on the west by Jordan and Syria. It is approximately 1390 km from north to south and 1250 km from east to west, covering an area of about 441,839 sq km. Its present boundaries were first drawn in 1918–1919 by British administrators who sought to construct a state there from former provinces of the Ottoman Empire following their military occupation of them in 1917. Their administration was granted international authority by the victorious powers in the First World War, especially England, France, and the United States, in a series of peace conferences beginning in 1920. These eventually gave Britain "mandatory" power over Iraq, recognizing the occupation of the land by the British military and abrogating a secret agreement made with France and Russia in 1916, according to which northern Iraq would be given to France after victory in the war.

"Mandate" was a new term put forward by England and France, in deference to the American war aim of self-determination for all peoples, to replace older words like "colony" or "protectorate." It implied that the British government would prepare Iraq for independence at a later date, as the British government believed that the peoples living the Arabic-speaking provinces of the Ottoman Empire should not be allowed self-determination as to what sort of government they wanted.

1

Like most international boundaries, the borders of Iraq were matters of convention and history. The convention behind them was a series of arbitrary decisions by British administrators as to where they should go. Their history was in part former provinces of the Ottoman Empire and in part the British administrators' awareness of the ancient past of the region: the modern boundaries included ancient lands such as Sumer and Akkad, Babylonia and Assyria, and had as well certain natural features that defined them.

The southern part of Iraq is a fertile alluvial plain created by the Tigris and Euphrates rivers, which flow across Iraq, the Tigris for 1418 km, the Euphrates for 1212 km, to empty ultimately in the Arab/Persian Gulf. As they approach the gulf, these two great waterways join 109 km north of the Gulf and branch out into myriad channels to form a vast marsh, most easily navigable by boat. Until recently, this marsh region was inhabited by a distinct people called the Marsh Arabs, or Ma'dan, whose culture was centered on a riverine way of life: fishing, trapping, bird catching. Their homes, utensils, and furnishings were made from the ubiquitous reeds of the marshes. Some of the earliest representational art from Iraq shows elaborate reed dwellings similar to those of the marsh Arabs, and ancient Mesopotamian poetry speaks of the inhabited world as if it were dry land heaped up by a creator god in a primeval marsh.

North of the marshes, the alluvial plain is well suited to agriculture. Rainfall in southern Iraq, as in most of the Middle East, is insufficient for agriculture, so artificial methods of watering crops are necessary. This means trapping and diverting the water from the rivers and redeploying it for cultivation. In southern Iraq, this was traditionally done by constructing channels and basins to carry and hold the water, and weirs or other barriers to catch, divert, or release the water where and when needed.

North of Baghdad, the plain gradually turns into a broad steppe, stretching to the foothills of the mountain ranges to the north and east, and continuing up the Euphrates in a narrow band into Syria in the west. The Euphrates rises in Anatolia and flows in a broad, curving, shallow channel south and east towards the Gulf, today drawing close to the Tigris near Baghdad. With its two main tributaries, the Balikh and Khabur in Syria, it forms a vast watershed plain, today known as the Jezirah, excellent for agriculture and animal husbandry, with easy communication along the river banks or between rivers by well-established tracks. The Tigris rises in Anatolia and flows through a more deeply cut channel south. Its main tributaries, the Upper and Lower Zab and the Diyala, flow into it from the east, cutting through mountain ranges to form natural lines of communication between the plain and the Iranian uplands. Because these tributaries flow directly from the mountains, the Tigris in particular is prone to massive flooding in the spring when the snow melts from the peaks.

The rivers of Iraq have determined its history in three main ways. First, the Euphrates has been an important channel of communication with northern Syria, Anatolia, and the Mediterranean. Second, the Tigris and its tributaries have been important channels of communication north and northeast. Third, the rivers made possible human life on the plain, blessed with rich soil annually renewed by the rivers.

Beyond the plain of Iraq, to the west, south, and southwest, stretch inhospitable desert for hundreds of kilometers. To the east, north, and northeast the plain rises to foothills that quickly turn into mountain ranges, whose upthrust dramatically separates Iraq from what are now Iran and Turkey. Small wonder then that human beings living in ancient times on the plains of Iraq thought that this was the center of the world, ringed by desert, mountains, and oceans. For them, all that lay beyond was foreign and strange, the source of exotic materials, strange beasts, and the abode of brutish men.

So it was that when the British administrators drew their boundaries, they were following the approximate boundaries of long-dead ancient cultures rather than the current realities of the region, with its patchwork of speakers of Arabic, Kurdish, Persian, and Turkish, its mixed Muslim, Jewish, Christian and pagan population, and its complex tribal divisions. To some, the ancient past of the region was a unifying factor in the face of many conflicting allegiances and ways of life. Indeed, the potential political and social usefulness of the remote, pre-Islamic, pre-Christian, and pre-Jewish past was soon to be seized upon by various states and peoples of the Middle East and the Balkans for their own political and cultural purposes. But this lay ahead. The land of Iraq, as it was created after World War I, was a product of colonial expediency, a desire to protect British interests, and, to a lesser extent, a desire to plan for exploitation of its oil (at that time most British oil was imported from the United States).

The word "Iraq" was first regularly used for this area after the Arab-Muslim conquest of 637. Though it appears to be an Arabic word, no one knows what it means. Medieval Arab geographers proposed various origins and significances for it, which show only they were making their explanation up by comparing Iraq to other words with the same consonants in them. One of the most widely accepted explanations is that the word means arable land along a major river, vaguely corresponding to English "alluvium," but this explanation may only have been reasoned backwards from the reality of Iraq itself. An ancient Greek term, "Mesopotamia," has also been used to refer to Iraq, especially by European scholars. Originally this word name referred to what is now northern Syria, specifically, the expanse of land enclosed by the big bend there of the Euphrates River, but gradually it broadened and moved east to mean roughly the plain and uplands between the Tigris and Euphrates, from the Gulf to the Taurus mountains. Many writers today use "Mesopotamia" when referring to Iraq before the Muslim conquest and "Iraq" for the land thereafter. Although this is a convenient historical distinction, similar to "Gaul" versus "France," a few writers prefer to say "ancient Iraq" instead of "ancient Mesopotamia." This is because they would rather draw no line of separation between the pre-Islamic and Islamic past of the region.

2. The Birthplace of Civilization

To visitors from parts of the earth with more temperate climates and more varied landscapes, the hot, featureless plain of southern Iraq may not seem like a place hospitable to the development of civilization. Nor are there splendid ruins to admire or reflect on, like pyramids or castles, such as could evoke a glorious past. In fact, the only features of the landscape that attest to the remote antiquity of human habitation there are hills or rises covered with debris, such as pottery and broken clay bricks, sometimes lying in the midst of faint outlines of ancient habitations, walls, and watercourses. These mounds are all that remain of once bustling cities and towns, home to a vibrant and long-lived literate culture.

The Tigris and Euphrates, like other restless flowing water, are likely to shift their courses to new ones, sometimes by many miles. By such a change, the Euphrates flows today far to the east of its course in historical antiquity, so that what were once cities, towns, and villages are now ruins left in remote desert. The advantage of this is that many of the most important ancient cities in southern Iraq were left unmolested for thousands of years, until modern times. Archaeologists can explore them unhampered by modern settlement, so they have yielded most of what we know about Mesopotamian history and culture. In more recent times, these remote fields of ruins have become easy prey to large-scale looting and destruction, so that most of their vast and rich historical record is now lost forever. In the north, where the river channels are more stable, ancient settlements and cities often underlie modern ones, so may be more difficult to explore.

Still, one may ask, why was civilization born on this featureless plain ahead of all other places in the world? There are at once many answers and no answer to this simple question. Numerous answers have come from exploration in the soil of Iraq and of neighboring lands, for the Middle East has been explored intensively for more than a century with this and other historical questions in mind. Some of these theories may be drawn together into a story that seems reasonable and convincing in its outline, even if the details are frustratingly vague. On the other hand, there is no answer, for we describe events and changes without really knowing why they happened, and refer to people whom we know very little about. New discoveries and reinterpretation of old ones give us fascinating evidence to work into the story, but leave the reader with a sense of incompleteness that only the imagination can fill in.

3. Production of Food: An Important Transition for the Human Race

Of the many ways to describe human beings of former times and how they lived, one long popular has been with reference to their technology.

One speaks of a "Stone Age," implying that people mostly used stone tools, or a "Bronze Age," when people mostly used bronze ones. Another way has been to focus on religious belief, such as "Christian," "pagan," "pre-Islamic." In older books one spoke of oriental and occidental peoples or the "great white race" versus the "Semites." More recently, a useful way of describing ancient human beings has been their mode of subsistence, that is, by what means they get the food and drink they need to survive. Some early cultures depended entirely on hunting game, for example, others on farming or stockbreeding. Still others depended on a combination of these strategies.

The importance of subsistence is that for nearly all of its history, the human race subsisted the same way, by hunting game and gathering naturally occurring plants. This mode of subsistence was very well suited for the human race and ensured its survival for more than 99% of its existence. Nor is hunting and gathering a demanding way of life; to judge from contemporary cultures, hunters need exercise their skill only two or three days out of seven to provide sufficiently for their community. They kill and collect only what they need to live and do not reduce their resources for sport or entertainment. Hunting populations, moreover, tend to remain fairly stable: hunters usually have small families, their children, especially girls, mature late; some hunting peoples even abandon infants to control population. Therefore, for most of its history, we imagine that the human population and its subsistence strategies achieved a balance, and that only major natural events, such as earthquakes, volcanoes, epidemics, famines, or major changes in climate, could cause a change large enough to be noticeable thousands of years later in the archaeological record. The best-known example of a major natural change is glaciation, the spread of polar ice across north America and Europe. The ancient inhabitants of Iraq knew nothing of this, but they did believe that very ancient peoples lived much longer lives than they did, perhaps a dim memory of a long-ago time in which change in human society was much less rapid. Unlike us, however, they believed that people as they knew them had always lived the same way, not as hunters, however, but in cities, because, as city dwellers, they thought that human life began in cities.

About ten thousand years ago, peoples in the Middle East gradually developed a different way of living based on farming and management of domesticated animals such as sheep and goats. Some historians refer to this momentous, irreversible change in human behavior as a revolution, thereby implying abrupt and dramatic change. But this change was abrupt only in comparison with the hundreds of millennia preceding when human beings had lived by hunting and gathering. One of the first places this change in behavior was observed and studied in detail was Iraq, in excavations of small settlements in the foothills or hilly flanks of the Zagros mountains. The change to a settled, productive way of life has also been studied in Iran, Anatolia, Syria, and Palestine, so this was a regional development throughout western Asia at roughly the same time, though it had local forms. What did it mean?

First, people settled in small villages in areas where certain wild grains, such as barley, and wild animals, such as sheep and goats, occurred naturally. These resources could be harvested in their natural state. They could also be managed: animals could be penned, herded, and bred. Preferred grains could be sown in specially prepared plots for greater productivity, away from less desirable plants. Domestication of plants and animals caused genetic and morphological changes in them through a process of selection: barley could be selected for preferred strains, such as those with softer husks and larger ears of grain; animals could be bred for quality of wool or hair, fattiness or yield of meat. Stable village life could be based on both sowing grains and managing animals, though in some dry seasons the animals might need to be taken away from the village to better pastures. Although this might describe the transition from hunting and gathering to pastoral and village life, it does not explain why this transition occurred when it did. In short, nobody knows why.

Change in the structure of human society accompanied change in subsistence. For much of the year, agricultural work is systematic and unrelenting: preparation of the soil, sowing, weeding, keeping off pests, harvesting, threshing, and storage. This pattern of life brings with it an ethos of working for what you gain, of saving, and of hopeful reliance on uncontrollable forces like weather and productivity of the soil and herds. There is less of the hunter's sense of participating in nature and more of the farmer's of manipulating nature. There is greater emphasis on fertility of field and herd than for the hunter, who need rely only on natural replenishment of what he takes. Larger families became the norm for farmers because even small children can be useful in field work and herding. With larger families come earlier physical maturity and steady, even exponential, population growth. Villages may become larger or more villages may appear, as people are not willing to walk more than half a day or so to their fields from their homes.

New technology appears as well: first, simple tools for tilling the soil and reaping, then, most important, pottery. Clay vessels allow storage, transport, preparation, and mixing of both solids and liquids. Pottery allows also cooking and thus diversification of food intake. One can soak or roast grains that would otherwise be inedible. One can make, transport, and store dairy products, including cheeses and related milk products. One can ferment grain into a powerful beverage, beer or ale, that goes beyond slaking thirst to altering mood and behavior, thereby acquiring social and ritual functions. Pottery can be used as a means of aesthetic expression in its shape, manufacture, and decoration. Ceramic production can be the work of a few for the use of many, as anyone can make a simple pot but large or fine ones require special skills.

So it was, in this period of change ten thousand years ago, in the foothills above the plains of Iraq, that small villages of mud brick sprang up, their houses consisting of a few rooms and an open area, pens for animals and storage bins for foods, surrounded by an agricultural hinterland extending perhaps several hours' walk. So forceful was this new trajectory of human life that in a few places, such as Jericho in Jordan and Çatal Hüyük in Anatolia, good-sized towns appeared with comparatively large populations and even specialized structures for some particular purpose in communal life. But these were exceptional cases. Most villages were small, with a few dozen houses at most. The houses were of the same size and plan, suggesting an egalitarian society with communal as well as individual household storage facilities. Perhaps, too, resources, such as fields, were managed communally.

4. Settlement in the Plains

A second important transition was the move of farmers and stock breeders down from the foothills onto the plains of Iraq. No one knows why or when this occurred, as the earliest settlements in the plain may be buried deep in the alluvium. One can guess that settled life on the southern plain began about 5000 B.C.E., much earlier in the north. Why move to the plain? No one knows. One guess is population increase, but no evidence has been produced from the foothills that the population had become too large to be sustained locally. The important point is that once human beings had mastered the skills of sustaining themselves, they could live in areas where the wild ancestors of the domesticated plants and animals they had come to depend on did not naturally occur. Humans could bring the new forms of plants and animals with them to the plain, thus causing a permanent change in its ecology. They were responding to the challenge of their environment and changing it and controlling it for their advantage.

In Iraq, moreover, this environment presented unique challenges that were not easily mastered. The dearth of rainfall required irrigation. In principle, irrigation need only be a matter of digging a ditch to bring water to a field. In practice, larger ditches require community participation in their construction and decisions about who is to receive how much water when. Irrigation in southern Iraq is complicated by the rising of the water in the early spring, and its low point in the hot season, when water is most needed, so decisions need to be made about the use of water that may affect more than one family. In any case, the availability of water from the rivers, if properly managed, meant that villages appeared along natural watercourses with regular intervals of distance between them. Even if the watercourses are long gone, the riverine pattern of settlement can be traced on the ground and maps drawn showing where ancient settlement was. Furthermore, quantification of the relative sizes of the settlements can reconstruct an emerging hierarchy among them, though the earliest settlements in the plain may have mostly been the same size.

5. A Durable Peasant Culture

The settlement of farmers on the Mesopotamian plain was a success, the first stage in a story of human activity there that continues to the present day. We need not imagine, of course, that the plain lay empty before people began to till its soil — there was game, such as gazelle, in abundance, marsh creatures such as turtles and birds, and especially fish in the rivers and swamps. Thus an ancient Mesopotamian fisherman's ditty invites the fish into his traps:

Let your acquaintances come,
Let those precious to you come,
Let your father and grandfather come,
Let the son of your older brother come, the son of your younger
    brother come,
Let your little ones and your big ones come,
Let your wife and children come,
Let your comrades and friends come,
Let your brother-in-law and your father-in-law come,
Let the group around your doorway come,
Do not leave anyone around you out, not a single one! *

But with agriculture and stock breeding, the land was changed forever. These two modes coexisted well and might be carried on by members of the same family. Flocks of sheep and goats could graze widely on the grassy plains in the spring, until the grass withered in the early summer. They could even graze off the first springtime shoots of the grain crops, thereby increasing the already high yields of the fields by causing a thicker second growth and fertilizing them as well. In summer the animals could be moved to higher pastures or fed on stored grain and its by-products from milling and brewing. In later periods for which written sources are available, the two main products of the Mesopotamian plains were wool and barley, supplemented by wheat and the fruit of the date palm, the abundant fish of the rivers, sheep and goats, and the hunting of game.

For centuries, then, stretching into millennia, a lowland peasant culture diffused throughout Iraq and far beyond into northern Arabia and the steppe of northern Syria. In northern Iraq, agriculture could be sustained by wells and rainfall, meaning less intensive fieldwork than in the irrigated south and the potential for more extensive cultivation. Even if the south had smaller fields under cultivation, those fields had much higher productivity per hectare than the northern steppe, which, however, had the advantage of greater potential area for cultivation. The south probably had a higher population than the north, so extensive areas of the north may not have been cultivated at all, even at later periods. In the south, settlements were strung along natural watercourses as the basis for irrigation and transportation. In the north, settlements tended to be spread far across the landscape where wells could be dug. Material culture, south and north, befitted a peasant way of life: simple tools, practical pottery. What these peoples called themselves, what languages they spoke, what social institutions, spiritual life, and traditions they had, we know not. Since their shrines resembled houses and the plastic arts that have come down to use are mostly exaggerated representations of the female body, we surmise that their religious belief and practice focused on the forces most important to their way of life: fertility, procreation, the safety of the home hearth. Two aspects of it strike the modern observer: the longevity of this culture, perhaps a thousand years or more, indicating that a viable way of life had been successfully transplanted and transformed in the alluvial plain of Iraq and beyond, and its over-all uniformity throughout Iraq, despite regional phases and variations. People might have continued to live this way of life indefinitely had not something extraordinary happened.

6. The First Cities

Nothing we see in the material remains of this nameless, long-lived culture gives a hint of the momentous changes that were to take place in southern Iraq. These led to the appearance of the first cities known anywhere in the world. An archaeologist of the future, studying the development of urban life on Manhattan island over a 300-year period, from 1650 to 1950, might well conclude that the massive and dramatic changes he sees in the archaeological record of the island began with the immigration of new peoples, then took off with incredible rapidity: a woodland culture gave way to cultivated fields, then a town grew to a metropolis, covering the entire island with human habitation, all within a few generations. In fact, an older generation of historians was wont to explain change by immigration of new peoples, so believed that the impulse that led from villages and towns to a huge, fortified city in the Iraqi plain, swallowing up the villages around it, had to be the result of an influx of new people, whom they suggested came by sea or down from the mountains. Historians gave a name to this new people, the Sumerians, and spoke confidently of their "arrival" in Mesopotamia, transforming the plain of southern Iraq as the European settlers did Manhattan island, and in about the same span of time, beginning around 3600 B.C.E.

Truth to tell, this invasion was imagined; there is no real break in the material culture visible between the modest agricultural settlements on the plain and the gigantic city that was to grow up there and send out its colonies throughout Western Asia and perhaps beyond. New types of pottery appeared, for example, but these seem to be in response to new conditions and not as imports from abroad, nor do alien goods, techniques, and styles suddenly appear in any media. Rather, there seems to be a kind of quickening, an intensification of the earlier way of life, a realization of certain potentials it offered for change into a new, powerful and dynamic, and fundamentally different trajectory. The better analogy would therefore be if modern Manhattan had been created within three centuries by the indigenous peoples living there in 1600. How and why this happened in southern Iraq, ahead of anywhere else in the world, is one of the most fascinating riddles of antiquity. We can watch this process happen, however, and measure certain aspects of it, through the patient labor of archaeologists who have carefully examined the remains of the earliest great city, Uruk, a place that has had the same name for at least five thousand years. Furthermore, archaeologists are tracing remains of the culture of Uruk in Syria, Iran, and Anatolia, where it spread rapidly and intrusively: for a short period Mesopotamian Uruk was the greatest city on earth. How did this happen?

Two kinds of information from the ground help explain this phenomenon. First was excavation in Uruk itself, concentrated on a series of major public buildings in the center of the city which must, in their day, have dominated the city and been visible from afar across the plain. While most of Mesopotamia was still a peasant culture in the fifth millennium B.C.E., monumental buildings were already under construction at Uruk. Around 3600 B.C.E. a large temple was constructed of stone laboriously transported from some 80 km away in the desert. More buildings were soon added or replaced the older ones. One of these was constructed on a gigantic irregularly shaped platform oriented to the points of the compass, over 12 m high, accessible by a ramp and staircase. It was evidently a sanctuary, perhaps to the sky god, consisting of a long chamber with an altar at one end and chambers to the side, its walls decorated with recesses. Close by was another great shrine where several large buildings, one for example 54.25 x 22.5 m on a side, were constructed as well. The walls and colonnade of one of these, the columns of which were 3 m in diameter, were decorated with cone mosaics (see Chapter 15). The countless man-hours of labor and resources that went into creating these structures had to be taken from other activities and compensated in some way: whose was the organizing and creative genius behind the planning and construction of these remarkable buildings?

Another approach to understanding the creation of the city Uruk has been to study the countryside that lay around it and to map settlements by size, historical period, and distribution. From this it appeared that throughout the plain a hierarchy of settlements was developing during the mid-fourth millennium B.C.E.: instead of villages of equal size across the landscape, some villages grew larger, and smaller settlements appeared to be dependent on them. One could even construct an index of villages, towns, and cities, calculating from their inhabited surface. This could be done because these settlements lay mostly away from modern habitations, often in open desert, so had not been disturbed for thousands of years. By this way of measuring, Uruk appeared just as extraordinary, a city surrounded by more than 10 km of fortifications, drawing into itself the neighboring towns and villages so as to leave a kind of empty corona of land around, a city many times larger than any other settlement observed in Iraq at the time. Thus evidence from within Uruk and from its rural hinterlands converge to suggest it was an unique agglomeration that transcended the millennial limitations of its environment, but had grown out of that environment, carrying further than other settlements changes that were occurring elsewhere in a more tentative form, both in Iraq and in southwestern Iran.

More clues could be brought to bear on this mystery. A spectacular innovation of this Uruk civilization, as we may call it, was the world's first representational art. By this is meant art that purports to show people, buildings, and animals as they appeared, rather than symbolically or abstractly. An assortment of images from early Uruk show us niched buildings, as the archaeologists had discovered, and hierarchically arranged animals, such as sheep. Other images show a male dignitary being drawn about in a kind of sledge or braining prisoners with a mace. Two of the most dazzling discoveries, the Uruk vase and Uruk head, are discussed in Chapter 15. Both were found in the temple precinct later sacred to the goddess Inanna, of whom a Sumerian poet wrote, comparing her to a thunderstorm with its pelting rain:

> *When you have spewed your venom on the land like a dragon,*
> *When you roar like thunder at the earth, nothing that grows can*
>   *withstand you!* **

No longer was this a world of small farmers. It was now dominated by an urban elite, with access to foreign materials with which to fashion its imagery, with control of specialized craftsmen to make this imagery, and the will and means to mobilize tens of thousands of human beings in its service. How, then, was this stratified society achieved and how did this elite maintain itself over vastly greater numbers?

For such a question only broad theories can offer answers, not art and architecture. A particularly persuasive theory is based on the capacity of the southern plains to produce an agricultural surplus. Decisions about how to deploy this surplus could lie at the heart of the new social stratification. The mechanism we see in action is referred to as "redistribution," a process whereby some people produce raw materials for food and others decide what is done with this production and oversee its distribution to people who do not produce food, either in raw form, as basic rations, or in prepared form, such as bread and beer. This would presuppose, in the case of a city, extensive capacity for management of people, sophisticated storage and accounting, and important facilities for mass production of prepared food, plus some way of distributing it.

Many writers on early economy believe that such a system as here envisioned could not effectively be imposed by brute force on human beings, rather, there must have been some ideological basis, a set of beliefs, that persuaded people where they belonged in a stratified society and impelled them to act on those beliefs. Some scholars therefore see the great investment in the temples at Uruk, and their dominating position in the city, as indicative that religious belief provided this non-economic means of regulating production and distribution. One does not have to look far in ancient Mesopotamian literature to find the notion that human beings were created to serve the gods, like so many workers or drones, and that human rulers were the vicegerents of the gods on earth, the stewards of their households, the shepherds of their human flocks. To some materialist modern scholars, these metaphors were merely excogitated to shore up an existing social order; to others, they reflect, however, dimly, the reality of this vanished world, in which human society and that of the gods were paradoxically a continuum with a sharp dividing line between them: human beings were mortal and of limited power, the gods were immortal and had unlimited powers.

Social stratification and the ability to command vast resources of human beings, livestock, and food, the means to obtain foreign commodities and to command the skill to work them, the will, sophistication, and talent to express a vision of one's society in symbolic visual imagery are but aspects of the Uruk achievement about which we wish we knew more. Two more aspects of this culture deserve our attention: its effort to colonize Western Asia, and the invention of writing, the most powerful tool ever conceived and applied by the human race.

One of the major surprises of the archaeology of the Uruk culture was the discovery of distant settlements that were unmistakably colonies of the city of Uruk. One of these in Syria, for example, on a promontory above the Euphrates, was planned and built on virgin soil, with fortifications, residential quarters, administrative buildings and material culture obviously originating in Uruk and having no prior relation to the existing culture of the region. This was not a long-lived undertaking, perhaps a century and a half, then it was abandoned and never thereafter occupied. Archaeologists soon traced a network of such settlements, some primary in the sense that they seem directly dependent on Uruk, others secondary in the sense that they may have been sent out from other colonies. Some have an admixture of local cultural remains, some, like the settlement in Syria, seem pristine. These colonies tended to follow natural riverine or overland routes and to be situated at key points along these routes, but in quite different environments. There seem to be many of these settlements, some of a large size.

What was the purpose of these colonies? One answer has been trade, the desire to secure resources not available in Mesopotamia. This seems a poor explanation for a settlement on the mid-Euphrates, however, which would have no resources Mesopotamia had not, nor, of course, is it necessary to have colonies to have trade. Other suggestions include an attempt to control as much territory as possible or a diaspora based on excess population in Uruk or some sort of social change or discontent. From the perspective of four millennia, the discovery of contemporaneous seventeenth-century English settlements in Holland and the north shore of Massachusetts might be equally perplexing and the explanations no less creative. The reality is, however, that the Uruk culture suddenly spread far and wide in the Middle East, and as suddenly collapsed and vanished.

The invention of writing was the most lasting and portentous achievement of the Uruk culture. Most people think that writing has been invented more than once, like other great inventions, in different places, but in any case the world's earliest writing is found at Uruk, at the beginning of one of the world's longest continuous traditions of its use. Speculations on the origins of writing abounded in the Middle Ages, the Renaissance, and modern times. They fall into two main categories, a belief that God gave people writing or that writing began with drawing pictures and developed from that to "true" writing. The second belief has been the most popular and is still found in many modern books. Uruk has provided the evidence that the pictographic theory is wrong.

We see now that the earliest writing was not pictures, but mostly abstract symbols and a few representational drawings. Furthermore, there were several principles at work in the earliest writing which were purely arbitrary, non-pictorial symbolic techniques: signs could be combined with other signs, inscribed within each other, reversed, inverted, tilted, or have certain parts of them emphasized with lines or other marks. These and other principles of writing are well known from the later descendant of this earliest writing system, referred to as cuneiform writing. The fundamental principles of the later forms of this writing are present already in the Uruk writing, so it must have been a system invented using a set of intellectual considerations, a deliberate and ingenious effort to represent language, not ideas or images, in symbolic form, across space and time. The system was complex and probably known only to a few. It gave its adepts a new kind of power and authority inaccessible to anyone else; as a Mesopotamian scribe expressed it, people could remind their rulers of what they had forgotten and frame their thoughts in a new medium.

Writing was not invented in a vacuum but appeared at roughly the same time as representational art, in the same place and social context. Thus this was a society in which the power of symbolism was appreciated and exploited to an exceptional degree. Furthermore, other symbolic systems of recording information already existed: clay tokens enclosed in marked balls of clay had been used to record quantities of goods in separate transactions, and seal impressions made in the surface of the clay indicated the authority or identity behind the transaction. This usage was ingenious but had important limitations, not least of which was that no independent concept of number had yet been arrived at, so separate forms and types of counters were required for each commodity. Depending on the commodity, the same symbol could stand for 10 or 18, for instance. Traces of this case-specific numeration survived in later cuneiform writing, but their historical importance was not recognized. Nor did this usage allow one to indicate more specifically even the basic nature of the transaction: income, out-go, balance. The use of tokens was not writing, but another technique of symbolic representation that was used parallel to writing for a while and later abandoned, though it periodically reappeared in Iraq thereafter. The technique of using tokens certainly influenced the invention of writing, most importantly in the shape of some of the numerals, the possibility that some counters were scored or marked rather the way later signs were, and in the fact that later rectilinear cuneiform tablets were in reality flattened spheres in which the surface of the tablet was regarded as continuous horizontally and vertically. Yet these tokens were not the ancestor of writing in the sense that writing grew out of the use of tokens. Perhaps we can say that writing was invented in response to some of the same needs met by the use of tokens, but in full awareness of the limitations of that usage. We know nothing of the inventor.

Surveying the culture of Uruk as a whole, we find that it developed and contained in some form many of the fundamental elements of later Mesopotamian culture: social, political, spiritual, material, not to mention the tendency to expand beyond Mesopotamia whenever circumstances permitted. The more we know, the more we see this period as the real beginning of Mesopotamian history. Yet, so far as we can tell, later Mesopotamian tradition had no memory of it. There was no recollection of the primacy of Uruk, her expansion and colonies, her fertile and accomplished use of symbols, her teeming thousands of workers or of their service to their gods and goddesses. All that we see of this marvelous efflorescence and mysterious collapse and disappearance is the discovery and reconstruction of modern archaeological investigation. Had the site of ancient Uruk not been scientifically excavated and the finds preserved and studied, none of this story would be known.

The site of Uruk, excavated by German archaeologists over nearly a century, has been spared extensive looting since the Iraq war owing to the protection afforded it by local leaders of tribes whose men have been employed for generations excavating the site; see also Chapter 14.

Bibliographical Note to Chapter I

For the earliest history of the human race, Robert J. Braidwood's *Prehistoric Men* (Glenville, Ill.: Scott, Foresman and Company, 1975) is still both readable and authoritative, though dated in many respects. For the Middle East, Hans J. Nissen, *The Early History of the Ancient Near East: 9000–2000 BC* (Chicago: University of Chicago Press, 1988) is good for the prehistoric periods. For early farming, Stuart Struever, ed., *Prehistoric Agriculture* (New York: American Museum of Natural History, 1971), though dated, contains a good diversity of essays. A more recent survey of the issues will be found in Andrew Sherratt, "Climatic Cycles and Behavioral Revolutions: The Emergence of Modern Humans and the Beginnings of Farming," *Antiquity* 71 (1997), 271–287. For the civilization of Uruk, Mitchell S. Rothman, ed., *Uruk Mesopotamia & Its Neighbors, Cross-Cultural Interaction in the Era of State Formation* (Santa Fe: School of American Research, 2001), will give an idea of ongoing research. Illustrated surveys of the periods covered by this chapter include Susan Pollock, *Ancient Mesopotamia* (Cambridge: Cambridge University Press, 1999) and David and Joan Oates, *The Rise of Civilization* (New York: Elsevier Phaidon, 1976). An excellent textbook account is Marc Van De Mieroop, *A History of the Ancient Near East* (Oxford: Blackwell, 2004), Chapter 2.

Translated Excerpts

*From the edition of M. Civil, *Iraq* 23 (1961), 156–157 lines 14–23.
**From the edition of William W. Hallo, *The Exaltation of Inanna, Yale Near Eastern Researches* 3 (New Haven: Yale University Press, 1968), 14 lines 9–10.

Chapter 2

Early City States and Empires

1. New Polities

After the contraction of the Uruk culture, its colonial achievement, at least, was not replicated for nearly three millennia. Perhaps this was because it was the first polity in world history to send out colonies; if the experience of colonization had not been positive for the local peoples, they were ready to resist them thereafter. There is nothing to tell us. Uruk itself sees no great change, and, indeed, continues to grow in size, but her colonies vanished forever. A certain diversification of cultures is detectable towards the end of the fourth millennium B.C.E., from the Mediterranean to the Gulf, as if local polities grew up, perhaps partly in response to the challenge of the city Uruk.

An interesting example of such a local polity is provided by the remains of a large palatial building at a place now called Jamdat Nasr (ancient name unknown), in northern Babylonia. The grand scale of this building tells us it was the seat of some major institution. The archival records, cuneiform tablets, scattered throughout this building tell us that it was the center of a manor of perhaps more than 2200 ha in extent and that its administrators planned its exploitation with care. They proceeded from an operative principle that the land should be divided into three main categories, land to sustain the manor itself, land to sustain the chief personage of the manor (whether priest or king we do not know), and land for the support of his retainers. This was decision-making on a high level and reflected a regional norm.

Selected records of choice foods found in this building were sealed with a great seal inscribed with the names of more than a dozen cities throughout Mesopotamia, though many of them can still not be identified for certain. Various other records in this archive were sealed with other seals, the seal being rolled across the wet clay to make a distinctive impression, as if it were an official letterhead, then the writing done. Yet the great seal, with names of cities graven on it, stands clearly apart from the others. We interpret its use to mean that there was a recognized cultural community on the Mesopotamian plains of cities that, like Uruk, used the Sumerian language for record-keeping and acknowledged a league or federation of cities, some perhaps politically powerful, some perhaps small cult centers. The establishment at Jamdat Nasr belonged to this league. Perhaps the choice foods were for offerings at a central sanctuary, maybe Uruk itself. We do not know the formal basis for a city's inclusion in this league or the consequences of being included, but we see evidence later at other cities, notably Ur and Shuruppak, that this or similar leagues of cities were a long-standing practice. Even more important, they show there was a concept of "our land," the Mesopotamian alluvial plain, which was seen as different from outlying regions.

2. Ur of the Chaldees

One important member of this mysterious league was the city Ur, to the south, home to a great temple of the moon-god Nanna-Sin, which dominated the city. The written records of this place, which are later than those of the palace further north, not only give us evidence of a league of cities, to which Ur belonged, they show another pattern of management of agricultural land that was typical of the irrigated zone: parcels of similar size set out in orderly blocks under individual overseers, each of whom reported to a supervisor. As important as produce was for the city's wealth, nothing in these records could prepare us for the astonishing discovery of the mass-burial tombs of the city's rulers and other dignitaries (see Chapter 15). Careful clearing of the remains by an English archaeologist, Sir Leonard Woolley, revealed details of human sacrifice that no unscientific digger of the scattered remains could have divined.

Woolley's excavations at Ur were carried on from 1922 to 1934 under the auspices of the British Museum and the University of Pennsylvania. They set a new standard in Mesopotamian archaeology for their meticulous technique and prompt publication. Woolley was also a successful popularizer and his discovery of the tombs was front-page news throughout the world. Woolley's excavations were also important for training a new generation of skilled field archaeologists. The site was damaged during the Gulf War. In 2003, an American military installation was constructed near the site of Ur, encroaching on the ruins.

3. The Rise of Kingship

Mesopotamian historical tradition was fascinated with royalty. Kingship was a gift from the gods, one story went, first bestowed on the northern city Kish, well outside of Sumer. Another story, however, insisted on the primacy of kingship in Sumer, long before the great flood. In any case, Kish was quite a different city from Ur, inhabited by people who spoke a Semitic language, belonging to the same great family as Arabic and Hebrew. The people of Ur spoke Sumerian, the language of the southern plain and the city Uruk. This language stands by itself, with no connection to any other known. If the Sumerians had taught the Kishites how to write, the Kishites taught the Sumerians how to rule — their city, not Uruk, was the first to have a great king. Most ancient Mesopotamian historians were satisfied with this historical tradition and repeated it for generations.

According to an ancient legend, kingship having come down from heaven, the first king, Etana of Kish, yearned to establish a dynasty by passing his diadem on to a son, but the gods had not planned for this, perhaps satisfied to bestow kingship wherever they willed. Etana therefore had to go up to heaven, clutching dizzily to the body of an eagle, to seek from the goddess Inanna-Ishtar a magic plant that would make dynastic succession possible by helping the king to beget an heir. Though the

Kishites saw descent from father to son as the natural devolvement of kingship, the same record of ancient kings that made Kish the beginning of royalty noted eight particularly interesting or successful kings of old, seven of whom were not of royal birth, so did not inherit the throne from their fathers. In fact, of these chosen eight, only a lord of Uruk was of royal birth!

The site of Kish has been explored repeatedly, beginning in 1852. The most important excavations were a French project in 1912 and a joint mission of the Ashmolean Museum, Oxford, and the Field Museum, Chicago, between 1923 and 1933. In 1989 a Japanese team began work at the site but their project was terminated by the Gulf War.

Mesopotamia had become, by the middle of the third millennium B.C.E., a land of kings ruling cities often of equal size and strength, banding against each other in leagues for protection, even if they may have had a common religious basis. The Mesopotamians therefore recognized both their common culture and their conflicting ambitions. Were there too many kings for the plain? Was the arable land not sufficient to sustain them all in their grand projects? Was there, as some scholars maintain, a progressive desiccation of the region, owing to a gradual change in climate and the hydraulic regime, so people were feeling increasingly competitive?

We can study the activity of a small city, Shuruppak, forming part of one of these leagues about mid-millennium or slightly later. This league was headed by the mighty king of Kish and included some of the same cities shown as allies long ago on the sealings from Jamdat Nasr. We can outline the "land," as the Sumerians called it, stretching from modern Baghdad to the Gulf. The southern half of the land was Sumer, the northern half perhaps called at this time simply the land of Kish, though no one knows for sure. Further north was, perhaps, the land of Subir, a term that may have included much of northern Iraq and parts of northern Syria. Syria beyond the upper Euphrates and around its big bend may have been referred to by the Mesopotamians as "the Upper Lands."

4. The City Shuruppak

Various languages were spoken in this region, including a Semitic language at Kish, but for long there was only one written, Sumerian. When the Kishites learned to write their own language, they not only used Sumerian signs, they even wrote Sumerian words that the reader was expected to translate into the language he was speaking. These they interspersed with words or parts of words in their own language but spelled with the intractable Sumerian script. So it was that Kishite students came to master Sumerian at Shuruppak, a place later famed for its wisdom and for having preserved writing from before the legendary flood. There they worked through the demanding curriculum of the time, memorizing long lists of signs and words and names, graduating to a point they could copy out elaborate hymns to Sumerian deities written out in abstruse orthography. Proudly they signed their names to their work.

We know this because when German archaeologists from the German Oriental Society cleared with care the remains of the city Shuruppak, in the early twentieth century, they found the schoolboys' work in the ruins of houses throughout the town. Perhaps the youngsters had boarded with and learned from local masters in their homes. The city had been abandoned for so long that its name would already have been only a distant memory to a Babylonian schoolboy a millennium before Herodotus visited Babylon, but the ruins and tablets were still there, undisturbed, in 1902.

At the time of their discovery, the archaeologists had no idea what the tablets said, nor the significance of hundreds of other tablets and fragments and bits of clay with seal impressions on them, scattered all over the site, but they collected all they could find against the day, which came more than two generations later, that new discoveries in Sumer showed what these tablets meant. Nor could anyone then have imagined that the Kishites, with their high Sumerian learning, taught people far off in Syria how to write and keep records, using the signs they learned in Sumer, as we now know from the discoveries at Ebla, south of Aleppo.

Shuruppak was a prosperous town of perhaps 20,000 souls, under the shadow of the king of Kish. Her administrators used no central suite of offices, so far as we can tell, but carried on their affairs in their own houses, writing vouchers, posting them to combined accounts, then carrying the combined accounts forward into larger accounts so the original vouchers could still be traced. Among other activities recorded, we learn that there was a staging area not far off where contingents from other cities, such as Adab and Umma, presumably allies and members of the league, converged for some military campaign.

Local consignments of goods were placed in special rooms, sealed ingeniously with clay wrapped around their door fasteners. When the doors or goods were opened, the broken sealings were tossed aside, but careful modern study of them has revealed the network of responsible people in town, men going from house to house on their business. Only the care of the archaeologists in preserving and noting the location of these modest objects allowed them to tell their story, as a hasty digger would ignore or overlook them. Most of the population of Shuruppak carried on their lives outside the purview of administrative records, which mention perhaps 1200 people all told. We assume that most were farmers, laborers, and stockbreeders, and that a few were artisans, merchants, and poets. A wealthy elite in town bought and sold urban lots among themselves, drawing up neatly written contracts that were stored in some central registry office in town. This group of documents was found by illegal diggers about the same time as the excavations and was scattered around the world, so we know nothing of their context.

Disaster struck. An enemy force took Shuruppak by storm, wrecking the whole town and leaving it a desolate waste where, according to a Sumerian saying, only owls moaned. Therefore in reading the records of this ancient city we have a snapshot, as it were, of the last year of its busy existence, before its men and women fell victim to the barbarities of warfare. Was it perhaps the troops of that same city Ur, mortal foe of the Kishite league, who burned their houses? A king of Lagash of roughly that time, Enmetena (see Chapter 15), claims that he became king of Kish, and the only way he could have done this was to conquer Kish and her allies. In the grim years that followed, former allies in the Kishite league, the Sumerian cities of Lagash and Umma, freed of the bond of alliance, fought, for generations, a bitter and destructive war over a strip of arable land between them. The dismal records of this conflict give us our first example of an extensively documented war. In the end, fire, defeat, and humiliation fell upon the proud city state of Lagash, whose ruler, in a last agonized appeal to heaven, cries for vengeance before his voice falls silent.

5. Lagash, Nippur, and Umma

The story of Lagash was, however, not over. Their rulers rebuilt their sanctuaries and walls and the city went on as before, always a prosperous place owing to her irrigated fields, her vast flocks of sheep, and her vital fishing industry. Moreover, merchants from Lagash traveled throughout the land and abroad: to Mari on the Euphrates, to the land of Elam in southwestern Iran, and by boat to the land of Dilmun, the island of Bahrein in the Gulf. Though this land was fabled as a kind of paradise in Sumerian poetry, to Sumerian merchants it was an entrepot where one could buy copper and tin, the two ingredients needed to make bronze. Bronze was the metal of choice for tools and utensils, being more durable than pure copper. Although Mesopotamia had no raw materials for making metal objects, she had learned, as have other resource-poor countries since, to refine the raw products of other lands, so her metal-working industry was professional, capable, and well supplied. Her craftsmen could make sophisticated castings using the delicate "lost wax" process; they could hammer and mold, they knew in precise detail about alloys, firing temperatures, and commanded such intricate skills as annealing and plating. To buy the raw materials, Lagashite merchants took shiploads of grain and wool to Dilmun, where seafarers from unknown lands brought ingots of copper and bars of rare and precious tin for them to choose from.

Nor was metal-working the only pyrotechnology the Sumerians mastered. They developed the art of making faience, a pre-glass material, that could be used to make beads and ornaments, as well as decorations for inlaying wooden furniture. This versatile substance could be formulated in various colors to resemble precious stones and molded into vases and figurines. It could be pressed into the features of composite statues to form lifelike eyes and smooth, gleaming eyebrows. From faience it was only one more step to glass, the first truly artificial substance made by the human race, for which even higher firing temperatures and pyrotechnical skills are needed. The Lagashites also knew the art of making perfumes, unguents, and aromatics from trees, plants, and animal fats, some for everyday use, some extremely precious.

Further light on the affairs of this energetic state is shed by a long series of inscriptions that tell of the concerns and achievements of her rulers. One of the most interesting group of these comes from the chancery of an enigmatic sovereign called Urukagina (or Uruinimgina), who somehow jockeyed aside the incumbent heir to become ruler. He boasts that he set aside the age-old ways of the city and instituted a new order in which the gods were paramount. Inspectors and fees were removed, even the costs of burial were altered, and powerful people could no longer bully their neighbors. He even took the title king, which rulers of Lagash did not normally use. We are fortunate in being able to see his reforms in practice: what Urukagina actually did was to take control of teams of workers and other resources belonging to the temples, reorganize them, and proclaim he was managing all on behalf of the gods. In this he failed, to judge from the documents, for it seems that he soon had to retreat from some of his more extreme measures. His strange, often incomprehensible proclamations suggest to some an original and dynamic leader, to others a vainglorious parvenu tyrant, but in any case one of the first rulers of history we see as an individual personality.

The sites of Lagash and the nearby city of Girsu have been so extensively damaged by looters that they look like the surface of the moon.

Nor was the day of Lagash's ancient rival, Umma, done. The example of Ur, and perhaps other cities, had shown the Sumerians that one city could predominate in the land by force and that it was possible to unite the whole region under one sovereign. The ruler of Umma, Lugalzagesi, a contemporary of Urukagina, nourished and acted on just this ambition. Early in his campaigns he sieged Lagash and she capitulated. The victorious Ummaite went further and further, telling us in a triumphal commemoration that he defeated cities throughout Sumer and commissioned a carved stone vase in honor of each of these conquests. These he deposited in the temple of the god Enlil in Nippur.

The site of Umma has been completely destroyed by looters.

Nippur was the main holy city of Sumer. Her principal temple, called Ekur or "mountain house," was home to the god Enlil, the chief god on earth by virtue of having chosen the earth when the gods chose their individual domains. The mythology of the god Enlil suggests he was often malevolent to the very human race that had been created to serve his needs. As to why this city, which did not have aggressive political leadership, occupied such a prestigious position in the beliefs of the Sumerians we are not sure; we know it later as a center of Sumerian learning and as the place triumphant kings went to be crowned king of the land. Therefore it was natural for Lugalzagesi to proclaim his victory there and ask the chief god on earth to look with favor upon his conquests and sovereignty, shortlived as they proved to be.

The site of Nippur, first explored by the University of Pennsylvania in the late nineteenth century, yielded thousands of tablets inscribed with works of Sumerian literature. These made possible the reconstruction of a totally forgotten chapter in the early history of world literature. The site of Nippur has been damaged by several deep pits made by looters.

6. Akkad: The First Empire

Some historians see in Lugalzagesi's conquests the culmination of several generations of efforts to unify Sumer by conquest from within. The unification of the land was, however, to come from without, through the new order initiated by a near legendary conqueror from further north, perhaps the region around the confluence of the Diyala and Tigris rivers. We know the name of this conqueror as Sargon, though it may have been a name he assumed upon becoming king. He was chosen as one of the eight most famous kings of the past given biographical notices in the ancient list of Mesopotamian kings mentioned previously, so already in the third millennium B.C.E., only a few centuries at most after his death, he was deemed of special importance. Moreover, a Sumerian story was early in circulation about his youth, according to which the goddess Inanna foiled a murder plot against him. Much later, in the first millennium, an Assyrian king adopted the name Sargon, perhaps out of admiration for his achievements, and a story of the first Sargon's birth and infancy was written that claims he was born in secret to a high priestess and set adrift on the river in a basket, whence he was rescued by a drawer of water. This is the first instance of the story of the exposure of the future leader, be it Moses or Cyrus the Great, and his subsequent rise to power despite this obstacle. This is difficult to square with the story of the early list of kings that says Sargon was not of royal birth, but the tales are clearly related. Some even said that the goddess Inanna-Ishtar had fallen in love with him, so from her came his strength and protection.

The importance of this accretion of stories is not their specific content so much as their unequivocal testimony that there was something especially remarkable about Sargon and what he did. Mesopotamian thinkers saw his age as a new departure, something glorious and worthy of special study. His surviving inscriptions were carefully copied by schoolboys. Heroic poems in the Akkadian language told of his campaigns to parts of the world no Mesopotamian king had ever reached, of his bravery and eloquence. This was the first period of Mesopotamian history about which Mesopotamian scholars of later periods knew authentic details. The expansion of Uruk was forgotten, but the birth, youth, and conquests of Sargon were vivid in historical and literary recollection until the end of Mesopotamian civilization.

Sargon harnessed the hitherto unknown forces of his land, Akkad, and set forth to conquer the world. Akkad was, it seems, the home of the easternmost branch of the Semitic peoples, somewhere around the Diyala valley. What occasioned the rise of these people, the Akkadians, to such power and prominence is unknown. The history of the Middle East shows numerous instances of rapidly expanding states having their rise in northern Mesopotamia and expanding across the northern steppes towards the Mediterranean, once their eastern and southeastern frontiers were secured. The ecological unity of this extensive northern region, the relative ease of communication across it, and the availability of supplies along the Euphrates and its tributaries certainly favored formation of large political entities.

Sargon's was not a case of colonies, as sent out by Uruk, but of a successful standing army; in one of his own inscriptions Sargon claims he fed 5400 able-bodied men in his presence every day. Speed and mobility may also have been factors, as the soldiery consisted of bowmen and lancers, lightly armed; the Sumerians seem rather to have favored dense formations with heavy spears, backed up by massive wheeled vehicles, no match for able bowmen. City after city fell before him; Sargon's army pushed far into Iran, defeating even extensive coalitions raised against him. He pushed up the Euphrates past Mari, no doubt reaching the Mediterranean. He put native Akkadians, he says, in governorships throughout Mesopotamia. Governorships imply, of course, a permanent presence, establishment of an apparatus for administration and the gathering of tribute, designation of provinces. Sargon built a great city, called Akkad (Agade), the same name as his land, and into this place flowed all the wealth of his conquests. A Sumerian poem waxes lyrical about its splendors. Inanna-Ishtar gave the place such wealth that treasures were stored up like grain:

> *She filled its very granaries with gold,*
> *She filled its gleaming granaries with silver,*
> *She apportioned copper, tin, and chunks of lapis among its granges,*
> *She even sealed them up in silos!* *

Sargon may have visualized some sort of religious reform whereby the Akkadian and Sumerian gods were brought close together and the sanctuaries of each part of the land received equal honor. In any case, he appointed his daughter, Enheduanna, high priestess of the moon-god at Ur. To this talented and fascinating woman we owe the first literature of any civilization that can securely be associated with a specific author. We owe to her, it seems, a traditional setpiece of hymns to the principal sanctuaries of Sumer. We owe her as well a long autobiographical poem in which she says that at some point she was threatened by a local rebel.

31

She prayed for help to the moon-god, Sin, whom she had served all her life, but he did nothing. Eneduanna tells us she even lost her power of speech in her fear and distress, a motif often used later in Mesopotamian literature. Then she turned to a goddess, Inanna, and begged her help, which came with terrible effectiveness. Her foes destroyed, Enheduanna resumed her offices and felt something stirring inside her, dark and private, which was her poem. She gave birth to it, she tells us, in an agony of creativity, then it stood apart from her as something independent in the light of day. Enheduanna wrote other poetry, including some ardent love lyrics. An image of her survives, now in the British Museum, and a seal belonging to one of her servitors was discovered (among those stolen from the Iraq Museum, see Chapter 15). Her work is so individual in stamp, though obscure and difficult to the highest degree, that she stands forth as a singular personality even in the dramatic times in which she lived.

No one knows how far Sargon's direct rule extended or how effective it was; we can judge the heaviness of his hand from a widespread revolt that broke out upon his death and the accession of his son, Rimush. Rimush was determined to restore his father's achievements. He moved first against the cities of Sumer, treating them with unmerciful cruelty. When the city contingents were defeated, he massacred them by the thousands and brought up men, women and children from the cities and made them undergo forced labor from which many died. The records of a concentration camp from his reign show free citizens and slaves, laboring together and dying, in some labor-intensive project far from their homes on the road to Iran, perhaps cutting stone. He was murdered in a palace conspiracy after a short reign and succeeded by a brother, Manishtusu. This king built on his brother's reconquest of Sumer to invade Iran once again. He tells in an inscription that he caused black stone to be brought from the mountain, reminding us of the labor camp of the preceding reign. This was diorite, a hard, dense, black igneous rock that his artisans worked to make a series of life-size statues of their ruler (see Chapter 15). Diorite became for generations thereafter the stone of choice for statues of rulers, difficult to obtain, difficult to carve, massive as their autocratic rule aspired to be.

By this time the land of Sumer had been reorganized into a new large province, designed to break down the boundaries of the old city states by creating a new entity administered ultimately by royal bureaucrats. The capital of this new province was none other than the ancient state of Lagash, which now prospered as the center of a much larger area than hitherto. A gigantic domain was carved out in Sumer and assigned to the support of crown officials, perhaps already by Rimush in retaliation for the revolt. Manishtusu himself purchased extensive lands to distribute among his own retainers. These were people who became directly dependent upon the king for support and largesse, so withdrew from the old ties of their community of birth. A new class of these people formed, scattered throughout the realm, seeking opportunity and preferment, their wealth and income derived from estates in the countryside. Like his brother, Manishtusu perished at the hand of conspirators.

The reign of Sargon's grandson, Naram-Sin, became a by-word in later Mesopotamian tradition for two thousand years. No other royal personality of the whole third millennium, save Sargon himself, left such an impression on history. We know Naram-Sin as a great conqueror, who boasts that the massively walled cities of northern Syria fell before him for the first time. He explored the sources of the Tigris; he fought a sea battle in the Gulf. There seemed no limit to his conquests. At the same time, he carried out administrative reforms. Standardized, easily understandable summary records were to be kept in each locality, for the inspection of royal officers, recording in full the harvest taken on their lands, the portion set aside for the royal household, and the expenses of cultivation. Many of these were written in the Akkadian language, especially in the land of Akkad, using an elegant new standardized script that was the hallmark of the royal administration.

The artistic output of this period still arouses our admiration (see Chapter 15): exquisitely carved seals, monumental statues and steles of the ruler, proclaiming his victories, with long narratives in Akkadian and Sumerian, replete with lists of defeated kings, their officers, and the number of their defeated troops. In these the king spoke directly to his reader, imagining the reactions of his enemies, challenging the future, giving for the uninitiated his own interpretation of the events he narrates. All this was a new imperial style, focused on the king and his entourage, the king a perfect hero and leader of his army and savior of his land. Later ages envied the supreme self-confidence and highly wrought self-expression of this time. In the meantime, boatloads of grain and tribute flowed into Agade, a new center for international trade, and Akkadian colonies were founded at Susa in Iran, as an administrative center and trading post, and far up the Khabur, for the management of agriculture there. As befits a great king, Naram-Sin also undertook building projects throughout his realm. One of the most lavish of these was a reconstruction of the Ekur, the Temple of Enlil at Nippur, under the supervision of the crown prince himself. No expense nor precious goods were spared in this great project.

But empire came at a price. Not everyone stood in awe of the serene arrogance of the noble Akkadians, whose domains lay astraddle the fields of the land, their manors away from the ancient cities in their own gardens of green. When the royal family passed through a region, they had to be entertained in extravagant style, wined and dined, seated on fine furniture in great pavilions while the laborers struggled in the field and the sharp-eyed scribes examined the contents of barges passing in review with goods to be taken to the capital. A Sumerian poet poured out his venomous hatred of this dynasty in an effusion claiming that the city Agade was to fall victim to the arrogance of Naram-Sin and succumb to hordes of barbarians. Some Sumerian cities, like Lagash, profited from the new order and flourished; we can imagine that some suffered as well, among them perhaps ancient Uruk. The people of Kish too perhaps looked on in envy at this upstart people who had usurped their ancient position. Sargon and his sons had called themselves kings of Kish, the greatest title of the day and one with international recognition, but Naram-Sin called himself king of Akkad.

What seemed a cataclysmic event to the ruling elite of the empire was a revolt, breaking out first perhaps at Kish, then joined, it seems by Uruk and Ur and a coalition of other Mesopotamian cities. They begged for foreign help as well. According to Naram-Sin's account, the foreign rulers were afraid to help; according to embroidered later tradition, a demonic horde of uncounted ghastly creatures was raised up against Naram-Sin. In nine major battles in a single year, he defeated his enemies, emerging as savior of his city and his imperial way of life. A brief administrative record of "booty from Uruk" gives us a hint of the fate in store for that rebellious city. Again according to Naram-Sin, the citizens of his city begged leave of the great gods and goddesses of the land to worship him as one of the gods of the land (see also Chapter 15). They agreed and his grateful subjects built a temple in his honor in Akkad. No other king had ever assumed the honors of the gods. Instead of kingship coming down from heaven, as the Sumerian history had it, Naram-Sin's kingship had gone up to heaven. Naram-Sin died after a long, eventful, and dramatic reign, the very type of the great king.

What happened thereafter is obscure. His son, Sharkalisharri, whose grandiose name means "king of all kings," was eventually crowned at Nippur and the work on the Ekur temple resumed. We know little of his reign save that the frontier seems to contract drastically and a people called the Amorites pressed hard on the southern settlements from their homeland up the Euphrates. So far as the Sumerian poet was concerned, Naram-Sin had brought a curse on his city by destroying Ekur and ignoring the diviners, who told him he must not touch the temple. Versions of this interpretation of his reign survived in later literature, in which a sorrowful and chastened Naram-Sin addresses future kings, telling them of his ordeals and enjoining them not to take the risks he did. To us, this sounds like wishful thinking. As to why the Amorites would press at this time, one controversial explanation has been that this was a period of severe drought in the northern rainfall zone of Syria, meaning first that the Akkadian installations there had to be abandoned, and second that the population, in order to live, had to press south to the irrigated lands or die. With savage glee, the Sumerian poet tells us of the destruction of the city Agade by vile mountain people called the Gutians. There were such people, stock-breeders in the Zagros uplands. They took advantage of the disorder to enter the lowlands and set up kingdoms there; venerable Umma was ruled by a Gutian, for example. The city Agade was rent by civil war and no doubt heavily damaged and looted, possibly destroyed.

But within a few years a prince at Lagash received a letter saying "There is a king in Agade!" and we know, in fact, of a dynasty that lasted there another century that gave gifts at Nippur and campaigned in Iran. However obscure and complex the period, we can be sure that the imperial ideal of the Sargonic kings was shattered forever, and we suspect that later ages looked back with nostalgia for those days, just as some people look back with envy on what seems in retrospect the calm assurance of the British, French, and German empires before the cataclysm of World War I smashed it forever.

7. The Kingdom of Ur

We think that Lagash was spared in the civil war and that she, of all cities, was in a position to take advantage of the decline of Akkadian power in Sumer. She was the seat of a large province and her rulers, respectful to whatever dynasty was in command of the land at large, presided over a compact and flourishing little state. One of them, Gudea, continued the practice begun by Manishtusu of carving himself in durable diorite. Under his aegis Sumerian literature blossomed: eloquent inscriptions, epic poetry, and hymns to the gods. One of the most elaborate of these is a florid composition that tells in great detail the story of how Gudea built a new temple and how even foreign nations were eager to proffer their goods to this undertaking. One would never know from its labored lines that there was any other place or power of importance on the horizon.

But Uruk was, at last, in a position to revive her fortunes. A vigorous new king by the name of Utu-hegal tells us that he drove the Gutians, those "snuffling snakes from the mountains," out of the land, so Sumer could finally come to life. How this squares with Gudea's beatific vision of the world we do not know. Indeed, soon a new version of the history of the land would privilege Uruk and avoid any reference to the grandeur of Akkad, much less collaborationist Lagash. When the national list of kings of the past was re-edited, Kish, Uruk, and Ur played leading roles, but Lagash was still not mentioned. Akkad, perforce, had to be included. Utu-hegal may have had in mind a revival of the former imperial order of Akkad, this time based at Uruk, but it seems his plans may have been cut short by his accidental death, and his brother, Ur-nammu, a junior officer apparently based at Ur, seized power, beginning the final chapter of Sumerian political history.

Of the five kings of the new dynasty of Ur, who bring us down nearly to the end of the third millennium, three may command our attention here. Ur-nammu, like his brother Utu-hegal, met an untimely death, in his case in battle, and a bitter outpouring of grief at his end suggests he was a charismatic leader of great potential. His son, Shulgi, succeeded to the throne at a young age and reigned for forty-eight years, a reign comparable to those of Louis XIV or Queen Victoria. Like them, his reign was an age marked by a certain style and many solid accomplishments. This was a golden age of Sumerian art, architecture, and literature. Shulgi's predecessor had dotted the land with new buildings, including the distinctive ziggurat, or stepped temple platform, associated with the major temples of the land. He too was a builder and patron of the arts and letters.

Under Shulgi's approving aegis, Sumerian poets turned out a whole series of elaborate hymns, glorifying his accomplishments in prolix detail. The kings of Ur claimed or revived no local tradition there, but rather associated themselves with famous kings of Uruk of the ancient past, such as the legendary hero-king Gilgamesh. They listened to long epic poems about the legendary figures of Uruk's past, as well as to stories of a king Enmerkar of old, the narrative replete, however, with witty references to current politics that to a savvy courtier must have seemed timely and amusing. There were daring jokes on the limitations of kingly power and the necessity to bluff in diplomacy, which we assume the king took in good part. This rich and delightful literature suggests a society sure of itself and of its values, ready for both fulsome praise and a light touch of mockery. There were masques or debates at court in which characters representing seasons of the year, raw materials, or domestic animals pitted themselves against each other in flowery eloquence to show which was the more useful to the human race.

Little of the splendid art of the period has come down to us, the carefully wrought furniture and awe-inspiring images worthy of royal commemoration. The carving of seals lost much of the vital exuberance of the Sargonic period and became confined to solemn hieratic scenes of a calm, ordered, status-conscious world. Some readers see in the literature of this period too an agenda, that of creating a literate hierarchy of people who had read the same compositions in school, and learned from them the importance of kingship and tradition, and who recognized in their peers the same education and values. We know it best from that center of Sumerian learning, Nippur, where students worked through a standard curriculum and glorified their own city in a ponderous, euphuistic hymn to the god Enlil, which, in its pompous verbosity, sums up the self-satisfied world view of the educated elite:

> *You founded it in the center of the world, as pivot point of earth*
> *and sky,*
> *The very soil of its bricks is the vitality of this land, the vitality*
> *of foreign lands,*
> *Its masonry is fiery gold, its foundations lapis blue.*
> *Like a wild ox, it tosses up its horns in the land of Sumer,*
> *While foreign lands droop their heads low in awe,*
> *And our people celebrate its great feast days in abundance!* **

The foundations of this society were teeming thousands of workers, sustained by a bare living of distributed raw ingredients of food and clothing, who worked long days in vast teams to meet fixed quotas of output. The king's bureaucracy could estimate to a nicety how long it would take to clear weeds from a given set of fields, how many workers would be required, and, ultimately what the field would yield. Thus they could compute their expenses and work needs exactly. Backbreaking work was a commodity, to be signed and sealed for like any other good. Moreover, the administration had a local and regional grasp of its tasks and output. The scribes knew for each major complex around the cities, the ancient temples, how much land they had and what condition it was in. They could compute the harvest in advance by comparing old records with the actual state of the field. They could work up calculations based on many such temple complexes, and could even compute regional expectations from past performance considering the land as a whole.

Agriculture was a matter of precise record-keeping; no detail of fieldwork was too small to escape the scribe's attention.

What they recorded reveals to us a disturbing trend. As the years went by, the royal establishment had moved away from the old, well-established mode of exploitation, based on extensive community involvement in matters of production. The Sargonic manor had relatively few workers and many lessees and beneficiaries of land grants. The crown received proportionately less income but the risks and labor of cultivation were widely distributed. The kings of Ur, however, initiated a radical approach whereby government teams of workers did as much cultivation as possible. This meant initially higher returns of harvests, as the crown was not sharing the harvest with lessees and dependents, but greater expenses, as the workers had to be supported with food and drink and lodging while they were working. Teams of thousands of workers had to be managed and sustained. Although the costs of such work were well known to administrators, they seem to have set them aside in the drive for greater control of productivity. Yet yields were dropping. Was it overexploitation, in a bureaucratic drive to increase production without due regard to traditional patterns of crop rotation? Was there in fact a decline in productivity? No one knows for sure, but it seems that the costs of greater agricultural management rose, while the yields began to decline.

During the reign of Shulgi, however, this was not yet apparent. The royal administration was subdivided and diversified for efficiency, using standardized writing and tablet shapes for its myriad records. A complicated system of rotating obligations, nominally for the cult centers of the land, coupled with certain taxes and benefits, laid the obligation to support the royal administration on local governors rather than the king's household. Merchants spread out across Western Asia, under commission from the royal household and any other interested party to secure foreign goods: metals, aromatics, oils, woods. The king's diplomats visited foreign courts and wrote frank appraisals of what they had seen. Shulgi, convinced of the usefulness of diplomatic marriages, sent off his daughters to grace the courts of foreign dignitaries; the girls' misery at such a fate can only be imagined. After a long period of peace, Shulgi was driven into an inconclusive war to the north and east, which never seemed to achieve its goals, despite the propaganda at home, and his scribes proclaimed the same victories, year in, year out. The Sumerian diplomatic service dispensed silver rings and fine clothing to an array of uncouth dignitaries, even as some litterateur wrote a letter in the name of a captive homesick monkey from exotic parts on display at the capital Ur.

Society seemed fixed and stable. We have the impression that the bureaucracy was omnipresent and efficient. To prevent too great a change in private status, it seems that land sales were forbidden, thus keeping individual financial initiative in check. There were plenty of economic opportunities, as interest rates were high and lenders happy to take advantage of them. Shulgi tells us the roads were open, well supplied with way stations, each with an agreeable garden around it. People knew their places and did their jobs.

There were ominous pressures, however, to the north and west. The Amorites, whom the Sumerians deemed barbarous people from the grasslands and cities of Syria, were a persistent presence, trickling into the alluvium. The Sumerians quipped that the Amorites lived in no houses and did not honor their dead. A military wall was constructed that would surely keep these infiltrators at bay, but they kept on coming anyway. Why? Was this another round of the alleged desiccation in the north, in which the choices became emigrate or die? Sumerian poetry begins to paint a grim picture of foreign invaders, pestilence, disorder, marauders in the ancient cities, loss of respect for the old ways. Clearly something was wrong. Inflation grew. By the reign of Shulgi's last successor, Ibbi-Sin, inflation was out of control. Productivity was down; how were the huge teams of workers to be disciplined and fed? The capital began to starve. Food was available, but at a price, from the Euphrates region, strange if, according to some scholars, this was where the problem of desiccation was worst. The price was high — suppliers wanted not only money but titles and authority that the king had to give.

The end came of a sudden. The great teams of workers broke down into disorderly rabbles. Country people pushed their way into the cities, buying, lending, or forcing their way into becoming a new, arriviste, urban elite. There was a breakdown in law and order. The Elamites, who had perhaps tired of listening to satirical poems at the court of Ur about how mythical Sumerian kings had triumphed over their mythical ancestors in the land of Aratta, swept down upon the capital, looting and wrecking it, and carrying off the last king of Ur to die in unhappy captivity in the land of Elam.

Bibliographical Note to Chapter 2

A fuller survey of this period will be found in Marc Van De Mieroop, *A History of the Ancient Near East* (see Bibliographical Note to Chapter 1), Chapters 3 and 4. An excellent account of Sumerian culture is found in Harriet Crawford, *Sumer and the Sumerians* (Cambridge: Cambridge University Press, 1991). For social history, J. N. Postgate, *Early Mesopotamia: Society and Economy at the Dawn of History* (London: Routledge, 1992) is excellent, as well as Marc Van De Mieroop, *The Ancient Mesopotamian City* (Oxford: Oxford University Press, 1999). For a more popularizing approach, Daniel C. Snell, *Life in the Ancient Near East* (New Haven: Yale University Press, 1997), may be recommended. The account of Shuruppak given here is based on the work of F. Pomponio and G. Visicato, an English summary of which will be found in *Early Dynastic Administrative Tablets of Shuruppak* (Naples: Istituto Orientale, 1994) and G. Visicato, *The Bureaucracy of Shuruppak* (Münster: Ugarit-Verlag, 1995). For the war between Lagash and Umma, see J. S. Cooper, *Reconstructing History from Ancient Inscriptions: The Lagash-Umma Border Conflict* (Malibu: Undena Publications, 1983). The interpretation of Urukagina's reign mentioned here is derived from the researches of K. Maekawa; see further B. R. Foster, "A New Look at the Sumerian Temple State," *Journal of the Economic and Social History of the Orient* 24 (1981), 225–241. For the Sargonic period, see M. Liverani, ed., *Akkad, The First World Empire* (Padua: Sargon SRL, 1993). There is no comparable collection of essays on the empire of Ur, so readers are advised to consult Van De Mieroop's *History* above. For Sumerian literature in English, see Jeremy Black, Graham Cunningham, Eleanor Robson, and Gábor Zólyomi, *The Literature of Ancient Sumer* (Oxford: Oxford University Press, 2004).

Translated Excerpts

*From the edition of J. S. Cooper, *The Curse of Agade* (Baltimore, 1983), 50–51 lines 25–28.
**From the edition of David Reisman, "Two Neo-Sumerian Royal Hymns" (dissertation: University of Pennsylvania, 1969), lines 68–73.

Chapter 3

The Age of Hammurabi

1. The Amorites and Their Way of Life

Despite the fortification wall and the best efforts of the kings of Ur, the flood of Amorites into Mesopotamia continued unchecked. Who were these people? From the point of view of the Sumerians, they were barbarous tent-dwelling folk without civilization, even though their leaders had been cultivated politely by the Sumerian diplomatic service. There were indeed some Amorites who were dwellers in tents in the pastureland along the middle Euphrates. They were divided into tribes and clans on the northern and southern bank of the river. There were also urban people in northern Syria, whom we would consider Amorites on the basis of their language, but to whom "Amorite" meant something like "pastoral nomad," even though to the Sumerians, in their literature at least, all Amorites were nomads. It was, indeed, the nomads and pastoralists who seem to have pressed hardest against the frontiers of the kingdom of Ur, rather than the city people of great urban centers like Aleppo. Perhaps their land was afflicted by drought, so they had no choice. Perhaps they saw opportunity in the alluvium, first as herders and workers, then as people with money buying their way into an ancient but unsettled urban economy. No one knows for sure. We do know that when events are once again visible behind the obscurity of the collapse of the kingdom of Ur, Amorites are everywhere: on the uplands east of the Tigris, in the major urban centers like Ur and Uruk, in proud tribal settlements outside great urban centers like Sippar. They spoke a new and vigorous idiom that was understood throughout the Euphrates valley, far beyond the horizon of the older Sumerian and Akkadian. The Amorites showed three different patterns of adapting to the new world in which they found themselves.

One was slavish imitation. Around 2000 B.C.E. a new dynasty emerged at Isin, a city near Nippur with a strong association with traditional Sumerian learning and the arts of healing. The founder of the new dynasty of Isin, Ishbi-Erra, came to power by demanding concessions from the beleaguered kings of Ur and he and his successors portrayed themselves as their legitimate successors. Thus, for example, they listened to their own praises in elaborate Sumerian hymns cranked out in their honor; they solemnly proclaimed the old titles of kingship; they added a new chapter, their own, to the ancient list of Sumerian and Akkadian kings; they cultivated a new, baroque style of Sumerian expression in their formal letters.

Another way of adapting took the form of pragmatic assertion of Amorite custom and business behavior. At Larsa, whose dynasty, after a century, replaced Isin in control of the land, we see an exclusively Amorite community, where, for the most part, only academics and priests had Sumerian names. These people had money to spend and did so, buying and selling urban house lots and gardens until, within a few generations, nearly all available urban land in Larsa city may have been bought up and the best quarter was filled with spacious mansions. They invested in labor, real estate, and raw materials, speaking the language of business and enterprise with only a vaguely Sumerian legal gloss. This was a world of first families, men of affairs who held responsible positions in the local chamber of commerce, who owned large homes in center city, whose sons studied Sumerian literature whereas their grandfathers had probably herded sheep. Their kings relied on them as notables to manage local affairs, like sheikhs of tribes, through some kind of central bureau. The king expected their help in collecting taxes, arranging military contingents, and administering local justice. In return, these men of affairs controlled local commerce, taxation, and agriculture, seized profitable opportunities, and bought themselves a new kind of urban social legitimacy that the new order allowed them.

A third way was proudly to proclaim one's Amorite background, to subscribe to an Amorite myth of origins that had nothing to do with the old Sumerian kings, but was based on ancient ancestors who lived in tents. For these people, the official means of expression was the new formal language, partly Akkadian, partly Amorite, with Sumerian influences as well, understood from Aleppo to Babylon, and a shared view of how international affairs should be conducted. In this respect, the Amorite world of Mesopotamia and beyond resembled the modern states of the Arabic-speaking Middle East. There were many claimants to power, deeply and with good reason distrusting each other. This was a culture of alliances, military and marital, with a strong sense of politics. We can single out, from among many, three personalities of this era: Shamshi-Adad, Rim-Sin, and Hammurabi.

An Amorite settlement near Sippar, called Sippar-Amnanum, has been intensively excavated by Belgian archaeologists.

2. Shamshi-Adad, King of Northern Mesopotamia

Shamshi-Adad was a dominating figure of the early eighteenth century B.C.E. He grew up in a world subservient to the great king of Eshnunna, Naram-Sin, who, like others of his dynasty, saw himself as a continuator of the grand tradition of the kings of Akkad, even taking the name of the great king of the former dynasty, just as the kings of Isin had seen themselves in the bright light of the kingdom of Ur. From what may have been his ancestral home, Ekallatum in Assyria, Shamshi-Adad went to Babylonia, all the while, it seems, biding his time. When Naram-Sin died, Shamshi-Adad's moment had come nor was he slow to seize it. He returned to Ekallatum and conquered the territory to the north and northwest, as far as the big bend of the Euphrates. Now it was his turn to think of himself as successor to the great kings of Akkad. He installed two of his sons as local kings, one, Yasmah-Adad, in the city Mari, on the mid-Euphrates, whence Shamshi-Adad had driven the ruling dynasty, and the other, Ishme-Dagan, as king of Assur. Shamshi-Adad himself set up his court at the city of Shehna in the Khabur region, renaming it "Shubat-Enlil," "Abode of Enlil," or chief god, perhaps an unsubtle reference to himself. His letters to his sons make fascinating reading, and in some cases must have been rather a trial for the confidential clerk to give utterance to:

> *Are you a child? Haven't you grown up yet? Is there no beard on your chin yet? When are you going to take charge if your household? Don't you have your brother's example, he who commands huge armies?* *

However much satisfaction it must have given this formidable man to address his sons as kings under his aegis, his days were numbered. After his death, his palace and new capital were overrun and looted, and his enemies, including young Hammurabi of Babylon, no doubt breathed a sigh of relief at his demise.

Letters of Shamshi-Adad, along with many other documents, were found in the ruins of the palace at Mari, Syria, by French archaeologists.

3. Rim-Sin, King of Larsa

Rim-Sin succeeded to the throne of Larsa in the nineteenth century B.C.E. This city's particular rival was Isin, proud of her assumed relationship to the kings of Ur, whereas the Larsa kings had a stronger sense of their Amorite roots. In any case, their competing objectives were control of the land, legitimation for which was recognition of their kingship at the city Nippur. Here Isin had the advantage, as it lay nearer Nippur than did Larsa, but Larsa was gathering strength. The basic technique of warfare in this period often included a march upstream from the enemy city, cutting off or controlling its supply of water if possible. This could be followed by a direct attack on the rival's army. During Rim-Sin's long reign, he gradually solidified his power over neighboring cities, then, in the climactic event of his reign, he attacked and destroyed the city Isin. This was perhaps the culmination of his ambitions, for most of the rest of his reign was dated by referring to this event.

4. Hammurabi, King of Babylon, and His Laws

Hammurabi of Babylon (eighteenth century B.C.E.) may be taken as the archetype of the successful Amorite ruler of his time. His name is most famous today because of his stele of laws discovered in Iran in the early twentieth century and now in the Louvre (see cover). It became a classic text in antiquity as well; there are many copies and excerpts from it dating as late as a thousand years after his death. Hammurabi craftily built his state using brute force, alliance, and betrayal. He solidified his hold in the south, respectfully maintaining an alliance with the king of Larsa, Rim-Sin. But he had a larger vision of his destiny than that king. When he deemed the moment opportune, he turned on Rim-Sin and conquered Larsa. This opened the way further north. Eventually he destroyed Eshnunna, a dangerous rival, Kish too, and many others. Marching up the Euphrates, he destroyed the great royal palace of Mari. In his inscriptions he boasts of his conquests, his ability to find his way out of many crises, and his lavish repairs to important cult centers. According to him, the gods of the cities he attacked were pleased with him and their subjects accepted his magnanimous offer of new dwelling places elsewhere. Therefore Hammurabi was undoubtedly a successful tactician of the first order. He succeeded in building a compact state in the center of the land and, in principle, breaking down the old pattern of independent city states forever. Although, according to him, rebels and trouble-makers appeared in various places, the fact is that the local city-state was gradually, during his reign and that of his son, Samsuiluna, absorbed into a Babylonian territorial state and Mesopotamia was making the transition to a new order.

Hammurabi's correspondence with his subalterns shows a man with close attention to detail; no local dispute over a field was too slight a matter to engage his attention. He frequently seems to be curbing administrators' abuse of their powers and insisting that previous rights and practices be upheld. Some scholars consider this evidence of a hard-working king, who did not shirk the burdens of effective management; others consider this evidence of an insecure man unable to delegate responsibility. In any case, he knew his realm well and had clear ideas and policies on how it should be administered.

Hammurabi's law stele is one of the earliest and most comprehensive collections of legal material from the pre-Classical world. It is mostly a list of hypothetical cases, from which we assume one could reason analogously to the circumstances of one's own case. The cases cover such subjects as wrongs to individuals, for example assault or rape; correct legal practice; management of fields held in tenure from the palace, marriage, witchcraft, and a vast range of other subjects, including medical malpractice. There is little evidence of the impact of the provisions recorded on the stele on legal affairs in everyday life. Some legal documents refer to a "royal edict," so the interest of the palace in legal matters was palpable, despite lack of reference to the stele itself, which may be more of a commemoration of the king's legal thought and activity than a "code" as that term is understood today. Local matters, such as disputes about property, were handled by local neighborhood bodies. Lawsuits could be heard by professional judges, apparently for a fee. Capital cases may have been referred to the palace for final disposition.

Nor was Hammurabi's stele the only collection of laws of this period; another large group of laws was discovered at Eshnunna, so promulgation of law was an important prerogative of the Amorite kings. Fragmentary collections of earlier Sumerian laws remain too, so the relationship between kings and collections of laws certainly antedates the coming of the Amorites to Mesopotamia. One fundamental principle of Amorite law was retribution in kind: if someone broke a person's tooth, his tooth was to be broken. Some offenses were punishable by heavy fines, and a considerable number by death. Efforts to arrive at the truth of a case were first by investigation. If that failed to establish the facts, one or both parties could take an oath. If even this procedure failed to establish fact, one could resort to the ordeal, such as plunging an accuser in the river to see if he came up vindicated or was about to drown, hence guilty of making a false accusation. Some Amorite laws sought to regulate rates of hire and prices as well.

Hammurabi's letters were found by looters in the early twentieth century; it is not known where.

5. Law, Society, and Literature

Parallel to the law collections is a large body of legal documents, such as witnessed contracts of sale, hire, or rental, and an assortment of court cases which sometimes record the actual testimony of the participants. Numerous suits at law give evidence for a litigious age. These often involved inheritance rights or social status, such as whether a certain person was free or a slave. Chattel slavery was a luxury for the wealthy, who mostly used slaves in domestic service. Chattel slavery was not important in agricultural production. Another form of slavery was debt slavery, in which people paid the interest on loans by working for the creditor. Since labor was scarce and expensive compared to the needs of the agricultural hinterlands, we assume that debt slavery was profitable to the creditor. Rates of interest were usually very high, from 18% to 33 1/3%, so in effect beyond the means of anyone in need. One possible reason for high rates of interest, besides pure greed, was that some types of debts and services could be annulled periodically by royal decree, thus in theory raising the risk of loaning money. Some loans may in fact have been foreclosures in disguise if creditors were seeking to seize property or able-bodied family members rather than realistically expecting repayment of the loan. From what we see in Babylonian business documents of the Amorite period, the early centuries of Amorite rule were times of considerable economic growth and activity, with much buying and selling of land; later, after Hammurabi's time, this seems to taper off somewhat, especially in the south, which became economically depressed and was even abandoned in some areas owing to protracted local civil war and a shift in the Euphrates during the reign of his successor, Samsuiluna.

Yet all was not business and politics in mid-second millennium Babylonia. What many would esteem as twin pillars of the good life, fine cooking and the arts of love, were cultivated by the Babylonians as well. A collection of recipes for elaborate cookery has come down to us, based on several stages of preparation, a variety of ingredients, and a sense of presentation at the moment of serving. While such pains and expense may have been as rare in private life as first-rate high cuisine is today, the discovery of these recipes opens an unexpected window into an otherwise unknown aspect of Babylonian life. Even for people in comfortable circumstances a roast of meat was only for holiday fare; dairy products, bread, dates, vegetables, and legumes were the usual diet. A varied literature on love illumines the tender passion with humor, ardor, and sometimes bitterness. In one passionate piece, a woman sings to her lover:

> *Your heartbeat is my reveille,*
> *Up then, I want to make love with you,*
> *In your smooth loins, as you come awake.*
> *How sweet your caress,*
> *How voluptuous your charms …*
> *O my loose locks, my ear lobes,*
> *The contour of my shoulders and the opulence of my breast,*
> *The spreading fingers of my hands,*
> *The love-beads of my waist!*
> *Bring your left hand close, touch my sweet spot,*
> *Fondle my breasts!*
> *[O come inside], I have opened my thighs!***

In this period originated the most celebrated work of Mesopotamian literature, the Epic of Gilgamesh. This told the story of a king of Uruk who tyrannized his subjects until the gods created a wild man, Enkidu, to be first his contender then his friend. The two friends set off on a quest to kill a monster and cut great cedar trees. They return to Uruk in triumph. When Gilgamesh rejects the advances of Ishtar, goddess of love and procreation, she sends a celestial bull to ravage the city, and the two friends kill the bull in an epic battle. The gods decree that Enkidu must die. Gilgamesh, overcome by the death of his friend, undertakes another, greater quest, to find a way to avoid dying, and this takes up the rest of the poem. This masterpiece was copied, studied, edited, and enlarged throughout the centuries that followed (see back cover). In the version of this poem from the Amorite period, Gilgamesh meets a woman tavern keeper far away at the edge of the earth, and she advises him to abandon his quest and to lead a happy, worthwhile life:

Gilgamesh, wherefore do you wander?
The eternal life you are seeking you shall not find.
When the gods created mankind,
They established death for mankind,
And withheld eternal life for themselves.
As for you, Gilgamesh, let your stomach be full,
Always be happy, night and day.
Make every day a delight,
Night and day play and dance.
Your clothes should be clean,
Your head should be washed,
You should bathe in water.
Look proudly on the little one holding your hand,
Let your mate be always blissful in your loins.
This, then, is the work of mankind.***

6. The End of Amorite Period

The dynasty of Babylon lasted more than two centuries and left its defining political and cultural imprint on the Babylonian landscape. The reigns of its last kings are obscure. The former empire may have shrunk considerably. The countryside, especially to the south, saw depopulation and abandonment. Local officials perhaps grew more independent of the palace and sufficiently well entrenched to pass on their offices and perquisites by inheritance, turning into local notables on the basis of their government office. Larger events, of which we know very little, may also have had their impact on Mesopotamia: a great kingdom forming in central Anatolia under a people we call the Hittites, the persistent migration into Mesopotamia from the east and north of a new people known as the Kassites. What pressures brought these people into the plain we do not know, but their names gradually appear in documents as workers and soldiers, almost as if the initial pattern of Amorite presence in Mesopotamia was repeating itself, but this time, unlike the Amorites, with a new people who had nothing culturally in common with the peoples to the north and west. The last king of Babylon was dethroned by a daring invasion of the Hittite king and his army in 1595. He withdrew soon thereafter, no doubt savoring this extraordinary triumph, but with no intent of occupying Mesopotamia. Into the resulting gaps the once immigrant Kassites were the first to take power, inaugurating a new phase of the history of Iraq.

The site of Mari, now in Syria, has been under excavation by French archaeologists for over fifty years. The extensive archives and correspondence found there are among the most important sources for the history of Western Asia in the early second millennium. The sites of Isin and Larsa were first explored by clandestine diggers in the early twentieth century. Later, systematic excavations were carried on by German and French archaeologists. After the Iraq war, both sites were effectively destroyed by extensive looting. Babylon has been explored by archaeologists since the nineteenth century, notably by Germans. The parts of the ruins dating to the time of Hammurabi lie below the present water table, so have not been found. Saddam Hussein ordered extensive construction and restoration at Babylon; see Chapter 6. Since 2003 Babylon has been greatly damaged by its use as a military base; see Chapter 14.

Bibliographical Note to Chapter 3

There is no comprehensive work in English on the Amorite period in Mesopotamia. In addition to the works of Van De Mieroop and Postgate cited above, Chapter 2, one may mention a fine study of Hammurabi and his times: Marc Van De Mieroop, *King Hammurabi of Babylon, A Biography* (Oxford: Blackwell, 2005) and another study by the same author of life in the city of Ur: *Society and Enterprise in Old Babylonian Ur* (Berlin: Dietrich Reimer, 1992). For another city study, Elizabeth Stone, *Nippur Neighborhoods* (University of Chicago: *Studies in Ancient Oriental Civilization* 44, 1987) is strongly recommended. A large selection of letters from Mari has been translated into English, with comments, by W. Heimpel, *Letters to the King of Mari* (Winona Lake, Ind.: Eisenbrauns, 2003). For Babylonian literature, see Foster, *Before the Muses* (cited below, translated excerpts). Babylonian laws have been translated by Martha Roth, *Law Collections from Mesopotamia and Asia Minor*, second edition (Atlanta: Society for Biblical Literature, *Writings from the Ancient World Series* 6, 1997).

Translated Excerpts

*After J-M. Durand, *Documents Epistolaires du Palais de Mari* (Paris: Editions Du Cerf, 1997), 1:138.

**B. R. Foster, *Before the Muses, An Anthology of Akkadian Literature*, third edition (Bethesda: CDL Press, 2005), 169.

***B. R. Foster, *The Epic of Gilgamesh* (New York: W. W. Norton & Company 2001), 75.

Chapter 4

A Babylonian Nation-State

1. The Kassite People and Their Society

An important legacy of the kingdom of Babylon had been to demonstrate that Babylonia could be the basis for a compact, powerful, and prosperous regional state. The Kassites brought to the crisis of its downfall a new population, a strong tradition of military service and organization, and an overarching concept of common identity that effectively displaced and rendered obsolete the old Amorite tradition. The Kassites spoke their own language, only scattered words of which remain today, so we know little of its possible relationship to other ancient languages of Western Asia. Kassite documents spoke of their "houses," a concept considerably broader than that of the Babylonian family and conveniently translated by "tribes." Entering Mesopotamia, first as soldiers, then as foreign conquerors from the east, the Kassites carved out great domains on the Babylonian landscape which appear tribal or feudal in structure and organization.

Like the early kings of Isin, the Kassites took their relationship to the indigenous Mesopotamian culture with the utmost seriousness. They adopted and supported the ancient Mesopotamian cults, rebuilt and restored the gods' temples, and maintained their rites, even if they never forgot their own Kassite deities. Within a century or so, the Kassite court at Babylon was the proud patron of not only Akkadian literature in its most elegant and carefully wrought style, it also revived the long-dead Sumerian language as a scholastic idiom. Kassite dignitaries carried seals with elaborate Sumerian prayers inscribed on them; royal inscriptions were worked up in that ancient tongue. The remains of a Kassite palace at Aqarquf (ancient Dur-Kurigalzu) yielded to archaeologists signs of an impressive tradition of sculpture in the round and wall painting. All of this suggests a reinvigoration of Mesopotamian culture for which the infusion of Turks, with their military culture, into the Arab-Persian Abbasid empire of the high Middle Ages provides a suggestive parallel (see Chapter 11).

Like the Turks, the Kassites were culturally highly adaptive and receptive, adopting the languages and traditions of Mesopotamia and making them their own, but still maintaining their own identity and values. Unlike Turkish, however, Kassite did not become a major written language of the new civilization into which its speakers had moved. There are ample indications that the Kassites kept their own preferences and styles in art, for example, though they adopted and refined the written culture of Mesopotamia with virtually no visible Kassite substrate.

The site of Dur-Kurigalzu was explored by Iraqi archaeologists during the years 1942-1945. The most important discovery was the ruins of a royal palace, from which various important works of art were retrieved. The excavations were never definitively published. All the finds were transferred to the Iraq Museum. Restoration work was later carried out on the ziggurat.

2. Kassite Government

The Kassite state, with its political capital at Babylon, and perhaps a second capital at Dur-Kurigalzu, to the north and west, depended in the first instance on governors of provinces, within which certain important cities acted as regional centers. At one of these, Nippur, an American expedition in the nineteenth century discovered a vast archive of administrative documents and correspondence dating to the fourteenth and thirteenth centuries B.C.E.. These give a picture of strongly centralized state, with extensive mobile work forces at its command. These could be moved from place to place as needed, especially for the extensive irrigation works that are discussed in detail in the letters. Perhaps there was some depopulation or impoverishment of local rural resources, an interpretation borne out by surveys of settlement patterns at that time.

On the local level, members of the Kassite nobility held extensive estates, which included many villages, bordering on crown lands and on the even greater domains of some of the Babylonian temples. The revenues of the government depended upon systematic taxation of agriculture and a series of dues on land and fees and tolls. Part of this income was invested in a professional military caste, also supported by land grants, some of whom were armored warriors skilled in the specialized warfare of the age, based on horse-drawn chariots. These weapons, like the phalanx, were effective in a single charge by which one tried to break through and scatter the lines of the enemy. The elite of the new army were men trained and disciplined in this mode of fighting. The horse, now being brought to Mesopotamia in large numbers, was a labor-intensive beast requiring extensive training of its own plus year-round maintenance. Thus while the Amorite kingdoms had made extensive use of seasonal levies and did support a class of professional soldiers by small land grants, in the Kassite period the professional warrior class seems to have expanded and become more expensive.

3. International Relations

The military power, extensive domains, and high culture of the Kassites entitled them to membership in the international club of great powers of their age. This was a new concept, unknown to Hammurabi and his successors, linking the whole of Western Asia, Anatolia, and even Egypt into a diplomatic and political network based on a fundamental acceptance of each other's frontiers. Relations were cultivated through treaties, correspondence, and exchange of embassies and gifts between courts. The members of this club, such as the kings of Egypt, Mesopotamia, the Hittites, and the king of Mitanni, a great state stretching across northern Syria and Mesopotamia, addressed each other as equals, and sent each royal gifts, such as gold and gems, weaponry, art objects, and textiles. They exchanged physicians, princesses, and singing girls and reassured each other constantly of their good will. The rhetoric of the time precluded expressing enthusiasm for a gift received, so one generally complained of its niggardliness while noting with satisfaction the sumptuousness of one's own rendering. No doubt the greatest king of all was the pharaoh of Egypt, who alone of the rulers of his age would bestow no native princess on a foreign ruler, though he accepted foreign princesses to his own harem. The Babylonians thought Egypt to be a land of gold; so plentiful was gold in this period that Babylonia itself went on a gold standard for the only time in its ancient history, as opposed to the silver standard that had prevailed in the past.

We know the names of various Kassite kings, such as Kurigalzu, who was evidently a city builder, and have some scattered references to their achievements, but as yet little is known of their reigns. So too we know little of Babylonian relations with her eastern neighbor, Elam, save that at least one Babylonian princess was sent to Elam to cement a diplomatic marriage. The Kassite king regarded Assyria (see Chapter 5) as a hinterland under his sphere of influence, but Assyria by the mid-fourteenth century was emerging as an independent power, and, to the irritation of the Babylonian court, admitted to the club of great powers.

4. Kassite Civilization

The Kassite period is often considered a high point in the development of the Babylonian sciences, religious expression, and literature. The science best known to us today was above all divination, the art of reading the future from phenomena of the past and present. The first extensive evidence for the arts of divination and the high status of the diviner comes to us from the Amorite courts. At the Amorite court of Mari, the chief diviner, a certain Asqudum, had been not only a major figure at court but also a trusted plenipotentiary who undertook the delicate task of negotiating the king's marriage to the princess of a near-by city. Perhaps from the house of a master diviner at Larsa comes a large set of carefully written tablets recording omens and their prognoses based on the inspection of the liver and gall bladder of sheep. This arcane and prestigious branch of the discipline involved framing a question, posing it, often to the gods Shamash and Adad as lords of divination, then sacrificing the animal to examine its liver and viscera. The location of certain telltale features and marks were charted and evaluated rather in the same style of reasoning used in modern graphology: one summed up the features potentially favorable and potentially unfavorable and reached a verdict. This type of divination was used prior to state decisions, as an appeal by Hammurabi concerning the outlook and command of an expedition to the north illustrates. Since the essence of the discipline of divination involved collection of phenomena that could be related to given outcomes, a large body of sources for reference was necessary. We have the impression that earlier collections, or local schools of material, were systematically gathered, evaluated, and standardized, beginning in the Kassite period. Thereby certain comprehensive works, running to hundreds of large tablets, could result, referred to as "series." From these, the scholar could look up prognostications, then could arrange procedures to avert the portended evils:

> *If there are green and red fungi in a man's house, the owner of*
> *that house will die;*
> > *(or) dispersal of the man's house.*
> *If half-green, half-red fungi fill a man's house, the man's son will*
> *enrich the father's house.*
> *If green fungi fill a man's house, the owner of that house will*
> *become poor.*
> *If a fungus keeps putting out protuberances, the government will*
> *have a claim on that house.**

Magic was a respected and related branch of the science of divination. Some magic was intended to ward off harm, whereas other magic was intended to harm people, especially people suspected of witchcraft themselves. This spell portrays the misery of headache prior to treatment:

> *Headache flashes like stars of the sky, it flows on like water at*
> *night,*
> *It has confronted the afflicted man and paralyzed him, as if it were*
> *a storm.*
> *It has killed that man!*
> *That man writhes around like one with intestinal disease,*
> *Like one disemboweled he tosses about.***

For some sciences that had flourished in the Amorite period, notably mathematics and mathematical astronomy, we have almost no information for the Kassite period, so it is not clear how much of the intellectual tradition of the first half of the second millennium was continued and cultivated in the second half. Since much of what is known about early mathematics may come from one group of tablets, again perhaps from Larsa, and much of what we know about later astronomy the same, from Babylon, this apparent gap may simply be a matter of chance.

Another important Babylonian science of the period was philology, the study of words and language. This entailed mastery of long lists of words and signs; a scholar could brag how many equivalences, that is, special meanings or values, he knew for just one sign. As in many educational enterprises, the knowledge had little or no practical application in writing; the important thing was that the would-be scholar had paid his dues to tradition by learning what was required of him. Babylonia was still formally a bilingual or translation culture, so the ability to translate to or from Sumerian into Babylonian was the sign of an educated person. At some point in this period, perhaps at Nippur, a school of translation was developed which tackled the problem of making Akkadian renditions of major works of Sumerian literature. These translations tended to be explanatory or dynamic rather than exact or literal. Their purpose seems not so much to have been for helping someone who could not read the Sumerian original (though they were a great help indeed in the decipherment of Sumerian in modern times) as they were a kind of recasting the source work in the target language as two faces of the same composition. In some instances the Sumerian original was altered to correspond better to the translation. The Amorite scholars too had developed a school and theory of translation, but at least some of this was purely speculative, based on morpheme-by-morpheme correspondences, rather like some early Jewish and Christian translations of the Bible into Greek or Aramaic from Hebrew. Some lovers of language of the Kassite period collected rare Akkadian words, devised commentaries on important works of literature, and delved deep into the significance of names and words by analyzing their constituent elements and how they were spelled. To a modern reader, much of this seems purely associative exercise of the imagination, exemplified in more modern times by finding hidden numerical or mystical meanings in ancient texts and claiming that these were the original intent of the author, but to the Babylonian thinker, this was all a fascinating expedition into the real meanings that objects and the words for them could conceal or stand for.

The Kassite archives from Nippur preserve various letters from court physicians. These prescribe treatments based on medicines and poultices, and make no reference to magic. Therefore we suspect that there were two branches of medicine, the physician who made use of a rich herbalist tradition, going back to most ancient times, and the magician or exorcist, who used magical means to deal with both physical and psychological problems. Later medical texts combine both approaches in one procedure, but we cannot be sure whether or not this was a later combination of two healing arts originally separate. Reference to surgery is known already from the laws of Hammurabi, but none of the procedures referred to in the Kassite letters involves surgery.

We know little of the specifically militarist culture of the Kassites. So great was the impact of Mesopotamian tradition on them that we have no record of any independent tradition that they may have had. Thus to stand for the cultural accomplishment of the period, we may turn to one of its most eloquent literary products, which Assyriologists have titled "The Poem of the Righteous Sufferer."

This is an extended self-narrative and lament by a certain Shubshi-meshre-Shakkan, who tells us he was a person of importance at the royal court. He was, he insists, a dutiful servant of his lord, a responsible householder and administrator, and a reverent worshiper of the gods. Despite his merits, he fell suddenly out of grace. He lost his repute at court, his family and friends deserted him, menials reviled him publicly:

I, who walked proudly, learned slinking,
I, so grand, became servile.
To my vast family I became a loner,
As I went through the streets, I was pointed at,
I would enter the palace, eyes would squint at me,
My city was glowering at me like an enemy,

Belligerent and hostile would seem my land!
My brother became my foe,
My friend became a malignant demon,
My comrade would denounce me savagely,
My colleague poisoned his weapons to shed blood,
My best friend made my life an aspersion.
My slave cursed me openly in the assembly of gentlefolk,
My slave girl defamed me before the rabble.
An acquaintance would see me and make himself scarce,
My family set me down as an outsider.***

His finances took a turn for the worse, base conspirators whispered together of taking his post, his prerogatives, even coming into his estate. All his efforts, using expensive consultants to find out what was amiss, served only to exhaust his resources. No chance had he to fight back, for he was struck down by a battalion of fell diseases. His powers of speech and concentration deserted him; speechless and gibbering, he wandered about, too oppressed to stay indoors.

My lofty stature they toppled like a wall,
My robust figure they flattened like a bulrush,
I was dropped like a dried fig, I was tossed on my face.****

Soon he fell bedridden, losing control of the functions of his body, and gradually lapsed into the coma of the dying. His family assembled at his bedside, his grave was dug and his grave goods were set out. The narrator sets forth his ills at great length and in intimate, distasteful detail, like an obsessive hypochondriac. His enemies glowed with pleasure at his imminent demise. He knew throughout, he says, that the god Marduk had struck him down from the pinnacle of his enjoyment of life, but he had no idea why.

In his last waking moments the sufferer sees a resplendent woman who promises him relief, followed by an uncanny exorcist with an elaborate name who says the words needed to banish his afflictions. Rising from his bed, the sufferer parades through the streets of Babylon, redeemed from misery, for all to witness. He even gives a feast at his gravesite, turning a funerary repast into a happy celebration of life. As Marduk was powerful enough to bring him low, so too the god's wonderful majesty could snatch him from the very jaws of destruction.

The content of this work invites comparison with various Mesopotamian compositions of different periods that confront the question of undeserved suffering. The biblical Book of Job is only the latest and most elaborate example of this group. But the Babylonian poem of the sufferer was also a product of its age, of exquisite poetic refinement and immense learning. The pride, passion, and artistic level of this extraordinary composition may stand for a mature and reflective civilization whose chariotry is now forgotten.

The preoccupation of the Babylonian sufferer's poem with power and life at court places it, of course, in the realm of the elite. The author gives no hint, however, of military prowess, so one cannot rush to make him emblematic of the success of his age. He was clearly a man of parts and authority moved by the fragility of his life's accomplishment. Whereas his interpretation of his own dilemma, that both suffering and redemption are signs of divine power, may not strike a chord with many modern readers, the deeply personal tone of this testimony speaks forth clearly from the broken tablets that preserve it.

These scattered threads from what was once a great tapestry of cultural achievements leave us wistful: no collection of scholarly or literary manuscripts has come down to us from what must have been great collections at Babylon and elsewhere. To judge from earlier and later ages, fine assemblages may have been in private possession of accomplished scholars and their families, but, as yet, no important library of the period has come to light in Iraq.

6. Hurrians in Mesopotamia

Outside of Babylonia itself, as one traveled north towards Assyria, one entered a different society, though one still heavily stamped with Babylonian custom. Between 1430 and 1330 B.C.E., the region around modern Kirkuk, north and east of modern Baghdad, was largely inhabited by people who spoke a different language and belonged to a different cultural tradition. They were referred to as Hurrians. Hurrian was a written language of first-rate cultural importance in the kingdom of Mitanni, a vast entity beginning at the Zagros mountains and stretching towards the Mediterranean. The capital of Mitanni lay in what is now Anatolia. The Mitannians shared with Kassite Babylonia a reliance on a professional military elite to sustain itself. To some scholars, the palace economies of this period and their demanding soldiery were a major factor in the decline and impoverishment of the countryside. Society was divided between the king's people, who served the king alone and had no particular ties to a town or village, and the citizenry whose livelihoods were based on the land, who acknowledged extended family connections, and whose allegiance was primarily to their family grouping.

However this may be, the kingdom of Mitanni was a formidable world power of the time, but the land around Kirkuk lay far on its fringes. Here illegal diggers in the 1920s discovered tablets at a mound that turned out to be the palace and surrounding town of a small kingdom, called Arrapha, which was loosely a vassal state of Mitanni. The population of this place was largely Hurrian in origin. Subsequent excavations at the site yielded many thousands of palace and private records, the study and publication of which has continued energetically for half a century since. The palace archives were of familiar types, muster lists for military service, for example, but the private ones show a very active local private economy, based on arable land.

Scattered across the landscape were small manors, the family members of which, in theory at least, held land in common and worked undivided shares. In practice, however, typically one family or one aggressive individual, often an eldest son who received a preferential inheritance, gradually took over the land through purchase or through loaning and foreclosure. Certain people amassed considerable estates this way. To circumvent the customary law that land shares could only be sold within extended families, the buyer and seller need only go through a fictive adoption procedure. These documents have shed a brilliant light on several generations of human business activity in this region, making possible many kinds of social, economic, and family studies, and giving rise to several important theories of the structure and functioning of the society and economy of the time. This was largely made possible by the systematic recovery of the documents in large groups found together in preference to the piecemeal appearance of scattered items on the antiquities trade. We are uncertain as to what brought the state of Arrapha to an end. Was it a rising Assyria? Since nothing of the politics of the time is mentioned in the archives of the time, we are only guessing in the dark.

The site of Arrapha, modern Nuzi, was extensively excavated by archaeologists from Harvard University. The numerous archives from this site are nearly completely published and are the basis for a vast scholarly literature.

7. The End of Kassite Rule and the Renewal of Isin

The end of the Kassite dynasty was marked by disaster, ruin, and collapse of the world order. The human race seemed adrift. Populations moved uneasily and destructively from one land to another; new settlements cropped up on the Mediterranean coast. The old palaces and courts where the kings of the age had exchanged gifts with each other were burned and looted. The Kassite royal house disappeared and eventually an Elamite claimant, through the marriage of a Kassite princess to an Elamite ruler, presented himself to the Babylonians, demanding coronation as their king and threatening reprisals if thwarted. This ultimatum the Babylonians rejected with scorn. Elamite troops thereupon invaded the land, destroying and looting some of its most sacred sanctuaries. After four centuries of dynastic stability, Mesopotamia was bleak, wrecked, and a battlefield of outlandish claimants to authority.

On to this scene a new dynasty at Isin arose, the most important ruler of which was Nebuchadnezzar I (not to be confused with Nebuchadnezzar of the Bible, for whom see Chapter 7). Later Babylonian tradition preserves a rich legacy of literature about this man. His first task was to establish a good claim to the Babylonian throne. Like the Isin rulers of a millennium earlier (see Chapter 3), Nebuchadnezzar chose to graft himself onto Sumerian tradition, so he claimed descent from a Sumerian sage who lived long before the Kassites or even the

Amorites had ruled the land. His next important task was to secure safe return of the statue of the Babylonian god Marduk, pillaged by the Elamites and in seemingly hopeless captivity in Elam.

In a surprise maneuver, Nebuchadnezzar invaded Elam in the hot season. Although his men and steeds nearly perished from the heat, he defeated the Elamite army and brought back the precious statue, amidst rejoicing, to Babylon. To the Babylonians, the return of the god to his home meant that all was well in their land again. A lengthy Babylonian poem, known today as the Epic of Creation, tells how Marduk became king of all the gods and reorganized the universe after his victory in battle over Tiamat, the sea. Some scholars think this nationalist composition, which places Babylon at the center of the world and considers it the gods' preferred dwelling place, was commissioned in honor of Marduk's triumphal return.

The site of Isin, including its major sanctuary, a temple to the healing goddess, Gula, has been destroyed by looters, especially after May, 2003.

During the centuries that followed, Babylonia went into decline once again, with perhaps a loss of population, a drop in prosperity, and abandonment of some areas. We know little of conditions in Babylonia for the next four hundred years.

Bibliographical Note to Chapter 4

A concise survey of what is known of the Kassites is J. Brinkman, "Kassiten," *Reallexicon der Assyriologie* (in English). International relations and diplomacy have been studied by Raymond Cohen and Raymond Westbrook, eds., *Amarna Diplomacy: The Beginnings of International Relations* (Baltimore: Johns Hopkins University Press, 2000) and Mario Liverani, *International Relations in the Ancient Near East, 1600–1100 BC* (New York: Palgrave, 2001). Letters from Kassite kings are translated in William L. Moran, *The Amarna Letters* (Baltimore: Johns Hopkins Press, 1992); other Kassite period letters are translated in A. L. Oppenheim, *Letters from Mesopotamia* (Chicago: University of Chicago Press, 1967). For a general study of agricultural life at Arrapha, see Carlo Zaccagnini, *The Rural Landscape of the Land of Arraphe* (Rome: *Quaderni di Geografia Storica* 1: 1979). For Hurrian society in general, there is an expert survey by Gernot Wilhelm, *The Hurrians* (Warminster: Aris and Phillips, 1989).

Translated Excerpts

*Adapted from Sally M. Freedman, *If a City Is Set on a Height* (Philadelphia: Occasional Publications of the Samuel Noah Kramer Fund, 1998), 199.

**Foster, *Before the Muses* (see Bibliographical Note to Chapter 3), 976.

***Foster, *Before the Muses* (see Bibliographical Note to Chapter 3), 397.

****Foster, *Before the Muses* (see Bibliograhical Note to Chapter 3), 400.

Chapter 5

The Assyrian Achievement

1. The Land and Its City

The city Assur sits high on a promontory above a bend in the Tigris. It is a natural fortress and crossroads for travelers following its west bank. The reasons and date for its first settlement are unclear. It lacked, for example, the rich agricultural hinterland of greater cities in northern Mesopotamia, such as Arbela and Nineveh. The name of the city and the name of its god were identical, so the promontory may have been itself an object of worship in remote prehistory; Assur remained a god for the most part without mythology or imagery even in historical times. Yet his name was destined to be the terror of western Asia.

As we recall, Upper Mesopotamia is a broad steppe stretching west from the foothills of the Iranian plateau to the Euphrates valley, thence to the mountain ridges bordering the Mediterranean; north to the foothills of the Anatolian plateau, and south to the alluvium. Besides rivers, the major physical features included Mount Sinjar, a cluster of mountains rising dramatically from the plain in the west. The Sargonic empire and Shamshi-Adad's kingdom in northern Mesopotamia, as well as the state of Mitanni, had shown, time and again, the potential and challenge of this region for the rapid creation of a broad political entity, but little in Assyrian early history hinted at the future destiny of this city.

Rather, in the last few centuries of the third millennium, Assur had been a provincial center, residence of a governor for the kings of Ur, later a compact city state, center of a vigorous international trade. This city state was ruled by a king, who served also as chief priest to the city god, Assur. The city largely depended on commerce for its prosperity.

Assyrian merchants set up colonies as far afield as Cappadocia in Anatolia, with local self-government focused in a chamber of commerce that oversaw legal and administrative matters of the community. Assyrian merchants often lived abroad for decades and carried on an extensive correspondence among themselves and with their families back home. The letters of their wives, many of whom remained in Assur, are the earliest large body of womens' writing from the ancient world.

Assyrian commerce was based on long-term contracts and partnerships, especially with relatives or trusted associates. The basic instrument was a caravan trade, bringing textiles and raw materials, such as tin, to Anatolia from Assyria, and selling them for cash. Tin was the most expensive import from Assyria and was one of the rarest and most valuable metals of the ancient world, a crucial ingredient for converting soft copper to harder bronze. No one knows where or from whom the Assyrians procured tin to bring to Anatolia. In any case, this caravan trade was immensely profitable to the Assyrians. No doubt ambitious rulers like Shamshi-Adad (see Chapter 3) had sought to control or divert this trade to serve their own interests.

Shamshi-Adad was, in fact, the first to introduce the title "king" into Assyria. No doubt he saw himself as heir to the great tradition of Mesopotamian kingship as set forth in an ancient list of kings and dynasties. Shamshi-Adad visited the city Agade, home of the Sargonic kings (see Chapter 2). A copy of the national list of ancient kings of Mesopotamia, called the "Sumerian King List," turned up at his capital, Shubat-Enlil, attesting perhaps to his desire to graft himself onto Mesopotamian royal tradition. Although he himself was no Assyrian, his name, as well as that of his older brother, Aminu, was incorporated into the official sequence of kings of Assur. This, unlike the Sumerian list of Mesopotamian kings, insisted that the only true kingship was that of the kings who ruled the city Assur. The older Sumerian list of kings included dynasties at Kish, Uruk, Ur, Agade, and other cities, but not so the Assyrian king list, which vested kingship in but one city alone, Assur.

Yet for most of the second millennium, the city Assur continued to be a small city state on the outer fringes of greater Mesopotamia. For a while Assur was vassal to the king of Mitanni, whose domains stretched across north Syria and Mesopotamia. But beginning in the fourteenth century B.C.E., a series of successful warrior kings laid the foundations in Assyria for an expansionist state that would soon become a member of the club of great powers.

2. The First Assyrian Empire

Assyrian inscriptions and literature suggest a determined imperialism, as already suggested by the notion of an exclusively Assyrian kingship. Any place outside Assur itself was a potential arena for conquest. In fact, the very coronation oath of the Assyrian kings had them promise to extend the land's dominions. The king was expected to lead his armies on campaign annually. Strategy dictated a secure southern boundary with Babylonia, and preventive and punitive raiding of the mountain peoples to the northeast and north. Thereafter expansion by conquest could reach the prosperous lands of the northwest and west, including the Euphrates Valley, the Balikh and Khabur, and, ultimately, the great natural boundary formed by the big bend of the Euphrates, the crossing of which was a major military and psychological advance. This region was dotted with urban centers ripe for plunder of manufactured goods, raw materials, livestock, and human beings. The going was not easy and there was a natural limit beyond which a seasonal campaign could not expect to go unless forward bases were available. Therefore during the later second millennium Assyrian military and agricultural colonies appeared in forward areas such as the Khabur Valley, where small garrisons remained to cultivate fields and stock supplies for the army. These enabled the Assyrian military machine to reach farther and farther into the west.

Best known of the early Assyrian warrior kings was Tukulti-Ninurta I (1243–1207 B.C.E.), who boasted at great length of his conquests and extensive building projects. He carried Assyrian military power even further west and north, solidified his provincial conquests, and brought home to Assur enormous quantities of booty and tribute. He constructed a major palace for himself in the city, then decided to build a whole new city across the river, called Kar ("port") Tukulti-Ninurta after himself. The strain on his overworked subjects must have been cruel indeed. Unlike his predecessors, Tukulti-Ninurta turned decisively against his ancient neighbor, Babylonia. He invaded the land, occupied the city of Babylon, and declared himself king there.

The Assyrians were justly proud of their ancient culture and political and social traditions, but they were well aware that their literature and scholarship were largely Babylonian in origin, even to the extent of using the Babylonian language, rather than their own Assyrian dialect, in their official inscriptions and other formal expression. Tukulti-Ninurta's attack had therefore religious and cultural repercussions which, according to later Babylonian historical tradition, led to his downfall. Assyrian tradition knows nothing of that; rather, Tukulti-Ninurta ordered that the Babylonian gods be brought to Assyria and that the Babylonian royal archives and scholarly libraries be looted. An erudite but bitter, paranoiac psalm in his name lamented that the world did not appreciate the new order and glory of his dominion. An extensive royal epic commemorated in turgid detail his war with Babylonia. Here Tukulti-Ninurta was a righteous and wronged monarch, the Babylonian king a scoundrel and coward. Their war was a trial at arms before the gods, who ruled in favor of the pious and obedient Assyrian. But Tukulti-Ninurta was imprisoned in his new palace and later murdered by one of his own sons.

Kar Tukulti-Ninurta has been explored by German archaeologists. German archaeologists have also found records of the forward military colonies of this period in the Khabur region of Syria. Early excavations at Assur turned up remains of Tukulti-Ninurta's palace and the fragments of the bilingual psalm. British excavations at Nineveh in 1929–1930 found many fragments of a large tablet which, once pieced together, preserved the epic of Tukulti-Ninurta. These fragments would have been discarded by looters as worthless.

This first Assyrian empire showed the potential and weakness of a major state based in this area. Assyria would always have to come to terms with Babylonia, politically and culturally, though her natural economic and strategic objectives usually lay to the west and northwest, where opportunities for expansion seemed nearly unlimited. Attacking Babylonia, a land which had a recognized northern border, was a serious and unusual measure requiring justification, whereas attacking anywhere else was a god-given, inherent right of the Assyrian king.

The same dark twelfth century that saw the collapse of Babylonia saw too the collapse of Assyria. Many associate these events with attempted invasions of Egypt by "peoples of the sea," and destruction at many urban centers in the Near East, as well as the collapse of the Hittite kingdom in Anatolia. Among other troubles, Assyria was invaded by tribesmen from northern Syria called the Arameans, who, like the Amorites before them, were largely village and nomadic folk. There are reports of famine, disorder, political instability and military weakness. Some see here a repetition of the events that brought the Amorites into Mesopotamia centuries before, and some speak of a regional convulsion, affecting the Mediterranean world as well, for which we have few written sources but a growing archaeological record. Assyria would not reassert herself as a regional power until well into the first millennium B.C.E.

3. The Second Assyrian Empire

During the first millennium B.C.E., although the history of Assyria and Babylonia ran parallel to those of ancient Israel, Egypt, and the Mediterranean world (including Greece and the Phoenicians), those regions lay on the periphery of Mesopotamian political, commercial, and even military concerns and were furthermore of virtually no cultural interest to the bearers of a proud and very ancient civilization. Of far greater impact, especially on Assyria at first, but later on Babylonia as well, was a new indigenous culture that evolved in northern Syria and southern Anatolia at the end of the second and beginning of the first millennium B.C.E. This was multi-lingual, but south of the Taurus and Anti-Taurus ranges Aramaic, a Semitic language related to Babylonian and Assyrian (as well as to Hebrew and later Arabic), was widely used. North of the Taurus, Anatolian languages, some associated with the extinct glory of the Hittite empire, such as Luwian, were still used, at least in inscriptions, but these gradually disappeared. In this region the Assyrians encountered a network of powerful and prosperous fortified urban centers with rich agricultural hinterlands and extensive stock-breeding, united by wide-ranging trade networks, various alliances and coalitions, and a sense of common culture. It was therefore to this region that renascent Assyrian imperial ambition turned, beginning in the mid-ninth century.

As in previous periods, the basis of Assyrian strategy was a secure boundary with Babylonia, pacification of the mountain peoples on the eastern fringes of Assyria, then a strong thrust northwest and west, up the Tigris, across to the Euphrates, and up the Euphrates and her tributaries. The next phase, especially in the eighth century, was to cross the Euphrates and invade northwest Syria, then Lebanon, and eventually Palestine. This typically entailed conquest of the great cities of northern Syria, such as Aleppo and Hama, the lands of Israel and Judah, with their capitals at Samaria and Jerusalem, and the maritime cities of the Levantine coast, such as Tyre and Sidon. To the north and west, conquest would continue into Cilicia, with the establishment of a presence on the Anatolian plateau. By the seventh century, Assyrian conquest extended even to Egypt, with the city Memphis and its riches falling into the hands of Esarhaddon, king of Assyria.

For various reasons, the boundary with Babylonia did not hold, so eighth- and seventh-century Assyrian kings invaded Babylonia and annexed it, one of them, Sennacherib, inflicting severe damage on Babylon itself. The Assyrians faced a complex situation in Babylonia. There were certain cities that deemed loyalty to the Assyrian kings a safe expedient; there were others that seemed continuously in ferment. The Aramean tribes, who had settled in Babylonia in great numbers and largely lived in rural areas, were difficult to subdue and presented no common cause with the cities in whose hinterlands they made their encampments. A new people heard of in the marshlands of the south, called the Chaldeans, not only effectively fought Assyrian domination but presented claimants to the throne of Babylon itself. Drawn into Babylonian affairs, Assyrian rulers reacted in different ways, some coming as conquerors as if they fulfilled some ancient destiny in the land, others coming as destroyers of a hated way of life, others presenting themselves carefully in Babylonian guise. Assyrian intervention in Babylonia increasingly drew her into confrontation with the land of Elam, in southwestern Iran, which tended to back opponents of Assyria and to give them haven, so eventually, in the seventh century, Assyria invaded Elam in force and destroyed it and its ancient culture forever.

No brief essay could dwell on any of these major historical subjects, the details of which are readily available in numerous excellent studies. Rather, what is important here are two main points. First, is the internationalization of Mesopotamia: the horizons of the land have widened to include all of western Asia, including significant areas of Iran, Anatolia, and Egypt. The city state of the third millennium was long extinct. The compact empire of Hammurabi was a significant achievement in its own right but was dwarfed into insignificance by the conquests of Sargon II of Assyria in the eighth century, which took him to lands of which Hammurabi knew little or nothing. Even the nation states of the second half of the second millennium had no realistic expectations of conquering each other, but now, the Assyrian king was reigning in Egypt.

Despite this internationalization, and this is the second main point, Assyria and Babylonia maintained parallel identities; Babylonia was never thoroughly Assyrianized, despite the presence of Assyrian garrisons, administrators, and a class of puppet rulers and informers. If Assyria had the greater military glory for the two and a half centuries between 860 and 612 B.C.E., Babylonia was not only to keep her identity but was to fall heir to the Assyrian conquests in the sixth and fifth centuries. Moreover, the city Babylon was long destined to be one of the largest, most prosperous and cosmopolitan cities on earth, thanks to her central position in the Persian and Hellenistic worlds. So it was then, that even when Assyria was utterly destroyed by the Medes and the last Assyrian king had fled his burning capital, native Mesopotamian tradition had centuries more to live in Babylonia as an international but independent cultural entity. We may choose two Assyrian rulers to symbolize the political aspirations and accomplishments of these centuries, Assurnasirpal II and Sennacherib.

4. Two Assyrian Kings

Assurnasirpal II (883–859 B.C.E.) was a founder of the new imperial order. As a warrior, he was effective and successful, extending Assyrian domains to the west, creating a powerful Assyrian military machine, and laying the foundations for a system of provincial government in certain annexed regions. Some of the annual campaigns were simply marches for booty; others were evidently to add territory to Assyrian dominion. His primary psychological weapon was one of terror, or "calculated frightfulness," as one modern historian described it. This was based on atrocities: mass executions, incinerating defeated civilian populations in bonfires, skinning defeated rulers alive, impaling their heads on stakes, leaving heaps of skulls as an admonishment to survivors. We need hardly be surprised, therefore, that on subsequent marches of this king, neighboring peoples hastened to buy their lives with gifts and tribute. Assurnasirpal describes his atrocities with relish in long detailed accounts, so unlike the more secret atrocities of some modern wars, this was a proudly proclaimed policy.

Assurnasirpal was fascinated by the royal palaces of the prosperous kingdoms of northern Syria he was invading and massacring. These were decorated by setting up slabs of stone in court yards, doorways, and major rooms, some with reliefs and inscriptions carved into them to commemorate the local king's accomplishments. The soft limestone of Assyria was ideally suited for this purpose, as it was easily worked, unlike the heavy volcanic rock of northern Syria, and Assyrian artistic tradition had a wealth of imagery and strategy to draw on to serve the king's need. Heavy stone slabs were therefore cut for the king's palace and carved with outsize, glaring images of Assurnasirpal, his massive muscles daunting the viewer with his ponderous, unopposable strength, surrounded by geniuses, stylized palm trees, and other symbols drawn from Assyrian religious and artistic tradition. The king's names and titles, plus summaries of his deeds, were engraved relentlessly across the face of the reliefs, again and again around the rooms and courts, bombarding the viewer with Assurnasirpal's self-predication to the ages. When freshly painted in bright colors and with the full decorative program intact, Assurnasirpal's new palace at Nimrud in Assyria, away from the old city of Assur, was surely a stunning, even overwhelming boast, to the present and future, of his personal power and cruelty.

Slabs from Assurnasirpal's palace were among the earliest large objects to be brought from Iraq to Europe and the United States, beginning in the 1840s; see Chapter 14. Individual examples are to be found in many museums. Numerous more were looted from Iraqi storerooms during the Iraq war, sawed into smaller pieces, and sold to antiquities collectors. The site itself was also damaged by looters.

The Assyrian king Sennacherib (ruled 705–681 B.C.E.) was born into the court of the Assyrian empire at a moment of its greatest glory. His father, Sargon, had dared to take the name of the great Sargon of the past, Sargon of Akkad (see Chapter 2), the first monarch to do so in more than a thousand years. He seemed destined to live up to this name, as he was the type of the warrior king, whenever possible marching on the frontiers of his far-flung empire, even vanquisher of the powerful kingdom of Urartu, a state which had emerged in the rugged intermontaine valleys of present-day Armenia, a remote and difficult objective for an Assyrian force. Following the example of Assurnasirpal and others, this vainglorious man envisioned an entirely new capital city built in his name, not far from the ancient city of Nineveh. On this site, now called Khorsabad, sprang up walls and monumental gates, temples, a palace complex and residential quarters. The king's correspondence shows how eagerly, amidst the pressure of the many campaigns and administrative tasks that confronted him, he followed the progress of the work, as reports arrived of construction quotas met.

Despite his successes on the fringes of his empire, Sargon had considerable difficulty controlling Babylonia successfully. Although it seems that he himself was an admirer of Babylonian culture and saw himself as fulfilling a very ancient Babylonian imperial tradition, there were many opponents to Assyrian rule, both in the cities and the countryside, men like the swamp fox, the Chaldean king Merodach-Baladan, who, from the marshes, pressed his own claim to the throne of Babylon, which

Sargon held proudly in his grip. The Chaldeans were a people who had settled in southernmost Babylonia, especially in the marsh regions, but who soon created a vibrant urban civilization there, difficult of access from the outside.

In this atmosphere of general triumph but some frustration in the south, young Sennacherib grew up. At the height of his power and achievement, Sargon was killed by a barbarian force, far from Assyria. So total was the rout that not even the king's corpse could be recovered for proper burial with his ancestors. Thus Sennacherib succeeded to the throne in a period of gloom, foreboding, and questioning: what had his father done wrong to receive such a disgraceful fate from the gods?

Sargon's city, Dur-Sharrukin, modern Khorsabad, was the first site in Iraq explored by archaeologists. It was extensively excavated by the French, 1843-1844, 1852-1854. Many of their finds were lost when the rafts carrying them downstream for shipment to France foundered. An important collection of reliefs, statuary, and many other objects from the finds are among the major exhibits in the Louvre today. Further excavations were carried out by the Oriental Institute of the University of Chicago, 1929-1935. Gigantic statues of winged bulls from Khorsabad are among the most impressive exhibits in the Oriental Institute Museum and in the Mesopotamian galleries of the Louvre. An Iraqi team cleared a temple at the site in 1957.

Sennacherib proved himself capable of meeting the enormous challenge presented to him. The demoralized and defeated Assyrian army was regrouped and made ready for a series of campaigns abroad, the best remembered of which today was a siege of Jerusalem in 705. Sennacherib abandoned his father's city, perhaps as a place of ill omen. By inclination an engineer, Sennacherib visualized not a new capital city, as had his father, but a magnificent palace the likes of which the world had never seen, to be built at one of the traditional Assyrian cities, Nineveh. While on campaign, he prospected for superior and innovative building stone to incorporate in this structure. His commemorative reliefs show swarms of men hauling gargantuan blocks and statues, with careful attention to the design of the sledges, the straining ropes, the flotation devices to bring them by water, and the triumph of putting them in place. Sennacherib expounds on his active interest in an experimental procedure for casting a huge metal statue, using the technical language of metallurgy. He tells us of a mysterious stone shaft he sank in the ground, and his aqueducts and waterworks have no parallels until the Roman period.

Finally, his "Palace without Rival," a microcosm of the world he ruled, was surrounded by a park set in exotic trees and shrubs, providing authentic habitats for exotic beasts and birds that bred there and raised their young, amidst artificial streams and marshes, grass and woodlands, the whole visible from pavilions at strategic intervals. He even seems to have constructed a mountain landscape watered by ingenious hydraulics that raised the water high enough from the plain of Nineveh to serve as mountain streams. He may further have experimented with the type of garden, seen from above and viewed as a living carpet, popular in the Islamic world and elsewhere, perhaps the original "hanging garden" that inspired one of the Seven Wonders of the ancient world.

No doubt Sennacherib planned his government and succession with the same flair and attention to detail. His eldest son, Assur-nadin-shumi, was groomed to succeed him by being given the sensitive role of king of Babylon, replacing various unsatisfactory and unreliable puppets that Sennacherib had tried before. This was no doubt a serious trial for the young man who, if he could meet the challenge, was ready for kingship at his father's death. Fate decreed otherwise, as the prince was deposed in a rebellion, with connivance of the Elamites, and was carried off to die in miserable captivity in Elam, beyond Sennacherib's reach. The bereaved monarch turned his fury upon the city Babylon. He tells us he destroyed the place so utterly that its site could hardly be identified, that he spared no one, man, woman, or child; that he carried off its dirt to Assur, perhaps to trample under his feet in a transplanted new year's festival there; that the debris he dumped in the river courses flowed far out into the sea to the awe of far-off island peoples. This was his violent solution to the problem of a restive province.

The death of his chosen successor raised the issue of which of his other sons was to succeed him to the throne of Assyria. Conspiracy and competition were in the air. Sennacherib himself fell victim to it, murdered by one of his own sons. To a Babylonian historian, this was a judgment, the same that had fallen upon Tukulti-Ninurta I (see Chapter 5), another enemy of Babylon.

The ruins of the great palace of Sennacherib at Nineveh were explored by British archaeologists in the nineteenth century, and much of its surviving decoration was brought back to the British Museum, where it is on display in the Assyrian galleries. The site was further explored by Iraqi archaeologists, and efforts made to preserve surviving parts of it. Statuary and reliefs from the site were put on display in the Iraq Museum in Baghdad. The site was damaged by looters in April 2003 and protective structures were stolen. Sennacherib reliefs still preserved in their original rooms were damaged or removed. Although American troops were camped only a few hundred meters away, they did not interfere with the looting. The Mosul Museum, where numerous Assyrian reliefs and other objects were housed, was also attacked by looters in April, 2003. A magnificent gate of the ninth century B.C.E., decorated with relief panels, was torn down and cut into pieces to sell on the antiquities market. The storerooms and offices were vandalized and many objects stolen or smashed.

5. Assyrian Culture of the First Millennium B.C.E.

The violence and cruelty that supposedly civilized states are capable of to enforce their policies and ambitions formed the subject of a long Babylonian narrative poem, drafted perhaps three generations or more before Sennacherib's time. How, in a world controlled by self-interested and all-powerful gods, could violence overtake the very cities that sustained them and their earthly homes, the great temples of the land? How could the city Babylon, center of the universe, the chosen dwelling of the god Marduk, built with the very labor of the gods, be given over to violence, plunder, and destruction? The poet, Kabti-ilani-Marduk, evolved at once a passionate portrayal and a complex theology of violence: the god of violent behavior, Erra, grows bored and discontented if he has no outlet for his horrible energies. At some pretext, however flimsy, fighting begins but grows quickly out of control, drunk on its own sacrifice of blood. The god of violence, Erra, boasts of his manic powers:

I will tear out the mooring pole so the ship drifts away,
I will smash the rudder so she cannot reach the shore,
I will pluck out the mast, I will rip out the rigging.
I will make breasts go dry so babies cannot thrive,
I will block up springs so the tiniest channels can
 bring no life-sustaining water.
I will make hell shake and heaven tremble,
I will make the planets shed their splendor,
I will wrench out the stars from the sky! *

This is but one monument of the rich and varied literature of the period, which includes narrative, devotional, and scholarly compositions, humor and satire, laments, love songs, in short, every form and style that tradition, imagination, and endeavor could command. An excerpt on untimely death in childbirth may suffice to show the range:

The day I carried the fruit, how happy I was,
Happy was I, happy my husband.
The day I went into labor, my face grew overcast,
The day I gave birth, my eyes grew cloudy ...
My husband, who loved me, uttered a cry,
"Do not forsake me, the wife I adore!" ...
All those days I was with my husband,
While I lived with him who was my lover,
Death was creeping stealthily into my bedroom.
It forced me from my house,
It cut me off from my lover,
*It set my feet toward the land from which I shall not return.***

Of Assyrian technology we have ample evidence. Mesopotamia had long been the center of pyrotechnology, centering both on the production of metals and the manufacture of artificial substances, such as faience and glass. The Assyrians were much interested in these arts, and produced elegant specialty glass, including a type known as "Assyrian red." Another esteemed industry was the art of perfumery: production of aromatic substances for a wide range of purposes. Scholars copied out recipes for these products as part of their encyclopedic training, but these were not really practical manuals for arts taught by example and apprenticeship, so we cannot reproduce any of them successfully. Assyria developed a taste for ivory work, including carving of individual ivory pieces and the incorporation of ivory into boxes and pieces of furniture (see Chapter 15). Perhaps the most celebrated piece of early glass from Assyria is the so-called Layard lens, an expertly ground glass eye lens, evidently to correct astigmatism, found in the royal palace at Nineveh in the nineteenth century and now in the British Museum.

6. The Fall of Assyria

A peculiar but fateful aspect of the internationalization of this period was the Assyrian practice of deporting large populations from one area of the empire to another. Mountain people were marched to the plains; villagers and townsmen were forced to forsake their homes and begin a long, sad march to some land they had never seen. By this means, the plentiful, Aramaic-speaking population of northern Syria found its way to new settlements in Assyria and Babylonia, even Iran. It is not clear if the purpose of this policy was economic development of underpopulated regions, for security, or a combination of these, but the result was the creation of a polyglot population in Mesopotamia drawn from the peoples of many lands, among whom Aramaic was the most widely spoken and understood idiom. This laid the groundwork for its role as the great world language of the Persian Empire and as a primary language of Judaism and Christianity.

The same fate awaited Assyria that she had dealt so harshly to so many other lands. During the eighth and seventh centuries, an Iranian people called the Medes had formed a state over the western half of the Iranian plateau. Their power seemed invincible as their archery and cavalry were more than a match for the less mobile Assyrian infantry and chariotry. Nor were the massive fortifications of the Assyrian cities proof against their siegecraft, which they had learned among the stone-built fastnesses of the highlands and mountains. The great prizes that lay before them were the Assyrian cities of Assur, Nineveh, Nimrud, and Arbela. These fell, one by one, not without desperate resistance, as shown by recent American and Iraqi excavations at Nineveh, which found the remains of defenders. The cities were given over to such a thorough slaughter, destruction, and plundering that nothing remained thereafter of Assyrian might and culture. As late as the Christian era, a few families in Parthian Assur kept at least a semblance of Assyrian names, but this only illustrates that scarcely a shadow of the past remained in a land that was largely underpopulated and impoverished.

Bibliographical Note to Chapter 5

For a comprehensive survey of Assyrian history and culture in English, H. W. F. Saggs, *The Might That Was Assyria* (London: Sidgwick & Jackson, 1984) may be recommended; more detailed presentations are in the *Cambridge Ancient History*, third edition. Orientation in current directions of research on Assyria can be found in S. Parpola and R. M. Whiting, eds., *Assyria 1995, Proceedings of the 10th Anniversary Symposium of the Neo-Assyrian Text Corpus Project, Helsinki, September 7–11, 1995* (Helsinki: The Neo-Assyrian Text Corpus Project, 1997). Readers interested in more information on Sennacherib's palace should consult John M. Russell, *Sennacherib's Palace Without Rival at Nineveh* (Chicago: University of Chicago Press, 1991). The same author has produced a comprehensive study of Assyrian palaces of the first millennium B.C.E.: *The Writing on the Wall, Studies in the Architectural Context of Late Assyrian Palace Inscriptions* (Winona Lake, Ind.: Eisenbrauns, 1999). For the gardens of Nineveh, the fullest study is Karen Polinger Foster, "The Hanging Gardens of Nineveh," *Iraq* 66 (2004), 207–220.

Translated Excerpts

*Foster, *Before the Muses* (see Bibliographical Note to Chapter 3), 907.
**Foster, *Before the Muses* (see Bibliographical Note to Chapter 3), 949.

Chapter 6

Babylon and Her Empire

1. The Land and Its City

The Medes did not follow up on their destruction of Assyria by invading Babylonia. Indeed, the Babylonian king, Nabonassar, had marched as an ally to the Medes and met for a moment of friendship and victory with Cyaxares, king of the Medes, in the field. To Nabonassar and his energetic son, Nebuchadnezzar, fell the task of forming a Babylonian empire on the ruins of the Assyrian, and this they set to with a will. The last remnants of Assyrian resistance in the west were quelled; an Egyptian force that came to their aid was annihilated. At Nabonassar's death, Nebuchadnezzar could look out over a dominion stretching from the Gulf to the borders of Egypt, secure in his alliance with the Medes, with no significant power to oppose him. When the city of Jerusalem revolted against him in 587 B.C.E., Nebuchadnezzar dealt out harsh punishment. The city was besieged. When it fell, the rebel king, Zedekiah, was forced to witness the execution of his sons, then was blinded, so he could retain this last image, before being led off into captivity in Babylon, along with many leading citizens of Judah. Thus began the long history of Jewish culture in Iraq, which continued well into the twentieth century.

Although Sennacherib boasted that he had ruined Babylon beyond recognition, now Assur was in ruins and Babylon was the greatest city of the age, enjoying a peace and prosperity she had not known for centuries. The great temples, including the temple of the national god, Marduk, were lavishly refurbished. The royal palace dominated the north end of the city, the great walls enclosed myriad dwellings and lesser temples. Many citizens owned strips of land and orchards outside the city, whence they drew income from their harvest. In the center of the city, a grand boulevard, the processional way, brilliantly decorated, was the avenue by which the god Marduk returned triumphant to his temple, amidst the rejoicing of his citizens, during the New Year festival.

The city of Babylon was heavily looted by local people in the nineteenth century for its baked bricks. European travelers expressed their dismay at the damage being done. The prospectors for bricks were happy to sell cuneiform tablets and other objects to dealers, once they understood their value, though countless were lost. A German excavation made a thorough exploration of the ruins in a series of excavations from 1899 to 1914. Iraqi archaeologists also did work at the site, beginning in the late 1950s, and rebuilt parts of the city. In 1987 and 1989, a joint Iraqi-Italian team excavated in a residential quarter. Beginning in 1978, Saddam Hussein ordered extensive reconstruction at the site, including rebuilding gates and walls, the Greek theater, the ziggurat, and a temple to Ishtar, plus an elaborate museum complex. He also built a palace for himself, as well as a series of lakes and channels in the area. During the Iraq war, American and Polish forces occupied the site. Soldiers drove heavy vehicles through the processional way, defaced monuments, and bulldozed parking lots, helipads, and other installations in the ruins. Archaeological material was excavated and dumped; outside materials, such as gravel, were brought in and spread on the site. See also Chapter 14.

Perhaps the most famous description of Babylon at this time was written by the Greek historian, Herodotus. He was interested in the history of Assyria and Babylonia as forerunners to the Persian Empire, and claims to have visited Babylon. He tells us, for example, that the walls were thick enough for chariot teams to drive on, and that every Babylonian woman had to prostitute herself once in her lifetime. Whether or not he actually visited the city, we can be sure that he knew next to nothing of Babylonian history and civilization, and that his celebrated story of prostitution is rubbish.

At this period the great temples at cities like Babylon and Uruk would have been dominated the landscape with their temple towers, vast temple enclosures, and extensive gardens. We know something of their affairs because at Uruk and Sippar thousands of documents were discovered that record administrative activities and correspondence of these great temples over many decades. These included management of agriculture, orchards, handicrafts, and livestock. They also contained the records of deliberations of temple officials, including trials of people on criminal charges, such as theft, assault, and matters of morals. The official correspondence of the high temple officials dealt with administrative matters and with such topics as the celebration of festivals in the temple or in outlying sanctuaries, some of which depended on the great temples for supplies and ritual materials.

Under the Babylonian kings, the palace took an increasingly active role in management of the great temples of Babylonia. A royal officer was placed on the temple staff to oversee crown interests and the top temple administrators were royal appointees. Although the great temples like the temple of Ishtar of Uruk were rich in land, orchards, and livestock, they did not have sufficient personnel to manage all these resources, so had to resort to renting out property to individuals in return for a share of the harvest. This worked well because only limited forced labor was available; the teams of temple workers were hard to control, not eager to work, and sometimes mutinous. The Babylonian kings, however, developed a practice of leasing vast areas of temple lands to private contractors.

At Nebuchadnezzar's death, the succession did not follow in an orderly manner. Like many powerful monarchs, he seems at various times to have entertained deep suspicions of his princes; one, who claims that he had been among his father's favorites, was, by his own account, jailed by his father because of untrue rumors fanned by his enemies against him:

> *He who manipulated me to benefit himself and to harm me, impose upon him a heavy punishment! O Marduk, be you the one to harm him! Single out for harm the one who stirred up harmful talk of me! O Marduk, the artful devices of humankind, who can thwart them but you?* *

He tells us that he was released from prison through divine intervention. We know that he ruled a short time under the name of Awil-Marduk (biblical Evil-Merodach) but was assassinated.

Eventually a military strong man by the name of Neriglissar took over. He had had a distinguished career as a field officer but may not have been so effective as a ruler. Family favoritism seems to have dominated to the point of impropriety, property was confiscated, corruption and greed may have cast a long shadow over his times. Under circumstances no one can explain, the throne passed to a man named Nabonidus, who was not of royal birth though his family was evidently at court. His redoubtable old mother, a priestess of the moon-god, who lived to be nearly a hundred years of age, tells us in her funerary inscription that she had lived through the reigns of seven Assyrian and Babylonian monarchs and still had excellent eyesight, hearing, and appetite.

Nabonidus has left a vivid impression on Mesopotamian history because of his eccentric religious views and the strong passions he inspired among his subjects. His enemies denounced him as insane, whence the legend of the mad Babylonian king of Jewish tradition, wrongly associated with his more famous predecessor, Nebuchadnezzar. It is clear that Nabonidus was eager to promote the cult of the moon-god over that of other Mesopotamian deities, and he took an increasingly hard line as resistance grew. He had special stone steles made, perhaps for placement in various temples. In a series of long, personal, and sometimes rambling prayers and inscriptions, he tried to explain his views, as in this pointed prayer to the moon-god:

> *The land you have resolved to make your dwelling, you will establish therein reverence for your great divinity for all time to come. The land you have resolved to shatter, you will remove reverence for you therefrom and you will overthrow it for all time to come.***

Even more extraordinary, Nabonidus moved his court for seven years to inner Arabia, to a place called Teima, which was an important caravan station and had a sanctuary to the moon-god. No one knows why he did this. Some consider this the act of a religious fanatic rusticating himself; others see a prescient vision of international affairs. If the Babylonian empire was to survive in the face of the great powers, such as the Medes, looking down upon it, as it were, from the uplands, the empire would need a second, more secure line of communication with the west, this one across the desert. This crossing was not easy, but could be done by camels, and preceding rulers had been surprised and impressed by the wealth they found when they invaded Arab territory. Nabonidus built a palace and enclosure at Teima and left his son, Belshazzer, to rule at Babylon as his viceroy. Belshazzer was not so imbued with the cult of the moon-god as his father, and seems to have acted with rather too free a hand during his father's prolonged absence. Belshazzer is mentioned in the Bible in the story of his feast, during which the mysterious writing appeared on the wall. In any case, Nabonidus suddenly returned and carried out a thorough shake-up of the Babylonian court.

The ruins of Nabonidus' palace at Teima were still clearly visible in the 1970s, but threatened by suburban development in the area, including a shopping center.

2. Babylonian Economy and Society

A tendency to allow close associates to take advantage of what would now be called government contracts expanded under Nabonidus's reign. A group of speculators contracted to manage all the arable land of the great temple at Uruk, for example, and even when it became clear that they were far from meeting the terms of their contract, the king insisted that they be left unmolested. Perhaps the temple officialdom had unrealistic expectations as to what the temple should receive from its resources, but it is clear that the results were not satisfactory and that the contractors were driven to embezzlement and default by the arrangement, as can be followed from the temple records. The original temple archive of Uruk, for example, may have consisted of several million clay tablets and wooden writing boards.

In the years before World War I, looters recovered many thousands of temple records from Uruk. Most of them were sold to the Yale Babylonian Collection, with important subgroups in Paris and the British Museum. British archaeologists discovered thousands of temple records at Sippar in the nineteenth century; study of this material has begun only in recent years.

Educated Babylonians at this time were well aware of the great antiquity of their civilization, by then more than three thousand years old, though they would not have used such a figure. An interest in ancient history flourished in professional circles, including a new style of chronographic history writing. This was focused on recent and current events, in which they were listed in the order they occurred (battles, deaths and accessions of kings, happenings of cultic interest), but was also extended to the remote past, so that chronicles of such long-ago kings as Sargon of Akkad were produced, such as the following excerpt:

> *Sargon, king of Akkad, arose during the reign of Ishtar. He had neither rival nor opponent, his fame spread over all lands, he crossed the sea in the East. In the eleventh year, he conquered the country of the West up to its farthest boundary and placed it under his sole authority, had his statues erected there and booty ferried across on barges. He made his courtiers dwell at a distance of every five leagues and governed the community of his countries as one.****

Nabonidus tells in an inscription that he restored a statue of Sargon discovered when a temple was being repaired, and insists in various places that he was restoring ancient rites and sanctuaries just as they had been in the remote past. He went so far as to revive the practice, first known under Sargon, of appointing a daughter high priestess of the moon-god, an office that had lapsed for centuries. He carried out excavations at the ancient Sargonic capital Agade. Collections of antiquities were formed. Scholars studied, copied, and displayed their decipherments of very old inscriptions. The official language of prayers and inscriptions became steeped in what were deemed old-fashioned or archaic expressions and were drawn up using archaizing spelling.

The literate person was supposed to have some knowledge of the ancient Sumerian language, so high literary expression could be salted with Sumerian loanwords. At the same time, Babylonian remained a supple and expressive idiom, in everyday life increasingly influenced by Aramaic, which was probably much more widely spoken than Babylonian in the land. Indeed, Babylonian may have become more of a formal language learned in school, as with Modern Standard Arabic today in Iraq, whereas Aramaic was generally spoken, like Iraqi colloquial dialect. Although legal documents were drawn up in Babylonian, some were docketed in Aramaic, which used a simple alphabet, to save having to read the cuneiform, which took years to master. Educated people wrote in Babylonian, had read major works of Babylonian literature, and honored the scholarly achievements of the past.

This education was often achieved through family training: certain families were repositories of scholarly, religious, and literary tradition and trained their descendants in what they knew. The sons, having achieved a certain competence, demonstrated it by making fair copies of the family collection of tablets to show their expertise, perhaps also in deference to the scholastic principle that for learning, writing is twice as effective as reading. Families had specialties. Some were diviners, whose scholarship was to evaluate data presented to them and to prognosticate from them, as well as, in some cases, to advise ways of averting portended harm. Some had mastered the long laments in Sumerian dialect that were sung in the major sanctuaries to appease the hearts of the gods. Scholarship naturally gravitated towards centers of wealth and power, where patronage and employment could be found. A small and highly trained guild was adept at mathematical and observational astronomy, compiling neatly written astronomical diaries at a center for astronomy at Babylon, in addition to the almanacs, astrolabes, and astrology known from the great libraries of the land. There may have been other such centers, such as at Uruk.

Much information has come down to us on Babylonian family life of this period, particularly among the wealthier classes, as these people have left us archives of their business affairs, records of their marriages and divorces, their suits at law, and their contracts. We know less about wealth in specie than we do about land, as prominent families built up patrimonies of fine homes in the city and gardens and orchards along the great canals at the outskirts. Since Babylonian inheritance practice dictated division of a parental estate, this often meant that succeeding generations had to work to reunite divided parcels or agree among themselves not to divide them. From dowries and inventories we see that a wealthy Babylonian enjoyed a good standard of living, with fine furniture (beds, chairs, chests, tables), textiles such as carpets and hangings, and sets of metal cooking utensils. Women treasured jewelry and expensive cosmetics and clothing. The better homes had domestic slaves, sometimes half a dozen or more. Only in this period of Mesopotamian history does slavery achieve some prominence, and then only in domestic capacities. Some slaves were domestic servants, others acted as business agents and confidential clerks and accumulated property of their own. Slaves could marry and have children of their own; slave women not uncommonly bore children to their owners, who would sometimes be of disputable status versus the children of free mothers. Although, in principle, marriage tended to be monogamous, concubinage could also be practiced among the wealthy, and there was no legal bar to bringing a second wife into the household. Divorced women and widows, as well as single women without dominating male relatives, enjoyed considerable social, legal, and economic freedom.

This was the world that Herodotus claims to have visited; if he spoke traveler's Aramaic, he could have communicated with Babylonians in public places, though Babylonian wisdom literature insists that it is bad to talk to strangers in the street. How he could have met priests or scholars we do not know and we may freely doubt that he did so. Herodotus's book was a best-seller in antiquity and remained the principal source for Babylonian history, manners, and customs until the decipherment of cuneiform writing in the nineteenth century.

3. Babylon and the World

Babylon was a truly cosmopolitan place in the sixth century B.C.E., for in her streets people of all lands carried on their business. Babylon was ideally situated for commerce, with easy access to the routes leading to the Gulf, thence to any place the sea trade could reach. Upriver, the traditional routes to the Mediterranean went along the rivers as always, and there was also the desert route west to the oasis of Palmyra, though how much this was in use is unknown. Desert routes led south into Arabia, no doubt linking indirectly by caravan with the urban and agrarian cultures of south Arabia, and perhaps west across the desert to Teima and from there to western Arabia, which also had caravan links north-south and east-west. Egypt could be reached either by crossing Arabia, to link with caravan and sea routes, or by the long route around to the Mediterranean, thence by land or sea. Egyptians were present in Babylonia, so we may assume that Babylonian merchants found their way to Egypt or at least had connections there. Certain families played a substantial role in international trade, dealing in such commodities as lumber, precious stones, metals, and textiles, though this is an aspect of Babylonian economy about which we are still poorly informed. We know, for example, that iron was in common use in Mesopotamia for tools, chains, weapons, and the like, but we do not know how iron was obtained or in what form.

Although Babylonians drew up maps of the world and speculated as to its shape and the distances between its different features, no Babylonian did what Herodotus did by making a journey and writing of the history and customs of foreign lands. No Babylonian wrote a description of a foreign landscape or people. So preoccupied were Babylonians with their own culture and their own affairs that it was sufficient for them to master the demands of their own world and pointless to inquire into those of another. Perhaps on a philosophical level they saw the world as unitary, with Babylonia at the center and all other peoples languishing in the periphery, though as soldiers, merchants, and businessmen they knew otherwise. Perhaps we err by seeing them through the dark glass of their elitist cuneiform written tradition; had we access to the rich, international Aramaic culture of this period we might have a broader and clearer perspective on what this dynamic and prosperous world was really like. Though grateful for the wealth of sources we have, unique for their time in quantity, variety, and distribution in time and space, the historian must remind himself to look beyond the brilliant illumination of his documentary surroundings towards areas still dark and unexplored. Of the lives of people beyond the reach of cuneiform writing we know next to nothing.

4. The Persian Empire

Word no doubt reached the Babylonian court of unexpected developments in far-away Media. A certain Cyrus the Persian, who had been a governor for the Medes in Parsua, a new name for the ancient land of Elam, had ousted his overlords and embarked on a series of military campaigns that placed under his control regions of which the Babylonians had scarcely or never heard. Nothing could stand in his way, as land after land fell before his forces. It was only a matter of time before the Persian armies appeared in Mesopotamia, marching down the Tigris in the spring of 539 B.C.E. The Babylonian army was routed and an advance Persian force entered Babylon. A few days later Cyrus himself arrived, according to his own account, to the acclamation of the populace, but this claim need not be taken seriously. As it proved, Cyrus was a humane and enlightened ruler by the standards of ancient conquerors, and Babylonia entered a new and vital phase of her existence.

The Persian Empire at its height stretched from Egypt to Central Asia, by far the most successful political experiment of its kind in antiquity. It was bound together by a rule of law, within which local laws could still be applied in their own fashion by local authorities. There was no interference with local religious or other institutions, no attempt to impose the Persian language. Rather, it was the destiny of Aramaic to become the principal common spoken tongue of this vast dominion, the language in which even the Persian nobility expected to communicate with the stewards of their far-flung estates. The empire was bound together by excellent road and post systems, carved up into satrapies or provinces, of which Babylonia was perhaps the wealthiest.

The provinces were ruled by Persian noblemen drawn from several great families and often related to the royal house. The basis of their power was the enormous Persian military, sustained in Babylonia by small grants of land, the holders of which were obliged to provide an armed soldier to the royal forces or to go themselves, a substitute being readily hired. The extensive Babylonian royal and temple domains passed into the control of the Persian crown and nobility. A file copy survives of a respectful and well-turned letter addressed to Darius, king of the Persians, by the officials of the temple of Ishtar at Uruk:

> *To the king of the world, our master, thus say your servants Amurru-dan, Kudurru, and Marduk-shakin-shumi: May Uruk and the Eanna-temple bless the king of the world! Every day, at opening the doors and closing the doors, we pray to Our Lady of Uruk and to the goddess Nanaya for a life long of days, health, happiness, stability of reign, and the downfall of the foes of the king of the world, our master. All is well with the administration of the Eanna-temple, the abode of your gods. We have begun the shearing in the abode of your gods. We have been praying constantly before Our Lady of Uruk and the goddess Nanaya for the king of the world, saying, "May this be the first of a thousand shearings at the pleasure of the king of the world, our master!"* ****

Important irrigation projects were begun for the further reclamation of arable land; the population increased and we have the sense that under the early Persian kings Babylonia continued to develop as she had under the last Babylonian kings, but with a much wider scope and an even more brilliant prosperity.

Babylonia was, after all, situated in the heart of the Persian empire and Babylon was a seat of Persian royalty. The city was dominated by a Persian fortress that served as the seat of the governor. There was indeed no place on earth better in a position to seize the initiative in international commerce. Although the tribute paid to the Persian court was a heavy burden, we have a sense that Babylonia profited from her commercial advantages, improved her agricultural base, and initially benefited in many ways from Persian rule. Some enterprising Babylonians sensed opportunity in the feudal organization of the countryside. They proposed to Persian fief holders that they sell the harvest rights on their fiefs for cash in advance; the business firm would arrange for the harvest and market it for its own profit. No doubt this left the producing peasant just as much at the mercy of speculators as he had been at the mercy of some distant Persian nobleman, and we may surmise that a large class of peasantry may gradually have begun to sink into debt and a kind of economic servitude from which there was no escape. Interest rates soared to 40–50%. The misery and burden of this large class of people were the dark foundation for the glittering superstructure of Achaemenid society, with its love of poetry, beautiful gardens, and knightly values. The very idea of nobility was foreign to Babylonia, which had always recognized the importance of certain families but had no notion that by the accident of birth a small percentage of the population was entitled to rule and enjoy a way of life inaccessible to others, whatever their achievements.

The Persian royal princes were ambitious and competitive and often had substantial forces at their disposal, so the Persian throne was by no means as stable as the extent of its dominions would call for. So too there were local rebellions, led by men desirous of removing the Persian overlords from their land. In Babylonia itself, a series of rebellions raised to prominence patriots who took the name of Nebuchadnezzar, so were perhaps trying to re-establish the Babylonian empire of some generations before. Under the later Persian rulers, such as Xerxes, conditions in Babylonia took a turn therefore for the worse. Persian armies suppressed the rebellions with severe reprisals and looting; the great temples were of course tempting targets and some of them probably sustained heavy damage at this time, possibly total destruction. We think that the gains under the early Achaemenids were lost under the later, as the land fell victim to rapacious factionalism.

As for Assyria, it remained one of the poorest provinces of the Persian empire, sparsely populated, with few important cities. So thorough had been the destruction by the Medes that nothing resembling the former Assyrian economy and agricultural regime seems to have reasserted itself.

Reading the literature studied by Babylonians in this period, one wonders what might have been the cultural impact of the new world of Persian rule on Babylonian civilization. In subsequent ages we will see that Iran exercises a strong cultural attraction on the lands and peoples around her, and in due season, the cultures of Iraq will be closely bound to those of Iran. This was an opportunity Mesopotamia had never enjoyed before: unfettered access as far east as the foothills of the Hindu Kush or the Indus Valley, for example. Yet we see nothing of this in Babylonian literature of the period. In daily life, some Persian words and technical terms creep into official parlance, and if we knew what buildings or the visual arts looked like in Achaemenid Babylon, we might see some Persian influences. But the age and durability of Babylonian literate culture may well have kept it isolated from important foreign influence. Babylonian historians noted, of course, the transitions of the Persian kings. An arcane literature of protest may have circulated among literati in which Elamite invasions of the time before Nebuchadnezzar I (late twelfth century B.C.E., see Chapter 4) were understood as foreshadowing the Persian invasion of Mesopotamia in the sixth century; the message was, of course, that a new Nebuchadnezzar might be expected to deliver the Babylonians from the Persians. That could be an additional reason that rebels chose the name Nebuchadnezzar: both of the former kings of that name were, in a sense, deliverers of Babylonia from "Iranian" rule.

The Jewish community of Babylonia went through an important transition in the early Persian period. Cyrus allowed the exiled Jews to return to their homeland from Babylonia, so some went and some stayed. The returning exiles under Ezra set about recreating a Jewish state; the Jews who remained in Babylonia continued their way of life, which was primarily based on small agricultural settlements, perhaps not much above subsistence level for most. On the other hand, a rich Jewish literature of this period centers more on urban life and adventures at court than on the village, but some of this may be the license of storytelling. Josephus, a Jewish writer of the Roman period, tells us that the Jews were an agricultural people without interest in the trade and traffic of the human race. Possible interplay between Late Babylonian culture and Judaism has scarcely been explored, though there are tantalizing hints that they shared a common medical tradition, for example, and Aramaic stories were the property of everyone. Thus the Jewish community in far-away Egypt told of a Mesopotamian wise man, Ahiqar, at the Assyrian court, long ago.

The Persian empire gave Western Asia and the Eastern Mediterranean a cultural and political commonwealth that it had never known. It showed that world rule by a great king was possible and could endure. For citizens of a poor and warring land, like Greece, the Persian empire offered unlimited opportunity for the ambitious, be it as a mercenary soldier or as a physician. Greeks were fascinated by the history of Persia as a kind of Arabian Nights land that had swallowed up the other great states of the past. Greek readers enjoyed accounts focusing on the wealth, love of luxury, and venality of the Persians, and on the endless court intrigues and succession struggles that plagued the royal house, a kind of royal decadent theater for Greece, which had no royal scandal worthy of the name to amuse itself with. Books purporting to describe conditions "inside Persia today" were popular reading. The shadow of Herodotus lay over any such enterprise, so the usual options were open to his successors and imitators: to say he was wrong, and that now the true facts can be told, or, to go him one better with even more outrageous and absurd stories about Persian decadence. The Greeks were not a nation of language learners, so no Greek read a Persian book about their history or religion and passed on what he had read in Greek. The near total disappearance of Achaemenid Persian written tradition leaves us only her enemies, detractors, and subjects to speak for the extraordinary achievements of the Persian empire, of which Babylonia was for long the jewel in the crown.

Bibliographical Note to Chapter 6

For Babylonian civilization in the first millennium, the following studies may be recommended: Joan Oates, *Babylon* (London: Thames and Hudson, 1979) and D. J. Wiseman, *Nebuchadrezzar and Babylon* (Oxford: Oxford University Press, 1985). Two more general works that are most useful for the later periods are Karen Nemet-Nejat, *Daily Life in Ancient Mesopotamia* (Peabody, Mass: Henrickson, 2002) and H. W. F. Saggs, *The Greatness that was Babylon* (New York: Mentor Books, 1968). For the Persian empire, the best source is Pierre Briant, *From Cyrus to Alexander: A History of the Persian Empire* (Winona Lake, Ind.: Eisenbrauns, 2002), though this does not give much specific information on Mesopotamia. For that, there is an excellent survey by Amélie Kuhrt in the *Cambridge Ancient History*, third edition, volume 4 part 2, 112–138; for Assyria specifically see the same author, "The Assyrian Heartland in the Achaemenid Period," in Pierre Briant, ed., *Dans les pas des Dix-Mille: Peuples et pays du Proche-Orient vus par un Grec, Pallas* 43 (1995), 239–254. More focused studies may be found in John Curtis, ed., *Mesopotamia and Iran in the Persian Period, Conquest and Imperialism 539–331 BC* (London: British Museum, 1997).

Translated Excerpts

*Foster, *Before the Muses* (see Bibliographical Note to Chapter 3), 854.
**Foster, *Before the Muses* (see Bibliographical Note to Chapter 3), 864.
***From Jean-Jacques Glassner, *Mesopotamian Chronicles, Writings from the Ancient World* 19 (Atlanta: Society for Biblical Literature, 2004), 268.
****From Albert T. Clay, *Neo-Babylonian Letters from Erech, Yale Oriental Series* 3 (New Haven: Yale University Press, 1919), no. 7.

Chapter 7

Mesopotamia between Two Worlds

I. Alexander the Great and His Successors

When Alexander the Great, in the spring of 334, crossed with his army from Europe to Asia, he may not have imagined that this journey would bring him to Babylon, a city that could have been little more to him than a fabled name. Victory after victory showed him that he, a young man from Macedon, could hope to topple Darius, the great king of all lands, and become great king himself. He marched the length and breadth of the Persian empire, a great personal achievement, but it is well to remember that he went nowhere the Persian kings had not been before him. Wintering at Persepolis, he burned the wonderful palace of the Persian kings, filled with the best treasures of the world. Some say he did this in a drunken orgy, some say at the urging of the beautiful Thaïs, who sought vengeance on her former masters, others say he was resentful that the Persians would not accept him as a successor to their king, so in defiance he sought to obliterate their kingship to found a new one. In any case, armed with the greatest treasury the world had ever seen, he set off for Babylon, and there gave orders that the ruins of the great temple of the Babylonian national god Marduk be cleared, no doubt for resumption of the ancient rites. Babylonian historians had taken note of his victories over the Persians but give us no hint if he imagined himself instituting a new universal kingdom based at Babylon. If so, it was a good strategic choice, as Babylon was still, despite her damage in civil strife, one of the largest and most important cities in the entire Persian empire. Situated roughly in the center of Alexander's conquests and with a long imperial tradition behind her that was not so closely identified with Persian tradition as was Persepolis, Babylon could well have once again ruled the world.

Alexander's death in Babylon on 11 June 323 (the exact day was noted by Babylonian astronomers), left his conquests in the hands of several marshals and followers. Whereas at first they maintained a pretense of waiting for Alexander's child, called Alexander IV, to come of age and take hegemony, as strife and betrayal broke out among them they soon abandoned even that, warring among themselves to be successor to the brilliant fallen leader. One of the strongest claims was raised by a marshal, Seleucus, who succeeded in taking power at Babylon. Seleucus's domains were extensive: the Iranian plateau, where Greek colonies were flourishing, Mesopotamia, and Syria, even parts of Asia Minor; of all the successor states, his most closely resembled the profile of the old Persian empire. Like Alexander, he married a princess from Central Asia, who raised their son, Antiochus, speaking her native language as well as Greek. But Seleucus's accession to power was fraught with challenges and setbacks. Another marshal of Alexander, Antigonus, based in Asia Minor, had hoped to wrest the kingdom of Asia for himself and invaded Babylonia for that purpose. Both sides fought hard and supported themselves by looting and terrorizing the local population. There were emergency taxes; holy places were pillaged. As a Babylonian historian noted, "there was weeping and mourning in the country."

Seleucus and his descendants were destined to rule in Iraq or Syria for two and a half centuries, down to the Roman and Parthian conquests. Before their kingdom was reduced, they faced the problems of how to rule such an enormous area with a relatively small Macedonian army to rely on. To complicate matters, they never gave up on the idea of expanding their domains to the west, to include all of Syria, Egypt, and Asia Minor, even Greece, as the sole successors of Alexander. Indeed, Seleucus himself met his death trying to return to Macedonia. Therefore Mesopotamia under their rule looked politically and strategically to the west as much as she had to the east under the Persians, and Babylonia was drawn directly and indirectly into the vicious politics of the

Mediterranean. In addition, Macedonian successors in Egypt, Asia Minor, and Greece and Macedonia were trying to establish their own hegemony, always hoping to outflank and protect themselves from the great king of Asia. At the same time, the successors of Seleucus hoped to maintain the old domains of the Persian empire in Iran, and this alone was a full-time struggle which in time they would lose. The eastern dominions became an urgent problem already in the first half of the third century, when peoples the Greeks called "Scyths" (Iranian Saka) invaded Iran in large numbers, overrunning some of the old Greek population there and posing a challenge that Seleucus's son, Antiochus, had great difficulty in meeting. The immediate consequence of the disorder in Iran was that various local chieftains there abandoned their allegiance to the Seleucid royal house and founded lineages of their own.

2. Life in Hellenistic Babylonia

The political and military strategy of the successors of Seleucus, referred to in history as the Seleucids, had western, Mesopotamian, and eastern programs administered from three capital cities: Antioch in Syria, with its near-by military base at Apamea; Seleucia on the Tigris, a new city built not far from Babylon, and Ecbatana in Iran. As the administrative capital of Mesopotamia and seat of the royal court, Seleucia must have attracted the ambitious and the colonist. This was a city in the Greek style of the time, with gymnasia, a theater, a palace, and Greek governmental buildings. It lay at the confluence of a royal canal and the Tigris river, about 60 km northwest of Babylon. The Roman writer Pliny claims that it was intended to draw population from Babylon. Although the growth of this place threatened to turn Babylon into a backwater and may have seemed dismaying to Babylonians who had hoped that once again their city would rule Asia, Babylon was still one of the most populous and important cities of the realm. Even at the height of the war with Antigonus, the clearance of the ruins of the major temple there continued. Greek civic and governmental offices must have been present there. The Greek theater at Babylon was still in use as late as 100 C.E., to judge from an inscription found at its site. Some Babylonians had both Greek and Babylonian names and occupied positions of responsibility in the local administration.

The remains of Seleucia have been explored by American and Italian expeditions since 1927. Although most of the architecture discovered was from post-Seleucid occupation, the burned remains of the Seleucid tax bureau were identified.

The Seleucids may have considered it prudent to support Babylonian cults and certain Babylonian deities, such as Nabu (Nebo), god of learning and wisdom, and Nanaya, goddess of love, seem to have gained followers in greater Syria, for example, perhaps partly as a result of Seleucid rule. A Babylonian hymn to Nabu was produced in a stilted though competent style, in honor of Antiochus:

> *O Nabu, foremost son, when you enter Ezida, the eternal house,*
> *may there be on your lips a favorable word for Antiochus, king of*
> *the world, and favorable words for Seleucus the king, his son, and*
> *for Stratonike his wife, the queen.**

A Babylonian priest named Berossus wrote a book for Antiochus, son of Seleucus, explaining Babylonian history and religion and giving a list of ancient kings, so he must have presumed that Antiochus had some cultural interest in his Babylonian domains. Babylonian astronomers continued to make their observations and record them carefully. Babylonian historians chronicled the deeds of the Seleucid royal house in some detail; we regret much that the tablets that contained these records are badly damaged. These scraps of evidence point to a cosmopolitan society in which men like Antiochus were prepared to be Hellenes in the Hellenistic world and great kings of Asia within their own domain, as well as local kings in the local style. Nor were they unique in this: the Ptolemies, Hellenistic rulers in Egypt, were pleased to be pharaohs as well as Greek kings.

3. Babylonian Culture and Economy

We do not know how much the Greek and Babylonian populations intermingled. The Seleucid royal house held large estates in Babylonia, for example, which must have been highly visible on the landscape and which may have been worked by native peasantry. Like the Ptolemies in Egypt, the Seleucids may have been wary of recruiting too much native soldiery, relying rather on Greek troops and foreign mercenaries to uphold their power. The Greek tax collector was of course everywhere, charging fees and tolls and duties to maintain the insatiable Seleucid war machine, which was scarcely ever idle. Although the Babylonians did note the doings of the royal house, there is no evidence they took much evidence in Greek culture; perhaps, as elsewhere, some did, but the proud old Babylonian families still read the Gilgamesh epic, recited Babylonian spells and hymns, and sang the ancient Sumerian laments in the old way for the cult. Sons of astronomers learned the art of observation and record-keeping on clay tablets in Babylonian, were examined for their skills, and promoted. The clerks of the great temple of Eanna at Uruk still kept their records in neat Babylonian script. A handful of magic spells in both cuneiform and Greek characters suggests that a few people, Greek or Babylonian, were interested in the possibilities of each other's writing systems.

But Berossus's laborious Greek book on Babylonian culture was probably a failure. Few people read it and copies of it were extremely rare even in antiquity. Native apologetics under colonial rule seldom make interesting reading for the ruling elite; they tend, rather, to cling the more strongly to their own, foreign, tradition when transplanted to a different clime. Few Greeks wanted to read a book full of strange, barbarous names and of a mythology that gave little evidence for the secret, alien wisdom they imagined lay hidden in the ancient books of the east. The treasures of the Babylonian temples were too tempting to leave untouched in time of need. So rather than projecting a grand synthesis of Mesopotamian and Greek, some historians are inclined to see classic patterns of colonial rule and a traditional Babylonian culture that was losing vitality and currency save in the careful work of a few learned families in major cities such as Uruk and Babylon. Perhaps they are too much influenced by such major instances as British rule in India, but the great complexity and extent of the Seleucid realm, its polyglot society, and the necessity that the rulers come to terms in some way with the ruled invite the comparison, if it is not carried too far.

The international character of exact science transcended the cultural insularities of the period. Greek-speaking scientists were aware of the superiority of Babylonian astronomy, for example, nor was it so difficult to translate astronomical tables from Babylonian to some other language directly, presumably into Greek. Scientific work, like military technology, has its own laws of circulation that often reach far beyond the range of other kinds of writing, so Babylonian astronomy made its way directly to the scientific treatises of the Hellenistic world and thereby enriched them considerably, some would say decisively. Babylonian astrology was also highly esteemed, at least in name, and may have traveled the same routes as astronomy, mingled with it. The vogue for astrology in late Babylonian culture certainly continued under Persian and Hellenistic rule; one could have a horoscope cast by a Babylonian specialist and the very word "Chaldaean" (see Chapter 6) came to mean "astrologer" to the Greeks. One could allude to the astronomers of Uruk just as one could later allude to the tables of Al-Khwarizmi, but only a few well-informed people would have any idea of their significance. Other forms of Babylonian divination, such as examining the entrails and liver of sheep, were known in the Mediterranean world but perhaps as an independent tradition.

We know even less of the eastern, or Iranian, orientation of Mesopotamia in this period. There are few written sources for Iran because the local tradition is lost and because the historians of the Hellenistic world were primarily interested in the Mediterranean and Syrian policies of the Seleucid rulers. The spread of Babylonian literature and culture to India, for example, has been suggested, perhaps during the Achaemenid or Hellenistic periods, conceivably through the medium of Aramaic or Greek translation or even translation directly from Babylonian to languages of India, but as with spread of Babylonian culture in Hellenistic western Asia, the evidence is challenging and disputable.

The economy of Hellenistic Mesopotamia was enhanced by the introduction of coinage, proceeding initially from the tons of silver and gold looted at Persepolis. Greek staters became standard currency everywhere and effectively replaced the old silver and grain standard of Mesopotamia. We imagine that many Greek colonists made their way to Mesopotamia and that adventurers from other parts of the world came there seeking their fortune. We surmise that a considerable amount of the best arable land in Babylonia was held by the crown and princes, who had taken it over from the Persian nobles they had displaced. The producing population would therefore have been peasants, many perhaps permanently tied to the land they worked and enjoying limited civil rights. The irrigation works of the early Achaemenids may have suffered damage in the civil wars of the late Achaemenid and Hellenistic periods, so there may have been an aggregate decline in agricultural output. But the Mediterranean world had an insatiable thirst for luxury goods from the east, such as fine textiles, aromatics, oils, and spices, not to mention precious and semi-precious stones, so we think that the commercial activity of the major Mesopotamian cities continued to be bustling and profitable. The main hindrance to economic development was surely the high cost of military adventure, east and west.

4. The Rise of Parthia

The Seleucids were not the only claimants to the traditions of the old Persian empire. In the steppe lands east of the Caspian Sea, where there is abundant seasonal pasturage for nomads, a new royal house of Iranian origin arose, in the region then known as Parthia. In later tradition, this royal house traced its origins to a certain Arsaces, who lived during the third century B.C.E., and even accorded him special honor as a deceased ancestor worshiped as a god. Thus some refer to this dynasty as the Arsacid dynasty and to their followers as the Parthians. Just as the Seleucid rulers numbered their years of reign from the beginning of Seleucus's reign, so too the Parthians invented an era commencing with the reign of Arsaces (beginning spring of 228 B.C.E.). They were therefore conscious rivals to the Seleucids in their own dominion, drawing on the same traditions the Greeks had, reaching back in theory perhaps to Alexander. Arsaces had been one of those local rulers who became independent at the time of the Scythian war of Antiochus and whom the Seleucids were unable to subdue thereafter. He and his successors expanded their realm at the expense of Seleucid claims over the next half century, founding a compact and powerful kingdom that effectively lay beyond the reach of Seleucid arms, despite temporary setbacks.

Yet the nomadic peoples of Inner Asia had no well-defined tradition of kingship. As nomads, they recognized their family leaders and chosen leaders (khans) in time of war, but no overarching royalty. Having chosen the Hellenistic model for kingship, the Parthian royal house could scarcely resurrect the Achaemenid royal line for themselves, thereby leaving that approach available to later rivals, the Sassanians. There was, though, something Iranian in the special veneration they accorded the deified founder of the house, which went beyond any honors accorded the deceased Seleucus but resembled the deification of Alexander in some areas. The nomadic peoples were difficult to subdue unless one could surprise them in their winter pastures on the hillsides, when they had less mobility. In the spring and summer they could move rapidly and evade direct assault. Control of the landscape could be achieved by imposition of fortress cities on key routes and controlling certain key districts. The Parthian fortress cities, such as Merv, were often circular, for optimal defense, and surrounded by massive walls that nomads without heavy siege equipment could scarcely hope to penetrate. We know little of the population pressures on this critical region, but we see time and again that the plains east of the Caspian and the pasturelands between the Oxus and Jaxartes rivers were the pressure points for peoples forced west by developments in Inner Asia and even China.

Greater Iran is a difficult land to conquer and rule, in part because of its distinctive geography. Settled life in greater Iran tends to be in towns and cities around the edge of the plateau, the inner part of which is largely desert, so Iran is like a bowl with its people living on the rim. The nomadic peoples could pass freely through the desert areas if they wished, but effective control over the entire region was hard to achieve and maintain because of the difficulty of communication and march. Most rulers of the region, from antiquity to modern times, have preferred to concentrate on a few key centers such as Merv, Bukhara,

Samarkand, Herat, Balkh, and Kandahar, leaving the countryside as more or less open space in between and seeking the allegiance of local chieftains to control it.

5. Parthian Society

The Parthian military strategy was based on elite units of archers on horseback, trained from childhood in the equestrian arts and marksmanship. The Parthian bow was accurate to a distance of about 200 m, with a drawing pressure of 30 kg, so could pierce shields and armor. The Parthians were famous for the so-called "Parthian shot," discharged backwards over the withers of a retreating horse, a feat requiring exceptional control and much practice. Parthian dress, trousers with narrow legs and baggy tops, clearly had its origins in horsemanship, and ancient images of Parthians, from as far away as China, often show them as horsemen. There were also heavy-armed tactical units of armored infantry. These were military techniques that could only be met in kind, as no field army could be proof against Parthian cavalry on its chosen ground, and the peoples of Mesopotamia and Syria had neither the horses nor the equestrian skills to face the Parthians on their own terms.

The strength of Parthia was also its weakness, some of the same weakness that plagued the Persian empire as well. The leading noble families, such as the great family of Surena, commanded large forces of loyal riders, were proud of their lineage, and often asserted claims to kingship for themselves. The Parthian king could control them only by force and guile, playing them off against each other, with an elaborate network of feudality and intermarriage, and sufficient outlets for their warlike energies. Many of these men, like the knights of the medieval Europe, thought of little beyond the arts of war and the intense joys of life between battles. Their feudal domains might lie far afield from the court and within them, even if they held a title as a provincial governor, the Parthian overlords reigned nearly as sovereigns. Thus the Parthians ruled more as a confederation than as a monolithic state. To Roman historians, approving of the heavy-handed, centralized, professional

Roman imperial administration, Parthia seemed loose and disorganized. They were to gain a healthy respect for Parthian military prowess but little for Parthian staying power, which lacked the tenacity of Rome's. Rapid Parthian conquests in Syria, for example, would be followed by withdrawal nearly equally as rapid. Roman specialists saw the Parthian royal house as inconsistent of purpose, treacherous, and liable to conspiracies and revolutions, and we owe most of our knowledge of Parthian political history to unsympathetic Roman historians and military men.

6. Parthian Mesopotamia

It was only a question of time before the Parthians broke the hold of the Seleucids on the Persian heartland. During the reign of the great warrior king, Mithridates I (171–138 B.C.E.), the Seleucid king, now Antiochus IV, was driven from Iran. The eastern capital at Ecbatana (ancient Media) fell under Parthian rule, and Parthian warriors poured into Assyria, Babylonia, and Elam (called by the Greeks Elymais). Therefore for most of the second century B.C.E., Mesopotamia, north and south, was under Parthian rule, and the Parthians dreamed of expanding to Syria, thus recreating the larger extent of the ancient Persian empire and replacing the Seleucids. The Seleucid model was closer to hand, so they struck coins in the Greek style and gave themselves the title "philhellene," meaning, presumably, "lovers of all things Greek." Mithridates was even crowned at Seleucia. Art and architecture were strongly influenced by Hellenistic styles. But in due course, a distinctive Parthian style developed, owing as much to Iran as to Greece.

But the Parthians too had their troubles with the Scyths, who were a constant threat to the east as the Parthians were pushing west, and whose nomadic way of life made them impossible to subdue effectively for long. The western frontier of Parthian control tended to stay near the Euphrates, meaning that western Asia was becoming divided a new way, between eastern control from Mesopotamia and Iran, and western control from Syria and soon Rome. The greater Mesopotamia of the early second millennium B.C.E., of the Achaemenids and of the early

Seleucids, was truncated by a frontier zone, a no-man's-land, that would tend to isolate Babylonia from her historical connections to the north and west. Being on the fringe of a great state, and a contested one at that, meant that Babylonia lost the central position she had enjoyed for centuries, and no doubt suffered as a consequence. Her major centers, however, such as Uruk and Babylon, continued to be important as trading centers under Parthian rule. Uruk, for example, had Parthian buildings as late as the second century C.E., and Nippur was dominated by a Parthian fortress. We know little specific of the city Babylon at this time, though one recent survey of its areas of occupation at this period estimates roughly a population of 20,000 people, perhaps a third of its population a few centuries earlier.

For the rest of the second century B.C.E. and into the first, the Parthians effectively held Mesopotamia as part of their dominion, while a Seleucid shadow state lingered on in Syria that made occasional unsuccessful attempts to retake Mesopotamia. Two major Parthian centers in northern Mesopotamia were at Assur and Hatra, the latter a new foundation located in the plain west of modern Mosul. Both Assur and Hatra had in common their location on important commercial routes; Hatra lay on the route overland from Assur to Syria and for much of Parthian history lay near the frontier, so was a focal point of trade. Hatra was a large town with an impressive mass of stone buildings forming a temple complex in the center, surrounded by six kilometers of walls with 160 or more square towers, well equipped to withstand sieges by the likes of Trajan and Septimus Severus. The place was aptly situated for trade, as a link between Palmyra and the ancient cities of Assyria (now Parthian centers), such as Assur and Nineveh (100 km to the northeast). Hatra was also of importance as religious center. There was a great temple to the sun-god, Shamash, whose name would have been familiar to any Babylonian, and temples to other local deities.

The site of Hatra, owing to its remoteness, was little visited by western archaeologists in the nineteenth century. The first systematic excavations were carried out there by the Iraqi antiquities service, beginning in 1951. Considerable architectural restoration was done on site. Important groups of statuary were removed to the Mosul and Baghdad museums, where they were smashed by looters during the Iraq war, apparently with the intent of taking the heads and selling them on the antiquities market as small sculptural pieces. At the site itself, many statues were beheaded as well. During the occupation of Iraq, explosive ordnance disposal in the area caused additional damage to the ruins.

To the visitor, the most striking aspect of the great Parthian-style buildings at Hatra, remains of similar buildings being also known at Assur and elsewhere, was the *iwan*, a high vaulted structure, often with one end left open so it looked out over a garden. The soaring inner space gave an impression of magnificence achieved in few ancient buildings prior to the development of domes. The design could be used for temples or for palaces. The decoration of Parthian buildings, including colonnades, could be strongly Hellenistic in style, using Corinthian columns, decorated porches, gates, and arches of Greco-Roman inspiration, but with a local accent. The Assyrian and Achaemenid tradition of using glazes in architecture was manifest in green glaze, the color of which seems to have been a Parthian innovation. These examples show the complexity and interconnections of this vast culture, with its local phases and developments, of which Mesopotamia formed an integral part and no doubt had much of her own to contribute. Perhaps the most celebrated innovation of Parthian art was its emphasis on frontality when portraying the human figure in painting or relief. It is more difficult to portray action in that mode than in profile and the viewer tends to look at the face, so the character and mien of the representation predominate. This trait spread west, through Armenia and Syria, and became one of the salient characteristics of early Christian and Byzantine representation of the human form.

7. Rome in Mesopotamia

The first century B.C.E. saw the definitive entrance of Rome into the Middle East. Rome had gradually expanded westward from Italy, first into Illyria (Croatia) then in a series of interventions in Macedonia and Greece. During the Punic wars, the great kingdom of the east seemed far away. When Roman public enemy number one, Hannibal, arrived at the Seleucid court and advised the great king, Antiochus III, of the danger posed by Rome, the Seleucid kingdom began to look like a Roman enemy, especially when she intervened in the various Macedonian wars. Rome's decisive defeat of Antiochus at Magnesia in Asia Minor removed for all the time the aura of invincibility the Seleucid kings had enjoyed, with their vast army and special terror weapon, trained elephants, before which it would take a brave infantryman to stand. A prodigious indemnity was laid on the Seleucid kingdom that went far towards destroying its economy. So it was that when Antiochus IV invaded Egypt in 169–168 B.C.E., he was met by a Roman delegation that insisted he depart, in the interest of Rome; thus his triumph, the moment he had at last fulfilled the dream of refounding Alexander's kingdom, was snatched from him. This was the moment the small Jewish state at Jerusalem chose to rebel against him and paid heavily for its temerity, as Antiochus vented his fury and disappointment on the Jews and sought to obliterate their kingdom and religion.

The decline and disappearance of the Seleucid dynasty left Rome and Parthia face to face across the Euphrates, each with a strategic and economic interest in greater Syria and each lacking the means to eliminate the other, as their centers of power lay too far apart. There were Romans, however, who imagined themselves latter-day Alexanders and who dreamed of defeating the Parthians as Alexander had defeated the Persians. The most tragic of these was a rich man, Crassus, who raised a Roman army and rashly invaded Parthian domains in 53 B.C.E., determined to make a hero of himself. The Parthians were at first incredulous at his venture and hoped terms could be reached, but when his determination became clear, a Parthian force lured him into a trap. The Parthian archers decimated the helpless Roman troops with showers of arrows. Crassus himself and his son were among the casualties; the small band of survivors was led home by Cassius, later renowned as one of the murderers of Caesar. This disaster weighed heavily on hearts in Rome. Parthia would thereafter be seen as the hereditary enemy of Rome though Crassus had been the invader. Intense Roman diplomatic efforts eventually retrieved the captives in

Parthian hands, as well as the captured Roman standards. As for the victorious Parthian general, he was executed by the Parthian king lest his stunning victory over the greatest military power of the world make him a rival for the throne.

In the decades that followed, the frontier swung back and forth as Parthians and Romans had their chance of victory and their moments of defeat. The local landscape, the once populous Euphrates Valley, must have looked more and more like a wasteland, crisscrossed by military roads and dotted with guard posts. Mesopotamia seemed further and further from the Mediterranean, despite a short occupation by Trajan (114–117 C.E.).

8. Parthian Cities

The Parthians placed one of their capitals at Ctesiphon, about 35 km south of modern Baghdad, in the vicinity of Babylon, in that same critical zone where once Babylon, Seleucia, and Agade had ruled their domains and later Baghdad would succeed them all. The Parthians thus in effect made the same decision Alexander and Seleucus had made, when he determined that Babylonia was to be the center of gravity of his new kingdom. The Parthian decision seems the stranger to us since the troubled heartland of their dominions lay far to the east, but makes sense if the Parthians in fact dreamed of re-establishing the Persian and Seleucid empires, with their domains in Syria, Egypt, and Anatolia. In that case, Babylonia would indeed have been the center of their new world order. At Ctesiphon, not far from Seleucia, they constructed their *iwans*, gardens, palaces, temples, and fortifications. As events proved, this left their capital open to Roman attack, but this could not have been a consideration when the site was first chosen. Once again, Babylonia was the center of a state that sought to rule Western Asia, but could not achieve this goal both because of its internal weaknesses and because of the Roman "iron curtain" cutting off access to the Mediterranean world.

Parthian Ctesiphon has been little explored by archaeologists. For an Arabic poem in honor of the place, see Chapter 8.

The Parthian kingdom lay astride the international trade routes that brought to the Roman markets some of their most prized and expensive exotic commodities, especially silk. It was much in the Parthian interest to promote this trade by providing security and way stations, exacting tolls and fees in the process. The secret of the Chinese miracle fiber, silk, was unknown in the Mediterranean world, but the demand for it was insatiable. The Chinese, for their part, had some interest in locating this market, which brought such a flood of specie into China, but a Chinese delegation made the journey only as far as Babylonia, where the Parthians advised them that it was not possible to get from there to Rome. The trading posts we call, too romantically perhaps, "caravan cities," especially Palmyra, on the desert route west from the Euphrates to inner Syria, soon capitalized on this lucrative market, providing guides through the desert tracks and all the goods and services required to bring exotic commodities from the Parthian frontier to inner Syria. Some trade may also have come up the gulf, easily linking India, Ceylon, and South Arabia with Babylonia. Indeed, the first and second centuries C.E. saw a lively commercial activity in Mesopotamia and from there north and west to Syria. Trading towns and small trading states flourished from the Gulf to the upper Euphrates. Their cultures tended to be Parthian in style and Aramaic in language.

The Romans obstinately pursued their vain efforts to subdue Parthia. Trajan's short occupation of Ctesiphon was perhaps the high point of this effort, though Septimus Severus triumphed by seizing the old Seleucid capital at Seleucia on the Tigris, which may still have had a substantial Greek population. Hailed by some as liberators, the Romans seemed to other citizens of that place merely a new tyranny of which they were an eastern outpost, so the occupation was not unmixed with difficulties. The siege of Hatra by the same emperor was a failure. In Roman thinking, the future of Mesopotamia seemed less important than the future of Armenia, which they saw as the key to Asia Minor. The Romans insisted on installing their own puppets as kings of Armenia, so too the Parthians, hence Armenia was even more of a flashpoint than Mesopotamia, which probably seemed to the Romans as legitimately within the Parthian sphere of influence, to be invaded only when the time seemed propitious. Armenia, however, was too important to be ignored for long.

9. The End of Mesopotamian Civilization and the Downfall of Parthia

During these poorly documented years, we assume that the ancient Mesopotamian civilization and its cuneiform writing became extinct. Knowledge of cuneiform may have persisted into the second century of the Christian era, but destruction in Babylonia had taken its toll. We may freely speculate that much of Babylon lay in ruins, with perhaps a town and market among the debris and a Parthian fort. Further south, at the ancient Sumerian center of Nippur, a massive Parthian fortress sat astride the ruins. Whatever survived of ancient Mesopotamian culture in Aramaic and Parthian is visible to us now mostly in hints and scraps: for example, a prayer of the Babylonian king Nabonidus in Aramaic, Mesopotamian deities at Palmyra, a few passages from Berossus's book quoted and copied from each other by orientalist historians. Magic, like science, traveled widely, so one need not be surprised if Mesopotamian spells turned up in new guises long after other forms of Mesopotamian literature were dead. Numerous magic spells are known, written on clay bowls in Aramaic and other languages. The bowls were buried, often in pairs, in front of houses to protect the families who lived there from black magic. The legacy of Mesopotamia in later periods is difficult to evaluate if only because it touched on so many different lands and peoples.

Numerous examples of bowls with magic spells appeared on the antiquities market after the Iraq war, indicating that Parthian and later sites were being dug clandestinely.

In the third century of the Christian era, a civil war in Parthia between rival claimants to the throne weakened the central government to such an extent that history could repeat itself in the old heartland of the Persian empire. In southwest Iran, that is, Persia proper, a rebel appeared in the spirit of Cyrus the Great, casting off allegiance to his Parthian overlords and laying the foundations for a new state that was decidedly Achaemenid in its ideology and claims. He traced his descent from a certain Sassan, a quasi-legendary personage about whom little certain is known, so we call this new dynasty, which brought the Parthian dynasty to an end in 227, the Sassanians.

Bibliographical Note to Chapter 7

For the history and civilization of Hellenistic Mesopotamia, see T. Boiy, *Late Achaemenid and Hellenistic Babylon, Orientalia Lovaniensia Analecta* 136 (2004); Amélie Kuhrt, Susan Sherwin-White, eds., *Hellenism in the East* (Berkeley: University of California Press, 1987); Susan Sherwin-White, Amélie Kuhrt, eds., *From Samarkhand to Sardis* (London: Duckworth, 1993). For the Roman perspective, see Fergus Millar, *The Roman Near East, 31 BC–AD 337* (Cambridge: Harvard University Press, 1993). For Parthian Mesopotamia, the sources are far scantier; for a good introduction, see John Curtis, ed., *Mesopotamia and Iran in the Parthian and Sasanian Periods, Rejection and Renewal c. 238 BC–AD 642* (London: British Museum, 2000). My remarks on Parthian archery are drawn from André Verstandig, *Histoire de l'empire parthe (-250–227)* (Brussels: Le Cri, 2001), 156 and M. Junkelmann, *Die Reiter Roms* (Mainz-am-Rhein: von Zabern, 1991), 3:163–169. For Mesopotamian tradition in later cultures, see Stephanie Dalley, ed., *The Legacy of Mesopotamia* (Oxford: Clarendon Press, 1998).

Translated Excerpts

*Foster, *Before the Muses* (see Bibliographical Note to Chapter 3), 866.

Chapter 8

Iraq between Iran and Arabia

1. The Sassanians and Their Subjects

The new Iranian dynasty called the Sassanians faced many of the same challenges that the Parthians had: how to deal with the unruly nomadic incursions in the east and northeast of Iran and how to assert control in the west against an implacable Rome. As with the Parthians, we have the same dearth of native sources: no native chronicles, few important historical inscriptions or major works of literature. What we do have is mostly filtered through later Islamic tradition. So, once again, we have to fall back on contemporaneous books written by authors who hated and feared the Sassanians and an imposing mass of later romance, most important of which is a narrative poem in 60,000 rhymed couplets by Firdawsi, of the late tenth century, called the Shah-namah, or "Book of Kings." This was based on authentic Sassanian tradition. Such varied sources as numismatics and archaeological exploration, rock reliefs and tombs have provided important information as well.

Although the Sassanians had risen to power in ancient Persia and probably viewed themselves as the authentic heirs of the Persian empire, they too established a capital in Babylonia, at Ctesiphon, once again placing Mesopotamia at the center of strategy to establish a single state throughout Western Asia. The first Sassanian ruler, Ardashir, was crowned there. The great *iwan* which may have served as an audience hall and throne room of the Sassanian kings still stands today, a forlorn ruin with no hint of the gardens, palaces, and bustling city that once surrounded it. Ctesiphon had a substantial population of Christians, Jews, and Zoroastrians. It was well fortified with walls and a moat.

A modern Iraqi poet reflects on the *iwan* of Ctesiphon, reviving a well-established Classical Arabic tradition on the same topic:

Despite the nights, the envious nights,
Your immortality indeed transcends death,
Defying through the ages any slap of obliteration's hand,
Though time itself had raised the threatening arm.
Time you withstood, firm as a towering peak,
With a stalwart strength a valiant warrior would wish were at
his side! *

The *iwan* at Ctesiphon has deteriorated markedly over the past century, especially because of flooding in 1908-1909. It was spared important damage during the Gulf and Iraq wars.

Adopting policies of forceful campaigning and building of key fortress cities, the ablest of the Sassanian monarchs were able to achieve an effective control of the Iranian plateau and the lands leading up to the Jaxartes river. There were always, however, pressures on the periphery so few Sassanian rulers had a free hand to pursue a consistent western policy that could achieve lasting results. When, in the fourth century A.D., the capital of the Roman empire was moved east to Constantinople, the eastern Roman empire's most important possessions were Syria and Egypt, with an increasingly tenuous hold on Italy, North Africa, and southwestern Spain. The Christianization of the Roman empire, beginning with the conversion of Constantine and the establishment of Constantinople as a purely Christian city, meant as well that such centers as Jerusalem and Antioch acquired additional importance because of their historical associations with the beginnings and spread of Christianity. Patronage of the church was a way for the emperor to show his wealth and power, so splendid basilicas were constructed in Syria and Palestine and Christianity gained an increasingly imperial character. After the fourth century C.E., the Christian Roman empire presented itself as the temporal kingdom of God on earth, the emperor the image or shadow of God to his subjects. All Christians, even if they were not under his direct rule, owed him fealty.

This lesson was not lost on the Sassanian sovereigns, but the religious situation in their own domains was highly complex. The best candidate for a "state" religion, if the Sassanian empire was to have one, would be Zoroastrianism, a revealed religion that had its origins in the Achaemenid period. Zoroaster was a prophet, thought to have lived in the sixth century B.C.E., whose teachings included a dualistic view of the universe as a battlefield between forces for good and evil, a human obligation to think, speak, and do good, and the necessity to perform certain rites of purification. Zoroaster's teachings had been later collected in a scripture referred to as the Avesta. Unlike the Christian and Jewish scriptures, these writings were scarcely accessible to the uninitiated, so a powerful class of professional Zoroastrian priesthood, referred to as "magi," had grown up over the centuries who were virtually a separate estate within Iranian society and who long antedated the monarchy. Thus control of the Zoroastrian religious establishment was not a simple matter, though Sassanian statecraft saw the church and state as mutually dependent.

Additionally, there were many subjects of the king who were not Zoroastrians, including Jews, Christians, pagans, and adherents to various Gnostic faiths and the cult of Mithra. The cult of Mithra had spread widely through the Mediterranean world in the ranks of the Roman army. Its teachings emphasized such soldierly values as courage, perseverance, and triumph; it had impressive ceremonies of initiation, and, to some at least, Mithra appeared a kind of savior god who could bring his followers through the trials and ordeals of their lives. There was also an ancient Iranian fire cult and among many nomadic peoples a cult of ancestors and the family.

The imperial Christian response, both to rival faiths and to divisions within the faith on points of doctrine, was increasing intolerance in the interest of a rigid orthodoxy with an explicit confession of its tenets. But there was less scope in the sprawling Sassanian realm, with its religious pluralism, for designing a strict orthodoxy such as the Roman emperor Constantine (mid-fourth century) and Theodosius (late fifth century) sought to impose on their own subjects. The Sassanian rulers would not tolerate any role for the emperor at Constantinople in the choice of church leadership within the Sassanian domains, and in Mesopotamia, where there were substantial Christian communities, there were several rounds of persecution and execution of church leaders. With the rise of the Nestorian heresy in the fifth century, condemned at Constantinople for non-orthodox views on the nature of Christ, many of its adherents fled to Mesopotamia and were allowed to practice their faith mostly unmolested, choice of church leadership lying ultimately with the Sassanian monarch, whether or not he chose to exercise it.

The Nestorian Christians of Iraq were a subject of fascination to European and American travelers and missionaries there in the nineteenth century. Nestorian missionaries brought their own faith across inner Asia as far as China, where traces of it were discovered by Catholic missionaries and later by travelers and explorers in China.

2. Sassanian Civilization

Sassanian society crystalized into an unequal three-part division of castes: the priesthood, a noble and warrior class including the ruling families, and, finally, the rest of the population, viewed by the first two classes as obliged to support them. This included the peasantry, many of whom were working land that was not their own but held in suzerainty by some nobleman, the pastoralists and nomads, and such people as craftsmen, administrators, and merchants. The Sassanian state was more centralized than the Parthian, relied on a professional army rather than tribal levies, and created a professional bureaucracy.

The most energetic and effective of the Sassanian rulers recognized that sound fiscality would be the best basis for a lasting and powerful state. There had to be a way to predict revenues and to collect them systematically. Since the main revenues of the state came from agricultural production in such fertile areas as Mesopotamia, royal agents compiled cadasters, or lists of arable land, and the income due from them. This allowed a professional administration to project a budget and devise ways to implement it. The preferred method did not involve extracting income directly from producers but rather relied on local headmen, notables, or squires to assume the responsibility for tax collection in their area based on a well-informed projection of the central administration. Although the basic practice may not have been a major innovation, the systematization of it was and this laid the foundation for administration and revenue collection in the subsequent Muslim states of the region as well, both in Iran and the Ottoman empire. In addition, there was the traditional patchwork of military fiefs granted directly by the crown or a great prince with specific dues to each, a pattern known already in the Achaemenid period. The result would be the growth of a sophisticated, professional, and powerful administration with well-established record-keeping techniques, which the king would need to keep subservient to his interests and the head of which should be a trusted and knowledgeable adviser.

Trade and commerce were also pillars of state, so enlightened Sassanian monarchs took steps to encourage them. The caravan trade was supported by the establishment of caravanserais, large enclosures at regular stages of march where the caravan could be brought into safety, the animals sleeping in the courtyard, the people using suites of rooms facing on the courtyard, a design not dissimilar to a modern motel. There were of course tolls and fees to be collected. The sea trade up the gulf from India and Ceylon was also of no small interest to the Sassanian rulers; the control of it depended on control of the major port at the north end of the Gulf, known as Spasinu Charax, which was probably located somewhere near modern Basra. From here it was only a step for the Sassanians to develop a maritime policy and to consider the possibility of trading posts or client groups in South Arabia. Mesopotamia, therefore, would reassert her position as the crossroads of Western Asia. The Romans had destroyed the city of Palmyra in the mid-third century because of the pretensions of the city's fascinating queen, Zenobia, who sought to rule as "augusta" of the east. This opened the way for other caravan cities, especially to the north, to profit from the trade, though the constant warfare between Parthia and Rome probably reduced its volume and value compared to the early third century. Only in the sixth century would the Christian Roman Empire discover the secret of silk production, which later flourished in Turkey, Cyprus, Lebanon, and parts of Greece, until late in the twentieth century.

Syria and Armenia, rather than Mesopotamia, were the principal battlegrounds between the two colossal states of Late Antiquity and the Early Middle Ages: the Eastern Roman (or Byzantine) empire, and the Sassanian empire. The economic loss, destruction, suffering, and depopulation brought about when either one of them resolved on a renewal of hostilities with the other is today incalculable but must surely have left the Euphrates Valley a forlorn remnant of what it had been before Mesopotamia had become politically part of Iran. This shows to what extent close connections with northern Syria were essential both for the prosperity of Mesopotamia and for the formation of successful large states there in antiquity. The new frontier had stabilized for centuries along one of Mesopotamia's major arteries with the result that even if the Parthian and Sassanian capitals were there, Mesopotamia could not prosper as she had, for example, under the early Achaemenids or in the most ancient times during the Uruk expansion.

3. The Sassanian Empire and the Eastern Roman Empire

The main stages of the conflicts between the Sassanians and the Eastern Roman empire can be summarized by two titanic struggles. The first, in the sixth century, pitted Chosroes Anushirvan against Justinian. Both were hard-working, calculating, brilliant rulers with visions of reigning supreme in the world. Justinian was convinced he could rebuild the ancient Roman empire. To retake its old provinces, such as Italy, Spain, and North Africa, from the barbarian rulers who had occupied them for a century or more, Justinian sought a lasting treaty of peace with his Sassanian counterpart and secured it at no small expense. This gave him a free hand in Italy against the Goths, though the campaign proved slow and discouraging. The Goths naturally for their part sought an alliance with the Sassanians, and the temptation proved too much to resist: Sassanian armies poured into Syria and even sieged the city Antioch, third city of the empire after Constantinople and Alexandria. The garrison behaved with great cowardice, accepting safe conduct to leave the city to the mercy of the Persian army, so the defenseless populace was put to the sword and the brilliant city, famous for its wealth, love of luxury, sophistication, and comfort, was destroyed, block by block. Chosroes may even have dreamed of a siege of Constantinople, but this seemed an impossible goal, as the city was well known to be impregnable, and the Sassanians lacked any Mediterranean sea power. A severe outbreak of the plague in Constantinople and Asia Minor claimed hundreds of thousands of lives before it ran its course; to campaign under such conditions would be madness. Justinian's achievements were a shambles, Chosroes had gained enormous loot and prestige, but the map of the Middle East remained essentially as it was, because the Sassanians showed no signs of following up their victory in Syria with a campaign of occupation.

The second of these wars, in the early seventh century, pitted Chosroes II versus the emperor Heraclius and was perhaps the closest thing to a world war in antiquity. The Sassanian emperor seized a moment of weakness in the Eastern Roman empire to launch a major onslaught, evidently designed to destroy the Byzantine state and to reestablish the old Persian empire. The invasion proceeded brilliantly: Syria fell rapidly into Sassanian hands, the Persian armies marched south to Jerusalem and captured it, making off with such sacred Christian relics as the true cross, which Constantine's mother, Helen, had miraculously rediscovered in the early fourth century. The Sassanian armies continued on to Egypt, laying that land under Persian control for the first time in nearly a thousand years. A major Persian force marched inexorably towards Constantinople. The Byzantine emperor, Heraclius, despaired and even thought of abandoning his capital and fleeing to North Africa, but when the patriarch of the church offered to melt its treasures to raise an army, he took courage. Since Egypt was the capital's major source of grain, immediate action was necessary.

Heraclius's strategy was daring and unprecedented. He brought his army across the Black Sea, thus outflanking the force on its way to Constantinople, and landed in eastern Anatolia, pushing south through the mountains directly towards Mesopotamia. The Sassanians were confident that the advent of winter would force him to retreat, but instead, Heraclius spent the cold season in the field, so was ready to march as soon as the spring thaw began. He emerged triumphant on the plain and marched south, as Cyrus and Alexander had before him. As he gained on the capital, Ctesiphon, the Sassanians abruptly withdrew their force attacking Constantinople and eventually their forces in Syria, Palestine, and Egypt as well. The Sassanian emperor was executed by his generals in 628 and they sued for peace. Heraclius returned victorious to Constantinople leaving the Sassanian empire seriously weakened and in disarray. Potentates all over the world hastened to congratulate him.

4. Arab Settlement in Mesopotamia

The depredation of the Euphrates Valley opened the way for new settlement, beginning perhaps as early as the late fourth century, of Arabic-speaking peoples from Arabia. Connections between Mesopotamia and Arabia have already been noted: the caravan route along the eastern edge of Arabia and through the deserts, probably ultimately connecting with the urban and agricultural regions of South Arabia; periodic invasions by the Assyrians, who garnered considerable plunder and were struck by the fact that the tribesmen could be led by queenly women; the residence of the Babylonian king Nabonidus at Teima. Arabs had settled in the southern Jordan Valley already in the Hellenistic period and by Roman times had gone from pastoralism to an exuberant urban culture deriving its prosperity from the caravan trade along the western coast of Arabia, among the most prized commodities of which was frankincense. This is easily harvested as a resin from trees that grow naturally in South Arabia and was an important element in rituals throughout the Mediterranean world. Arabs had also moved into southern Syria, where the Byzantine rulers gave them titles and police functions along the frontier. The Euphrates Valley was therefore part of a larger region of Arab settlement. The Sassanians found good reason to encourage the development of small Arab principalities along the Euphrates to perform guard and police functions on their behalf. Hira, a town the stood on the east bank of the Euphrates just south of modern Kufa, the capital of a dynasty known as the Lakhmids, was particularly noted as a center for early Arab culture.

The site of Hira has not been explored by archaeologists.

The Arabs as a population in Arabia were predominantly nomadic, organized into tribes and smaller groupings that gave the individual his identity, community, family, and social hierarchy. The most important cultural expression of the Arabs was not material but linguistic: the arts of poetry and rhetoric. Poets were people of special importance whose work brought special esteem to their tribes and whose greatest achievements were treasured by later generations. Although the Arabs living in the Jordan Valley and Syria had learned to write in a form of Aramaic, and the South Arabians had their own language and writing system, the Arabs of the Euphrates Valley began to experiment with writing their own language, Arabic, in a distinctive, connected, cursive form of the same alphabetic script used to write Aramaic and Greek. This was the ancestor of the present-day Arabic script, which may first have been used at Hira, the Lakhmid capital in Iraq.

5. Western Asia in the Seventh Century

The Sassanian invasion of the early seventh century and the Byzantine riposte had the short-term effect of throwing out of alignment the network of vassal tribes and kingdoms both in southern Syria and along the Euphrates. While the Arabs in these regions did not disappear, their allegiances were disrupted and some of the little kingdoms, such as the one at Hira, may have suffered heavily or been destroyed in the Sassanian advance, as if the emperor imagined that they would no longer be of strategic use in the new empire. Thus, at the beginning of the seventh century, the southern reaches of the two exhausted warring states were not so well guarded as formerly.

Heraclius too seems to have given little thought to Arabs. He wanted to create a resilient frontier along the southern reaches of Anatolia, taking advantage of the mountainous frontier, so reorganized the historic provinces into military districts commanded by men who knew the local terrain well and had considerable discretion, including their own treasuries. This was in due course to prove a durable barrier against the Muslim conquerors, but left Syria and Palestine as provinces defended by garrisons outside of the military districts of his core state. With the defeat of the Sassanians, he could see no threat in that quarter; the agenda was to protect the heartland of his empire.

There was another line besides that of the military districts. That was a doctrinal or confessional one. Already in the fourth century the emperor Constantine had to deal with dissension in the church over such varied issues as how to treat Christians who had sinned by denying their faith and, much more complex, how to define the nature of Jesus Christ. When one spoke of Jesus as the son of God, did that mean that Jesus was younger and subordinate to God? When one spoke of his being born of Mary, did that mean that he was human or partly human? If he was in fact divine, then his suffering and earthly mission seemed to some to lose their immediacy. If he was in fact human, then he was to that extent imperfect, born in time and place, and inferior to God. These were not easy issues to resolve. Various church councils, the most important at Nicaea (325) and Chalcedon (410), had defined orthodoxy in these matters (Jesus had both a human and divine nature, separate but indissoluble), but this left important groups of sincere, practicing Christians, belonging to ancient and well-established Christian communities, beyond the pale of the imperial order. The largest and most important groups of these excluded Christians lived in Egypt, Syria, and Mesopotamia. Historically they are referred to as "Monophysites" because they continued to insist that Jesus had but one nature, not two distinct human and divine ones. Although Orthodoxy was strong among the Greek-speaking population of the Middle East, for example in the coastal cities of the Levant, once one crossed the mountains into the interior, the Aramaic-speaking population was overwhelmingly Monophysite in faith, though with significant doctrinal disputes among themselves. The native, non-Greek population of Egypt, called the Copts, was also Monophysite, as was the independent Armenian church, founded in 301 by Gregory the Illuminator (hence claiming to be an apostolic church antedating even Nicaean orthodoxy).

There was thus a division across the Christian Roman empire running along doctrinal, linguistic, and ethnic lines. Although relatively few even devout Christians today have any detailed understanding of the difference between Monophysite and Orthodox Christianity, these battles were as hard fought as those between Catholics and various types of Protestants in Europe during the sixteenth and seventeenth centuries and the doctrinal disputes were no less urgent and militant. Heraclius was well aware of this, as had been his predecessors, and tried to find a compromise solution, suggesting that perhaps one could agree that Jesus and the Father had but one will, thus papering over the question of their joint nature, but this ingenious effort satisfied no militants on either side and made no headway. With the wisdom of historical hindsight, we see the weaknesses in both the Sassanian and Byzantine empires at the heady moment of Heraclius's triumph. He was to live to see his fairest provinces taken away forever by a people who scarcely figured in his strategic thinking: the Arabs, afire with a new revealed religion that claimed to replace all others, even the imperial orthodoxy that had helped his state through some of its darkest hours. For the present, however, the true cross and other sacred relics were returned to Jerusalem amidst ceremony and rejoicing.

Bibliographical Note to Chapter 8

There is little in English on Sassanian Mesopotamia. For a brief but authoritative introduction, see Richard N. Frye, *The History of Ancient Iran* (Munich: Beck, 1984), Chapter XI. More detailed accounts are found in the *Cambridge History of Iran*, especially volume 4, with extensive bibliographies. See also the work by Curtis cited in the Bibliographical Note to Chapter 7, especially St John Simpson, "Mesopotamia in the Sassanian Period: Settlement Patterns, Arts and Crafts" (pp. 57–66).

Translated Excerpts

*Hadi Muhy al-Khafaji, in Ali al-Khaqani, *Shuara' al-Ghari* (Qom: Bahram, 1987), 12:400–401.

Chapter 9

The Muslim Conquest of Iraq

1. The Mission of Muhammad

In 570 a child known to us as Muhammad was born in Mecca, a city along the caravan route along the western coastal zone of Arabia, about halfway between South Arabia and the Jordan Valley. Muhammad's father died before his birth. Since Arabian custom required a father to acknowledge his children formally at their birth, Muhammad was therefore deprived of any inheritance from his father's property. He grew up, therefore, as a poor relation and ward of uncles. Mecca was a bustling commercial center. Its leading families were active in the lucrative north-south caravan trade to Syria, so it was only natural that Muhammad learn that business, and perhaps even ride with some of the caravans trekking north to Jordan and on to Syria. He had little or no opportunity for formal education. A wealthy widow, Khadijah, invested funds with him as her agent, and in due course they were married. The couple settled down to what might have been the anonymous and comfortable life of everyone else of their station in the city.

Mecca was also a pilgrimage center, with all the vested economic interests that invariably are found in such a place. Each year a major fair and pilgrimage attracted people from other towns and tribesmen from the desert. Custom allowed them to set aside any feuds and differences for the duration of the fair, so they could freely buy, sell, exchange news, attend poetry recitations and competitions, arrange marriages, and the like. Mecca possessed several sanctuaries with idols representing the astral and celestial pantheon of the region, as well as a "black stone," said to have fallen from heaven, which was an object of veneration. The town had a good agricultural base and some local industry, especially leather and metal work. The commercial and religious advantages of Mecca, therefore, were intertwined and mutually sustaining. The patterns, allegiances, and opportunities of the first forty years of Muhammad's life in Mecca allow no hint that he was to become one of the most influential men in all human history.

Muhammad had withdrawn occasionally to meditate in a small cave on the outskirts of Mecca. Of a sudden, the angel Gabriel announced to him there that he had been chosen to be the messenger of God to the human race. He was to recite or read aloud the words he found in his heart:

> *Recite this! In the name of your lord who created, created humankind*
> *from a clot of blood,*
> *Recite this! For your lord is most bountiful, who taught the use of*
> *the pen, taught humankind what it did not know.**

The first of these were short, rhymed utterances, some proclaiming the oneness and beneficence of God, some pleading for his protection, others urging mortals to be grateful to God for their existence, to be worshipful of him, to be generous to fellow human beings, and to fear a day of judgment:

> *When the trumpet is sounded, that day will be a day of trial, nor*
> *remotely easy for those who do not believe.***

Muhammad confided his experiences to a few and recited the words as the angel had ordered him. His circle of followers grew among those ready to respond to a message of goodness and mercy and to accept Muhammad's mission and leadership. These did not include, however, the leading merchants of Mecca, some of whom began to see a threat of social unrest in Muhammad's teaching. Others suspected overweening ambition on the part of someone they had had known all his life, far too ordinary to be chosen of God for a new prophetic mission to all people.

The messages from God continued, grew longer and more elaborate, and in some instances seemed critical of the obstinacy and inherent selfishness of those who would not believe but who thought mostly of their own gain. There were even attacks on the venerated gods and goddesses and condemnation of the veneration of the idols at the center of Meccan religious life. Muhammad claimed that there was only one all-powerful God, and that he, Muhammad, was the messenger of God:

He it is who has sent his messenger with right guidance and the true religion, to exalt it above every other religion, even if those who do not believe are opposed.***

The response among leading Meccans was increasing anxiety and suspicion. Muhammad was threatened and his extended family shunned in the hope that they would bring him back to his senses. This, of course, was impossible, as the dictates of God were too compelling for him to ignore, so the solution was for Muhammad and his followers to go elsewhere.

In 622 Muhammad and a group of his followers moved to the city now known as Medina, about 320 km north of Mecca along the caravan route. Civic life in that place had deteriorated, owing to stubborn feuds among the leading tribes and families, such that outside leadership was needed to bring it stability. There was also a substantial Jewish community among whom Muhammad hoped his message would be received as a fulfillment of what he saw as their expectation for another prophet. Muhammad's followers came to be known as "Muslims," meaning people who submitted only to God and who acknowledged that Muhammad was God's messenger. Communal prayer was instituted at Muhammad's house in Medina, at first involving prostration in the direction of Jerusalem as holy city, later towards Mecca. The prayers were at regular intervals throughout the day and night, announced by a public call.

Muhammad did not envisage setting up an isolated religious community in exile. His message was for all human beings and if God chose to leave some of them unaccepting of his mission, that was because God had marked them for destruction. When the Jewish community at

Mecca refused to accept his mission, he massacred them. He also preyed upon the Meccan caravans, the economic lifeblood of that city. The Meccans sent armed forces against him. Muhammad had no military training and experience, but the fervor of the men and women who fought on his behalf brought victory in every confrontation. It became obvious to the Meccans that their cause was lost and they must submit. Thereupon in 630 Muhammad returned in triumph to Mecca, forgave all his opponents in a general amnesty, and destroyed the idols, though he adopted the black stone as the most sacred object in Islam. He set about first to build a Muslim community and second to spread the message of Islam throughout the world, beginning with the recalcitrant Arab tribes. These had never known any form of unified rule. Though their religious beliefs did not readily allow them to adopt a new, strict regime of faith and submission to Muhammad's teaching, a basic appeal of Islam, to join a new community of allegiance transcending family, clan, and tribe, invoked a fundamental Arabian value that individual worth was based on solidarity with a larger group.

Not long before Muhammad's mission, South Arabia, though not the region of Mecca, had for a time been a zone of confrontation between the Sassanians and the Byzantine empire. Central and Northern Arabia were of little interest to either side. To Heraclius the emperor at Constantinople, who might even have received a letter from Muhammad calling upon him to submit to Islam, Muhammad would have seemed like one more heretic or false prophet in a Christian world that knew of and had condemned many such. So numerous were they in fact that Christians of his generation would need books to contain all of them and the orthodox arguments refuting their errors. Although there were Christians living in Arabia, it was not a Christian land but the range of uncontrollable tribesmen. Therefore an organized attack coming from Arabia was unthinkable to the strategists of the great states of the period.

The discipline and zeal of the Muslim armed forces soon accomplished what no sheikh or king had ever contemplated, the unity of the tribes of Arabia in submission to Islam and the diversion of their warlike energies towards lands that had still not submitted. The obvious targets were the Eastern Roman empire, with its key provinces in Syria and Egypt, and the Sassanian empire, with its capital in the heart of ancient Babylonia. The message of Islam was to be carried throughout the world.

Muhammad died in 632, having made no formal provision for a successor who was universally recognized as such by the Muslim community. The Muslim community did agree among themselves that there should be a successor to Muhammad as spiritual leader of the Muslim community, commander of its armies, and warden of its resources, but not as a prophet; the line of prophecy ended with his mission. The words that the angel had instructed Muhammad to say were soon collected into a book now known as the Koran, or "recitation." Its rhymed prose made it easy to learn by heart, especially in a culture that placed high value on reciting poetry and lengthy genealogies from memory. The Koran did not promulgate a fixed system of belief so much as it guided in ethical, social, political, and ritual matters.

2. Arabian Caliphs and the Conquests of Iraq

At Muhammad's death, leaders of the Muslim community agreed that he had no successor as prophet and messenger of God, but that a successor should be chosen to exercise political and moral leadership of the Muslims. Some Muslims believed the successor should be chosen by common consent from among Muhammad's early followers. Others believed leadership should pass automatically to members of the prophet's family, especially his son-in-law, Ali (see below, section 4). The first caliph chosen was Abu Bakr, an early convert to Islam and father-in-law to Muhammad. As the new leader of the Muslim community, he was called "caliph," meaning "successor." The office of caliph was to have a long and complicated history, the last vestige of it being abolished only in 1924. At the same time, various of the Arab tribes renounced their allegiance to Islam, claiming that they were bound only to Muhammad himself. But the Muslim community, led by the new caliph, marched against them and they were once again brought into submission and unified within the community of Islam.

Now a large fighting force was available to the Muslims, which soon coalesced into an army. The Arabs had the advantage of swiftness and mobility, a good knowledge of desert terrain, and could disappear into the desert after a swift and devastating raid. They had the added advantage of capable military leadership, stemming perhaps in part from the nomadic tradition that leadership was to be earned by ability, courage, and fairness rather than preferment. Leading Muslim generals, such as Khalid ibn al-Walid and Amr ibn al-As, were brilliant strategists and highly effective commanders. Muslim armies moved rapidly north against Byzantine Syria and northeast against the Sassanian kingdom.

In 637 the battle of Qadisiyyah, not far from Hira on the Euphrates, southwest of Babylon, doomed the Sassanian dynasty. The Persian forces fought with valor but were no match for the Arab forces who took advantage of the heat and dust to overwhelm their foe. In a surprise maneuver, Arab forces had crossed into Iraq by the desert route from Arabia, perhaps following the same path in reverse that the Babylonians had used to enter Arabia some thousand years previous. The Muslim armies were joined by many Arabs who had settled previously in Mesopotamia. Some were no doubt sincere converts to Islam seeing conquest as a religious duty, while others were opportunists on the look-out for booty. The Christian peasantry of Iraq accepted the new regime as they had accepted Persian rule, and were slow to convert to Islam.

The collapse of the Persian army left the capital, Ctesiphon, open. There wondrous riches awaited the Arab armies, as stunning to them as the treasures of Persepolis had been to the Macedonian warriors. Not only were the buildings and gardens beyond the experience of a tribesman from Arabia; they were furnished with carpets, ceramics, furniture, metalwork, and decorations of a kind they had never seen or imagined. Since the Sassanian king had not submitted to Islam but fled, later to die abjectly in a remote part of his former kingdom, his goods and lands were forfeited to the Muslim community. Suddenly administrators were needed, to understand the management of the vast estates now under their control, to collect taxes, to keep records. A treasury was needed to control and deploy the gold and silver that had fallen into their hands. Small wonder, then, that in Iraq the Sassanian administration was taken over and redirected under Muslim leadership. The very word for treasury among the Muslims, *diwan*, was borrowed from the centuries-old traditions of Persian government. The Muslim forces continued into Iran until they had reached and crossed the frontiers of the old Persian empire, far into inner Asia and to the foothills of the Hindu Kush. Thus the Muslim conquests, in barely a century, would create a polity vastly larger than the empires of Cyrus the Great or Alexander, and would do so under continuing changes in leadership.

Meantime in Syria, the Muslim armies advanced rapidly. Damascus fell in 635, Jerusalem in 638. Heraclius had at first forced them to withdraw, as he had the Sassanian invaders, but at the battle of Yarmuk in 637, the Arab armies were victorious and the routed imperial forces had to flee. Heraclius rode with the remnant of his forces back over the mountains into Anatolia, where the military districts were better prepared to face this new threat, and sadly looked for the last time at one of his fairest provinces. Syria had suffered in the last centuries of Byzantine rule, even beyond the divisive doctrinal disputes and the Sassanian invasion. Some of her major cities, like Antioch and Berytus, had been shattered by earthquakes during the sixth century. The Roman frontier lines had been neglected. Important changes had taken place in society there over the past three centuries: the circus and the bath, centers of Roman public life, had been replaced by the church. A new Christian elite, often composed of clerics or local holy men, was in some areas the most important or even the only form of authority. This meant that doctrinal disputes had great impact and that some communities were not loath to shake off what remained of orthodox Byzantine rule and to submit to the seemingly invincible Muslim armies. Those that did so were allowed to retain their property and to carry on their own religion as they wished, for some, both Jews and Christians, an improvement over their circumstances under Byzantine rule. They were required to pay a poll tax as non-Muslims, as well as a land tax, but taxation was scarcely a new experience to them. In Syria too, local administrators were called into Muslim service, the records still even kept in Greek, for Arabic had as yet no vocabulary or usage suitable for complex administrative tasks. The Muslims gradually reorganized the patchwork of administrative practices and exemptions they encountered into a simpler, more uniform regime.

So it happened, then, that Muslim governmental and cultural traditions in Iraq were heavily influenced by the Sassanian (and so ultimately Achaemenid) background of Mesopotamia, whereas in Syria, Greco-Byzantine governmental and cultural traditions molded the ways of the Muslim conquerors in the captured territories. Architecture, coinage, ceramics, ways of living, were in the first instance to draw on what the Arab conquerors found before them, as Arabia had little in the way of material culture to rival those of Syria and Iraq. In Syria, for example, local church architecture, which used domes and mosaics to create imperial sacred space, were to be the example for the earliest mosques at Jerusalem and Damascus, whereas in Iraq it was to be the *iwan* of the Parthians and Sassanians.

Egypt too fell before the Muslim armies, then all of North Africa to the Atlantic, then most of Spain. Egyptian, Berber, Christian, Jewish, and Andalusian communities fell under Muslim rule and in most cases converted. The ancient Christian communities of North Africa, for example, which had been home to Augustine and Tertullian, disappeared through conversion and immigration, leaving the landscape dotted with the ruins of abandoned Christian churches.

3. Islam and the Arabs in Iraq

These important local influences on the merging Muslim state were met and molded by strong Arab traditions that arrived with the conquerors. The first of these was of course Islam itself, a faith that seemed at once demanding in its public ritual requirements: prayer, alms-giving, a month of fasting during daylight hours, and, at least once, pilgrimage to Mecca, but humane and straightforward: a simple profession of belief in God and his prophet. The tenets of its faith had at first none of the doctrinal intricacies that had divided Christianity for more than three centuries, especially the problem of the relationship between Jesus and God, the orthodox solution to which Muslims scorned as polytheism. On the social level, the Arabs tended to maintain their sense of tribal allegiance and origin, even when they had long settled in urban areas. These allegiances left a subtle, complex network beneath the surface of Islamic society, at once durable and taken for granted but difficult for an outsider to detect or evaluate strategically. So strong was tribalism in the early years of Islam that non-Arab converts often felt obliged to join a tribe as clients or dependents.

By far the most important export from Arabia, besides Islam itself, was the Arabic language. Arabic was rich in its structure and vocabulary and was readily adaptable to the new domains. It was the main cultural treasury of the Arabs. It was the language of the dominating faith and of its sacred book, the Koran. This, unlike the Jewish or Christian scriptures, which had circulated in translation for centuries, was deemed untranslatable: every Muslim should study the Koran in its original words. Arabic effectively replaced local languages in most of the areas conquered by the Muslims, including Syria, Iraq, Egypt, North Africa, and Andalusia. Only Persia was able to maintain its native language in the face of Arabic, though adopting its script and in due season much of its cultural and religious vocabulary. Persian was destined to become the second Islamic language in both prose and poetry, enriching Islam with the prodigious intellectual, historical, and aesthetic traditions of Persia. Although Persian remained largely at home in Iran and became known as a second language to the cultivated Muslim, Arabic was soon to become the only world language of the Middle Ages, understood far more widely than any other tongue.

Within the first two centuries of Islam, therefore, Iraq had become an Arabic-speaking country with a large Arab population in both cities and countryside. The second successor to Muhammad, the caliph Umar ibn al-Khattab, combined strict piety with extraordinary administrative skills and insight. One of his fundamental policies was based on the premise that where possible, the Muslim communities in the new territories should maintain a separate identity from the indigenous, non-Muslim population, to guard against dilution of their faith and to keep the tribesmen from damaging the agricultural and urban bases of the new empire. Western Asia could prosper once again, as the Euphrates was no longer a contested frontier. Now Syria was once again linked to Iraq by trade, and Iraq to Iran and Central Asia. New settlements were founded, organized along tribal and quasi-military lines. From these settlements have grown some of the greatest cities of the Muslim world, such as Cairo in Egypt or Kairouan in Tunisia; in Iraq, they were Kufa and Basra. These were purely Muslim cities in the same way Constantinople had been a Christian city without a pagan substrate. In them the Muslim faith could be practiced and elaborated free of foreign influence, and the nascent scholarly arts of Islam and Arabic could flourish. They were also centers where the booty and revenue of the conquered lands could be distributed among the conquerors. Northern Iraq, on the other hand, had lost her important markets in Anatolia, so its major city, Mosul, declined, and nomads were free to prey on villagers.

Kufa, in southern Iraq, became an early center for the historical and analytic study of the Arabic language, including its grammar and vocabulary. Although this may have been seen by some scholars as proceeding from the necessity to understand the Koran correctly and precisely, the rapid growth of Arabic as a language of poetry, humane letters, religious expression, government, science, and imaginative and lyric expression gave this undertaking a much wider application than scriptural study. However, the dominating influence of the Koran and the language arts associated with it kept formal Arabic expression from breaking into dialects across the Muslim world: the same Arabic prose or poetry could be written and understood from Seville to Tashkent, all through the long history of the language. Local spoken idioms, of course, began to diverge from each other, so a distinctive Iraqi spoken Arabic evolved that was quite different from the spoken Arabic of Egypt or Morocco. The formal Arab language is learned by all Arabs who go to school; this formal language is the common property of the entire Arab world and unites all Arabs in a sense of common linguistic culture and heritage even when they cannot understand each other's colloquial dialects, which may be as different as Italian is from Portuguese. In the written tradition of the Middle Ages, the formal Arabic language was universally used, so we know little about the history and development of the Iraqi spoken dialect of the language.

4. Leadership of the Muslim World

The Muslim conquests did not achieve all their objectives, however. The greatest prize of all, Constantinople and the rest of the Byzantine empire in Anatolia, eluded their grasp. Several Arab armies laid siege to the city, especially in the eighth century, backed up by the newly developed Muslim navy, for important groups of Arabs had become seafarers. The natural and manmade defenses of the city were too strong. Prior to the invention of gunpowder, there was no way to break through the massive land walls. The Byzantine navy was armed with a terrible secret weapon, Greek fire, a substance similar to napalm which could be launched in a fiery stream from a short culverin on the deck of a ship to envelop enemy ships and their crews in sticky, unquenchable flames. The Arabs were ill-prepared for the cold Anatolian winters and the defenders were valiant, resourceful, and determined. Had Constantinople fallen in the eighth century, most or even all of Europe, certainly the Slavic-speaking world, would have become Muslim. As it was, until the fifteenth century Constantinople held her position as the world's greatest city and as the bulwark of Christendom against repeated Muslim onslaughts. In the west, Muslim armies reached the Rhone river and Poitou but did not establish a permanent presence beyond the Pyrenees.

The vast extent of the Muslim domains and the sophisticated cultural traditions now incorporated into the larger Islamic polity meant that Arabia was increasingly a political backwater, important primarily as the birthplace of Islam and the source of Arab immigrants. Already in the early years of the successors, discontent and dissension grew among Muslims over various questions. Some were social: what was to be the status of non-Arab converts in relation to the Muslim Arab tribesmen? Some Muslim leaders obviously favored their relatives in the distribution of appointments and resources, some of whom might even have opposed the prophet in his own lifetime, whereas deserving Muslims were passed over. The booty of the conquests allowed elderly Muslims in Mecca to receive handsome pensions, but the soldiers garnering the booty received comparatively little. The best of the conquered lands were being distributed among the same favored groups — the usual complaints of those in the field versus those at home who reap the profits of their victories.

Some issues had to do with leadership. Not everyone had agreed on the succession of caliphs. Here consent was the main concern, as Muhammad had left no son, for example, who might have claimed his mantle. He did, however, have male relatives by his various marriages. Of these, his son-in-law, Ali ibn Abi Talib, who had married his daughter, Fatimah, had been one of the most persistent in pressing his claim to leadership. Ali had supporters in the Muslim community but not enough to prevail in the early debates over who should succeed to leadership. Ali also had opponents, as, for example, he had once questioned the virtue of one of Muhammad's wives, Aishah, and she, as the last surviving of them, strongly resisted his claim.

In 656, a force of discontented Muslims marched on Mecca to protest and present their various social and economic grievances to the then ruling caliph, Uthman. He was a pious but ineffective old man who seemed to succumb too easily to the pressures of his relatives in the old Meccan aristocracy, many of whom had been opponents of Muhammad but were now being given lucrative posts in preference to the Medinans and others who had been early supporters of Islam. This march broke into violence and the caliph was murdered as he sat reading his Koran. A wave of revulsion and guilt swept over the Muslim world: what had happened to their morality and polity that made such a ghastly crime as this possible? What were solutions to the issues it raised and who was going to present them and on what basis?

To Ali and his followers, this seemed the moment for him to take leadership and to try to rebuild the Muslim community, based on his close personal relationship with the prophet himself. To others, however, the day of the old generation of Meccans had passed and the time was ripe for leadership drawn from the vigorous and increasingly sophisticated men administering the conquered lands, who would have a broader experience and sense of how to deal with the new pluralism of Islamic society. To them, the Meccans had shown their ineptitude, even venality, and no choice from among the ruling class of Meccans was going to heal the divisions opening within Islam. No doubt simple ambition played a role in this as well. Ali had always had local enemies at Mecca who did not trust him. In any case, though Ali succeeded to the caliphate, armed resistance broke out, especially in Syria, led by a man named Muawiyah, who was at best a distant relative of the prophet but a cousin of the murdered caliph, whose death he sought to avenge. Ali's critics accused him of doing nothing to save Uthman, even abetting in his murder. The Muslim community fell into civil war.

Ali's army moved into Syria and met Muawiyah's followers at a place called Siffin in 652. As the tide turned against Muawiyah, his followers clamored for a truce and arbitration on the basis that it was evil for Muslims to be fighting each other. Ali accepted, to the disgust of some of his more militant followers, and as talks dragged on his support began to weaken and evaporate. Finally Ali was stabbed to death by a disaffected follower for private revenge, leaving his faction leaderless and allowing Muawiyah and his followers to establish a new caliphate, this one based at Damascus under the long shadow of imperial Roman and Byzantine tradition. According to legend, Ali's body was placed on a lone camel and buried where the camel first stopped and knelt. This was at Najaf in Iraq, near Kufa. Later Najaf was to become one of the most sacred shrines in Islam. Ali was canonized by his followers as a martyr, a noble, eloquent, generous, and chivalrous leader. Some followers believed he possessed secret knowledge that no other Muslim had; others asserted he was sinless and infallible. After his death, therefore, Ali came to be a figure in Islam second in importance only to Muhammad himself. He was later thought to have transmitted his secret knowledge through generations of leaders called *imams* among his followers and descendants. Many sayings of Ali are preserved, such as

> *He who looks to his own fault takes no heed of the fault of his neighbor. He who is satisfied with what God provides regrets not whatever has passed him by.*****

In the meantime, the followers of Ali, condemning the new Syrian caliphate as a usurpation, next pinned their hopes on Ali's younger son, Hussein, then a boy in his teens. A small force was mounted in Arabia and marched into Iraq, presumably in the hope of establishing a power base there, away from Syria. This small force was met and cut to pieces at Karbala by a much larger force loyal to Muawiyah, and Hussein was killed. His remains were interred at Karbala; this too became a pilgrimage spot, a site of grief and reflection, where the martyrdom of Hussein was thereafter re-enacted in passion plays and mourned in public demonstrations of grief.

5. Divisions within Islam

In the generations that followed, and until the present day, those Muslims who accepted the succession of Muawiyah and his family, known as the Umayyads, to the caliphate, were referred to as Sunni, "orthodox." Those who believed that the succession rightly belonged to Ali and to his descendants were referred to as Shi'i, often understood as "sectarian" or "protestant" Muslims. The deep differences between the two groups developed throughout the history of Islam in many different ways, over fundamental points of doctrine and theology, over religious law and its authority and interpretation, over the interpretation of the Koran, and over how the Muslim community should be led. Orthodox Islam continued to accept the spiritual leadership of the caliphate. In Iraq and Iran, where there were many Shi'ite communities that did not recognize the orthodox caliphate, leadership often clustered around individual religious leaders and teachers, some of whom taught that a descendant of Ali would someday reclaim leadership of the Muslim community. Iraq contains two of the most sacred cities for Shi'ite Muslims, Najaf and Karbala.

As in Christianity, sectarian differences within Islam were based on many factors besides purely doctrinal disputes, but the doctrinal disputes were the most important fault lines. These formed the basis for contesting leadership and moral authority among Muslims, resulting in various rival caliphates of the Middle Ages, but they did not prevail over a common sense of Muslim identity, especially where non-Muslims were concerned. The struggle against Christianity for control of still hard-fought parts of the Mediterranean world such as Sicily, Cyprus, and Crete, or the mountains of Armenia, or Anatolia, continued, was pressed vigorously by Muawiyah and his descendants, the Umayyads.

6. Commerce and Business

The Muslim city of Basra, in Iraq at the north end of the Gulf, was built near the site of more ancient commercial centers and was a natural commercial center. Here the Arabs learned the ways of international seafaring trade. The city soon had a diverse population and was also a key center for export of textiles produced in Iraq, as well as the import of goods from India, China, and Iran. If the population was originally soldiers, the conquerors gradually became artisans, sailors, and merchants. Within a century of the conquest of Iraq, the separate identity of the Muslim ruling elite was breaking down and amalgamating with other groups to form a new Muslim, Arab-speaking society internally differentiated according to way of life, wealth, education, and social mobility.

7. Developments in Arabic-Islamic Culture

A vigorous new Arabic-Islamic culture emerged among the ruling elite at court and in the cities. This was based on the indigenous cultures of the conquered regions and was expressed in such arts as painting, material culture, research, theology, and a new court literature. The court at Damascus, for example, saw a new kind of Arabic culture develop: supple and elegant Arabic prose, poetry both in the old manner, with themes of desert, camel or horse, and lost love, and in new manners: praise of the ruler, the pleasures of strong drink and of both sublime and courtly love. Many of the best poets of the Umayyad court were, in fact, natives of Iraq rather than Syria.

One popular theme of the new literature was love, and one of the most famous of all Arab love stories has a Romeo-and-Juliet quality. It tells of the doomed love of Qays for the woman Leila. Unable to recover from his disappointment, Qays wandered the desert, known as the "madman" or the "possessed." In this excerpt he imagines Leila, long married and many times a mother and grandmother, still longing for her true love:

They say that Leila is heartsick in Iraq,
Oh would I were the cure to heal her wrack!
Though Leila's sons and grandsons gray with age,
Leila's passion burns with ever keener rage.
I vow could I meet Leila in some far retreat,
I'd pilgrim to the holy house on naked feet! *****

New Muslim-Arab building styles developed from the old churches and basilicas, lighter, more ornate, with intricate carving and brilliant tile and mosaic work. Even the desert was no longer a place of passing encampment but became domesticated and sentimentalized from the perspective of palaces and fortresses. Thence one could sally forth to a desert hunt but return to a Roman-style bath and a splendid meal served in a hall vividly painted with secular themes, amidst music and dancing.

For a hundred years, until 750, the Umayyad caliphate prevailed, giving a strong western secular accent to Muslim government as the Arab successor to Rome and Byzantium there, and a strong worldly tone to a new vigorous Arab culture as successor to the old Meccan religious leadership of the Muslim community. Iraq was a key province of this new Muslim state, ruled by governors from a new settlement called Wasit, but it was still only a province, many residents of which felt alienated from the Umayyad Arab aristocrats of Damascus.

Bibliographical Note to Chapter 9

A brilliant, modern survey of all Arab history is Albert Hourani, *A History of the Arab Peoples* (Time-Warner Books, 1991). More old-fashioned, with more detail and giving a strong flavor of the original sources, is Philip K. Hitti, *History of the Arabs*, eighth edition (London: Macmillan's, 1964). For society and government, I have drawn material from Ira M. Lapidus, *A History of Islamic Societies*, second edition (Cambridge: Cambridge University Press, 2002). Of the various English translations of the Koran, A. J. Arberry, *The Koran Interpreted* (London and New York: Macmillan's, 1955) remains the classic. A useful literary introduction to the Koran will be found in James Kritzeck, ed., *Anthology of Islamic Literature* (New York: Holt Rinehart and Winston, 1964), 22–51. Of many biographical studies of Muhammad, one may still recommend W. Montgomery Watt, *Muhammad, Prophet and Statesman* (Oxford: Oxford University Press, 1961).

Translated Excerpts

*From Koran surah 96 (after Arberry).
**From Koran surah 74 (after Arberry).
***From Koran surah 9 (after Arberry).
****Caliph Ali ibn Abi Talib, *Nahj al-Balaghah*, from Bassam K. Frangieh, *Anthology of Arabic Literature, Culture, and Thought from Pre-Islamic Times to the Present* (New Haven: Yale University Press, 2005), 449.
*****Qays ibn al-Mulawwah, "Majnun Layla," from Frangieh, op. cit., 437.

Chapter 10

The Age of Baghdad and Samarra

1. The Abbasid Caliphate

The revolution against the Umayyads was a complex event. From the religious aspect, the Umayyads were charged with being too worldly and for having forsaken the teachings of Islam. To the Shi'ites, of course, they were the usurpers and murderers of Ali's line. The new claimants to leadership, the Sunnite Abbasids, claimed descent from an uncle of Muhammad, Abbas, and further claimed that a great-grandson of Ali had transferred his interests to the cause of their family. The Abbasid claim was for their family rather than for a single individual, so gained strength thereby. The Umayyad dynasty was weakened by significant defeats, east and west, in their increasingly unsuccessful efforts to continue Muslim conquests of new lands. From the geographical standpoint, this was a revolt of Iraq, supported by Iran, against Syria, driven by the sometimes harsh rule of the Umayyad governors in Iraq. Therefore the Abbasids were able to mount a broad coalition against their enemies, enough to topple their dynasty, but this coalition was, ultimately, more anti-Umayyad than pro-Abbasid, so the Abbasids soon turned against many of those who helped bring them to power, including the Shi'ites. The last surviving member of the Umayyad dynasty fled to Spain, where he founded a new Umayyad ruling house that eventually claimed the title of caliph for themselves.

The new Abbasid dynasty, which came to power in 750, ruled at first from a town near Kufa and quickly eliminated rival claimants to power within the family, even leading officers who had helped to engineer their victory. The first Abbasid caliph, Abbas, promised a new era for all; even the Shi'ites could feel avenged with the massacre of the Umayyad house. In seeking a basis for their power, the Abbasids began to turn away from the old Arab aristocracy, with its pride in lineage and tribal affiliation, to seek broad support from within the greater Muslim community, especially among Persians, who had been instrumental in bringing them to power. The result was a rapid internationalization of Islam, even though the Abbasids themselves, Arab aristocrats, were to be the longest-ruling Arab dynasty in the Muslim world: descendants of this family were to hold the caliphate in Iraq for 500 years.

Certain parts of the Muslim world were not, however, under effective Abbasid control, so for the first time the Muslim polity was divided. Egypt and North Africa, for example, were ruled by dynasties that gave nominal allegiance and payments to the caliph but were otherwise effectively independent. The Shi'ites were politically marginalized. The far east of Iran, as well as Afghanistan and Central Asia, gradually began to see the creation of hereditary governorships that in time would become local dynasties.

Iraq itself was diverse in its population. The majority of the settled population had been Christians and Jews, who spoke Aramaic as their first language. Aramaic is related to Arabic, so it was presumably not difficult for these people to develop at least a speaking knowledge of Arabic in the new society in which they found themselves. There were probably numerous speakers of Persian, especially in the larger cities and towns. The Arab town and city population of Iraq prior to the conquest had been largely Christian but Arabic-speaking. There were also nomadic, tribally organized Arabs in the steppe country. The Muslim conquerors had mostly settled in the south, at Kufa and Basra, as well as at what became the Umayyad administrative capital, Wasit. Others had settled in Mosul, the largest city in the northern steppe, which had replaced Nineveh and Assur as the marketing center of the region. There were presumably Kurds and other ethnic groups as well, but we know little of them in this period.

2. Baghdad and Its Civilization

The Abbasid caliph Mansur (754–775) completed the suppression of resistance and went on to expand the frontiers of Islam in Iran and India. On 30 July 762, a favorable day chosen by his astrologers, he founded a new capital city, Baghdad, "city of peace." The name of the place was inherited from Sassanian times, and is of unknown meaning, though many fanciful etymologies have been proposed. The new city consisted of a separate, fortified complex for the ruler in a circular shape, a pattern known from Parthian and Sassanian Iran. The caliph's "Golden Palace" was entered by a golden gate; a vast dome covered the main hall. The palace was served by its own mosque. In addition, there was a military quarter, a special settlement for the crown prince, and a market district. Construction materials were brought from near-by Ctesiphon, symbolizing the transition to a new era. Baghdad was favorably situated where the Tigris and Euphrates channels come close to each other, allowing excellent connections to both Syria and Iran, as well as to Egypt by the desert road; this was soon developed as a pilgrimage route to Mecca. As a new city, Baghdad was free from the tribalism of the Arab cities of Kufa and Basra, and people drifted there from all over the Muslim world to seek their fortunes. It supported a substantial Jewish community, with its own market district, and there were important minorities of Christians, especially Nestorians, and of Mandaeans, a Gnostic sect that emphasizes the importance of John the Baptist. There were Shi'ites and Sunnites. Thus no group could predominate and the Abbasids, skillful politicians, could provide the unity for a pluralistic society. Arab writers lavished their praises on this great city, claiming it had 30,000 mosques, 10,000 public baths, gardens, a zoo, and 6000 streets. The streets were swept daily and to ensure cleanliness, beasts of burden were forbidden in the enclosure. The commercial and manufacturing areas were laid out outside the walled caliphal city. Among the most famous was the book market, where scholars congregated and poetry recitations were held. The city, really an agglomeration of several cities on both banks of the Tigris, was renowned for its schools, four universities, libraries, hospitals, musical conservatories, and an observatory, and may have supported a population of close to half a million within a century of its foundation, hence the largest city in Western Asia and far larger than any city in Europe. The Mustansiriyyah University, founded about 1230, stressed religious sciences.

One of the buildings of this university still stands in modern Baghdad, having been converted into a customs house for the city in 1823. It was restored as a historic monument in the twentieth century.

Baghdad became a center for Arabic scholarship, theology, historiography, medicine, and philosophy. For example, the ninth-century philosopher Al-Kindi, who pioneered the formation of a language of philosophical discourse in Arabic, was a native of the city and taught and wrote there for most of his life. The early tenth-century historian al-Tabari, whose universal history is one of the most impressive and important works of its kind from the Middle Ages, spent much of his career in Baghdad.

The rich hinterland of Baghdad was served by an elaborate canal system inherited from the later Sassanian rulers. Baghdad had therefore replaced Ctesiphon, Seleucia, and Babylon as the major metropolis of the region. The city grew apace, as did the Abbasid court and governmental apparatus.

The nearest model for government was provided by the Sassanian state of the seventh century. The caliph, like the Sassanian king, was an absolute ruler, with an executioner ready to hand, though the caliphal government was rapidly diffused and elaborated into a series of bureaus or ministries. The caliph was served by a confidential adviser, or vizier, a Persian office, and a series of bureaus, called by the Persian word *diwan*. Among these was a rapid and effective road and postal service, already begun by the Achaemenid kings, an intelligence service, a judiciary, and the religious establishment, which last included education through religious schools, often attached to mosques. Sassanian writings on the art of rule and statecraft set the tone for the new government. Arab writers lavish their praises, and sometimes perhaps their imaginations, on the wonders of the caliphal palace, with its 22,000 carpets and such curiosities as a marvelous tree with movable gold twigs and mechanical jeweled birds. Persian practices of the good life, with its love of comfort, beauty, and pleasure, predominated. Hence the Arabs learned the enjoyment of gardens, pools, and baths; elegant cuisine, music, and sophisticated equestrian sports such as polo, not to mention the arts of falconry and the hunt.

The most important interaction between the government and its rural subjects in Iraq was through taxation. The central administration followed the Sassanian practice of estimating local yields and taxing on the basis of that estimate. Government lands, often the best, were exempt from taxes. Actual collection of taxes on the local level was often left to local headmen, landowners, or other notables. Though such men were not administrators, they gained power of patronage and prestige by representing the central government. Thus the administration remained centralized and professional but relied on non-administrators to implement its policies. This pattern, already very ancient in Iraq, was to remain normative until modern times.

The climax of this early phase of the Baghdad caliphate was the rule of Harun al-Rashid (786–809), whose name is now associated with the irascible tyrant entertained by the stories of the Arabian Nights. He led the last great caliphal campaign against the Byzantine empire (806) in the hope of taking Constantinople, the major objective of the Muslim conquests that had never been realized. Perhaps hoping to open a second front against Byzantium, Harun sent exotic gifts and an embassy to Charlemagne, in far-away France. The extravagance, culture, and wealth of the Abbasid court reached an apogee in his time, the mores of which are epitomized for educated Arabs today by the sensuous verse of Harun's poet and carousing companion, Abu Nuwas, whose name still refers to a riverfront district in Baghdad once famous for its waterside restaurants. In his wine songs, he was outspoken about his vices:

Offer me no wine to drink unless you tell me, "This is wine."
Don't make me drink in private, let the public binge be mine.
What's life without that drink sublime?

If it's long with drink then short's the time!
Yes, what's the loss unless you see me walking a straight line,
And what's the gain unless you meet me staggering and blind?
Do you proclaim my loved one's name and mince no words with me,
There's no delight in getting tight, if you do it secretly.
I signaled for the barmaid after waking from my doze,
By now the stars had faded and there an eagle rose.
She said, "Who knocked?" We said, "A crowd!"
*"It won't take aught to please them if a drop of wine's allowed."** *

Although there is a rich literature and numerous works of art surviving from this period, no significant architectural remains of early caliphal Baghdad have been identified.

3. Samarra and the Growth of Local Dynasties

The achievements of the early Abbasids were undermined by a disastrous civil war after Harun's death between two rival claimants, his sons Amin and Ma'mun. Ma'mun was eventually the victor, from his capital in Central Asia. In this period began regular recruitment of soldiers from Iran and Central Asia, Turkish and Iranian, who were formed into ethnic military corps with personal allegiance to their commanders. These became a troublesome presence in Baghdad, as they had no basis for a productive relationship with the local population. After Ma'mun's reign, to achieve greater security for the ruling house, the caliphate was moved to Samarra, 96 km north of Baghdad, where it remained from 836 to 894. There a sprawling settlement developed, comprising some 57 sq km, including two major palace complexes and various smaller ones, mosques, a grand boulevard, six military cantons, a town, and extensive grounds for polo and horse races and hunting parks. Today the ruins of this once bustling metropolis are dominated by a helicoidal minaret, belonging to its major mosque, in its time the largest in the Muslim world. This tower was clearly inspired by the ziggurats, or temple towers, of Babylonia.

Samarra was extensively excavated by German archaeologists in 1911 and 1913 and beginning in 1936 by the Iraqi Directorate-General of Antiquities. The site was damaged during the Iraq War and the American occupation. Troops used the minaret as a sniper's lookout and a bomb wrecked its top in 2005.

The move of the caliphate to Samarra soon placed it at the mercy of the local military. This in turn encouraged local governors in remoter regions to declare independence or to withhold payments and tribute expected at the capital. This allowed local forms of Islamic culture and society to flourish in many parts of the Muslim world. The courts of these local dynasties were often centers for patronage of arts and letters, including poetry, theology, astronomy, mathematics, and other exact sciences. Mosul, for example, prospered under independent dynasties in northern Syria and Iraq during the tenth and eleventh centuries, then fell under Seljuk rule. In the early twelfth century it was a major center of resistance to the crusades. It was taken and pillaged by Saladin, whose dynasty held the city until 1272.

A twelfth-century minaret, the so-called "leaning minaret," is one of the few important medieval architectural monuments left in Mosul.

Another consequence of the move to Samarra was that the religious establishment also grew more independent of the caliphate, though it was always charged with formulating religious justification for caliphal rule. Religious skepticism found its voices too, especially in the verse of Abu al-Ala' al-Ma'arri (tenth century), who wrote prolifically expressing his doubts about the faiths of his time:

Pagans are stumbling, Christians all astray,
Jews bewildered, Magians far on error's way.
We mortals are composed of two great schools,
*Enlightened knaves or else religious fools.***

A further consequence of the weakening of the caliphate was that the foreign trade of Iraq, overland to Iran and Syria, by sea to Africa,

India, and China, became dominated by individual merchant families and venturers, whereas the earlier caliphate had followed the Sassanian example by trying to control international commerce. The importance of international trade for developments in Muslim art and culture can hardly be overestimated. Imported spices, for example, became staples of a new and more varied diet for the upper classes. Exotic woods, such as teak, presented new possibilities to joiners and wood carvers for furniture and architectural elements such as doors and lattices. Some scholars associate the rapid development of Islamic ceramics, with its spectacular glazes and applied decorations, with the stimulus provided by the regular importation of fine Far Eastern wares into Iraq, beginning in the ninth century. Iraq did, however, have long pre-existing local traditions of glazing and experimentation with vitreous materials to build on, including tile work and glass. Furthermore, the raw materials and firing technology needed for Chinese ceramics were not accessible in Iraq, so local potters first experimented with their own glazing styles then gradually developed a distinctive luster ware, made by applying mixtures of copper and silver to the first glaze then fixing it with a second firing. The innovative ceramic traditions of Iraq spread to Syria, Egypt, and Iran, so within the Muslim world local styles and techniques developed rapidly.

4. Medieval Iraq

The main economic basis for Iraq under the caliphs was, as in antiquity, agriculture. The principal revenues of the government came from tax on land or crops, paid by all subjects, supplemented by a poll, or income, tax, levied on non-Muslims, plus import and export duties and a manufacturing tax. The early Abbasid caliphate reaped enormous benefits from Iraq's rich agricultural potential, then the greatest in the Muslim world. Southern Iraqi agriculture depended on the extensive canal system perfected by the Sassanian rulers of the sixth century. The main Nahrawan canal, for example, passing near Baghdad, ran for 225 km and made possible the economic development of the whole region around Samarra and south as far as Kut. There was a barrage on the Tigris below Tikrit which drew water off towards Baquba. Part of this channel was called "Qat al-Kisra," "Chosroes' Cut," because of its Sassanian origin. By all indications, however, agricultural production in Iraq declined sharply in the mid-ninth century, and did not recover until modern times, when many of these areas, for example the region east of the Tigris from Samarra to Kut, were not cultivable.

The reasons for this decline are much in dispute. Certainly the civil war of the ninth century and the subsequent weakness of the central government contributed to the neglect of the canal system, which required large resources and constant maintenance. The natural courses of the Tigris and Euphrates are also subject to abrupt change, though there is no evidence that such a change took place at this period so as to have such a disastrous effect on the hydrography of the region. Some scholars think that great canal schemes can lead to overexploitation of the landscape, hence salinization and loss of productivity. Though salinization is a fact of Iraqi agriculture, other scholars believe its historical importance has been exaggerated. Further dislocation was caused by a lengthy slave rebellion in the ninth century in the south (868–893), where Africans, called by the Arabs "Zanj," had been brought in to reclaim marshland for farming.

On the positive side, the Arab conquests had brought dramatic developments in agriculture because the great extent of the Muslim domains opened new possibilities for plants and trees to be introduced to new environments. Thus, for example, the orange, as well as apricot, peach, sugar, and saffron made their way west as far as Spain under the Muslims; rice was extensively cultivated in Iraq for the first time. The new crops of fruits, nuts, and hitherto exotic plants brought high profits to both the landowners and the cultivators in the early centuries of Islam, and continued to do so in areas outside of Iraq with a more stable agricultural regime.

5. The Translation Movement

One of the most important cultural achievements of the early Abbasid caliphate was the collection and translation into Arabic of works of philosophy, philology, and exact sciences from Greek. This was a sustained effort, begun already under the caliph Mansur, that lasted for about two centuries. There was a school of very accomplished translators at Baghdad. The translators and their patrons saw themselves as collecting and saving for posterity the scattered scientific literature of antiquity, and took as their model a comparable collection and translation said to have been carried out under the later Sassanian rulers. Translation served important ideological purposes as well, for groups who had sought to revive Persian religious and cultural traditions against the Muslim state had used translation of Zoroastrian works as a way of gaining recruits to their cause. Therefore it was in the interest of the caliphate both to respond and even to co-opt translation into Arabic for its own purposes. This was because the caliphate was being positioned in Iraq as the legitimate successor to the Sassanians and it was important to keep Persian support. The earliest translation at Baghdad was, therefore, probably from Pahlavi, the language of the Zoroastrian scriptures, into Arabic. In due course translation from ancient Greek served different purposes. Mansur's successor, Mahdi, was interested in the systematic defense of Islam in polemic, the use of systematic argumentation to attack heresies and other religions, so commissioned a translation of Aristotle's *Topics*, a work on argumentation and debate, as an important source for the necessary techniques. Harun's son, Ma'mun, was not only personally interested in ancient writings, but also as the victor in a destructive civil war, he turned to doctrinal correctness as a way to uphold and justify his rule, even instituting an inquisition. For him, religion and the state went hand in hand, so it was for the state to enforce correct religious belief, and religious dogma was to be put in the service of upholding and explaining his government and its policies.

Most important for western culture, the Muslim government and its translators chose to see the ancient, pagan Greeks as imbued with much knowledge worth recovering. They considered that their Greek-speaking contemporaries, the Byzantines, though they used the same Greek language, were far inferior to the pagan Greeks in wisdom, owing to their adoption of Christianity. This put the Abbasids in a comparable position to that of Europeans who, in the nineteenth and twentieth centuries, grafted ancient Near Eastern cultures, such as those of Mesopotamia and Egypt, onto the foundations of western civilization, but excluded Islam and Byzantium as later and inferior. For the Abbasids, there was a polemic purpose against their major political and military enemy and cultural and religious rival, whereas for later Europeans a comparable attitude towards past and present was in effect a polemic against Islam and against eastern, Greek-speaking Christianity. The works of Aristotle, therefore, offered the Baghdad scholars, who understood them well, rational tools to be used for the benefit of the caliph's government, for the systematic defense and propagation of the faith, and as cultural weapons against a rival polity and culture. Translated works could open the secrets of astrology, alchemy, philosophy, and natural and exact sciences, and could serve to educate a new managerial class in service of the government. Inevitably, the impact of the translation movement led to a broader sense of scholarship and education in Abbasid Iraq: philosophy and the sciences were truly international, to be sought among the written traditions of non-Muslim peoples as well as Muslims, to be elaborated, understood, and transmitted in Arabic in the context of Muslim civilization. To put it simply, Aristotle belonged as much to the Muslim world as he did to the Christian world, in the ninth century more so, as there was no one in Charlemagne's empire, for example, who could read the works of Aristotle in Greek and there was no translation of them available in either Latin or the vernaculars of northern Europe.

So it was that the first contacts of Latin Christian scholars with the works of Aristotle, for example, were through Arabic translations they studied in Spain and Sicily, the lands where, in Medieval Europe, libraries of translations and scholars able to read them were to be found. A twelfth-century student bored with lectures on Christian theology and biblical exegesis at Paris or Oxford could go to Cordova to read, in Arabic, works of Classical Greek antiquity, and to translate them into Latin for those who could not read Arabic, the universal cultural language of the medieval Mediterranean world. In this way, the Abbasid caliphate was directly responsible for the transmission of major components of Classical Greek civilization to the Latin-speaking world.

Through the translation activity at Baghdad, ancient Greek philosophical and scientific writing became truly international, not bound by any culture, time, or language, and thereby ultimately a cornerstone of Latin-speaking civilization of the high Middle Ages and the Renaissance. In addition, elegant court literature in Arabic developed, in prose and verse, strongly influenced by Persian styles, taste, storytelling, essay-writing, and concepts of useful and interesting knowledge.

The rapid expansion of learning under the Abbasids was also stimulated by a new invention, paper. Prior to the use of paper, books were copied on much more expensive materials, such as vellum, or papyrus, which was mostly exported from Egypt. Paper was introduced to the Muslim world in 751 by Chinese prisoners and had the advantage that it could be milled anywhere. The Abbasids were quick to realize the potential of paper and soon it became the standard medium of publication. It was cheaper, easier to produce, and lighter in weight than other media, so many more people could own books copied on paper than could afford vellum or even papyrus rolls. The Abbasid government was also the first to adopt the use of paper for official record keeping. Baghdad was to remain a center for paper production throughout the Middle Ages.

6. Decline and Fall of the Abbasid Caliphate

The decline of Abbasid civilization that began in the tenth century seemed to proceed on many fronts at once. Political power slipped away in several directions: to Iran and Central Asia, and to Egypt, where a rival, Shi'ite caliphate, called the Fatimid caliphate, emerged beginning in 969. Many would associate this with the decline of Iraqi agriculture, as the great canal systems of Iraq fell into disuse and only local irrigation works were maintained. So weak did the caliphate become that an Iranian Shi'ite dynasty, called the Buyids, extended their power over Baghdad itself for better than a century (945–1055). The Buyids, however, were content to recognize the religious leadership of the caliphate over all Sunnites and to base their legitimacy as rulers on caliphal recognition.

The conversion of the Turkic peoples to Islam, however, was to prove decisive in the reassertion of orthodoxy. The Sunnite, or orthodox, tradition was vigorously reasserted by a Turkish dynasty referred to as the Seljuks, who combined a strong tradition of military life with a self-perception as guardians of orthodox Islam. As champions of the faith, they renewed the long-dormant policy of attack on the Byzantine empire. In 1071 their efforts were met with brilliant success under the command of Alp Arslan at Manzikert, near modern Ankara, where the Byzantine army was decimated and the emperor himself taken captive. This opened much of Asia Minor to the Seljuks. As they pushed ever westward towards the Aegean and Constantinople, they began a Turkification of the region and its conversion to Islam. The grateful caliphs had granted them the title "sultan," meaning a person with political and military power who owed allegiance to the caliph. In the early twelfth century, in fact, the caliphate began to revive and showed signs of regaining its former power and prestige.

By the twelfth century, local rule in Iraq was evolving away from the central government, however, into a pattern resembling European feudalism of the same period. Grants of land to support military men, for example, gradually became private property passed from generation to generation. Local war lords, nomadic leaders, and commanders of slave soldiers usurped many of the day-to-day functions of government, but still recognized the supremacy of the caliphate and its institutions. The religious composition of Iraq was still complex, including Sunnites, Shi'ites, adherents to mystical Muslim brotherhoods (Sufis), not to mention eastern Christians, Jews, and Zoroastrians.

Yet Baghdad and the caliphate were doomed. A terrifying, invincible force appeared from the far east, the Mongols. Their numbers were overwhelming; they could cover long distances rapidly on their sturdy, tireless horses. They were fierce fighters, absolutely loyal to their leaders. They took little interest in the lands and peoples they conquered, often massacring the entire populations of cities they overran, as well as destroying them to the ground. They even sent back small expeditionary forces a few weeks later to places they had decimated to kill anyone who had somehow escaped them and was trying to reestablish life in the ruins.

In 1258, under the chieftain Hulegu, a Mongol force approached and laid siege to Baghdad. The caliph had ignored warnings of their advance and the city soon fell. Hulegu entered the caliph's palace and, to judge from an account written by a Persian historian, Rashid al-Din (d. 1318), who wrote under Mongol rule, enjoyed himself by toying with the fears of the caliph and his vast court:

> *He commanded that the caliph be brought and said, "You are host and we guests, show what you have that would be suitable for us." The caliph understood the real meaning of these words, so began to tremble in terror and became so frightened he could not recall where the keys of the stores were. He ordered that some locks be broken and offered as a tribute two thousand robes, ten thousand pieces of gold, and various precious objects studded with gems and decorated with pearls. Hulegu-khan paid no attention to them, gave all to the commanders and those present, and said to the caliph, "The wealth you have above ground is obvious and belongs to my servants, but you show the hidden stores, what and where they are." The caliph revealed the reserve full of gold in the center of the palace. They broke it open and it turned out to be full of pure gold, all in 500-gram bars ...****

Next the caliph was forced to make a choice among his family and household, and was finally cruelly executed, along with his grown sons.

For the great city there was no hope. Her mosques, universities, palaces, public buildings, schools, homes, libraries, and gardens, half a millennium of human accomplishment, were looted and burned and her people put to the sword (estimates of the killed vary from 800,000 to two million). According to one account, the stench of the corpses of the massacred population became so intense that the Mongols soon had to withdraw from the city. A thirteenth-century Arab historian who, as a Shi'ite, rejected the Abbasid caliphate, wrote a long history of it, full of detail, but when his narrative reached the destruction of the city, words failed him, so he contented himself with a verse of poetry:

> *What then occurred, I cannot bring myself to say,*
> *Imagine it, but ask for no account, I pray.*****

To the modern historian, the cultural loss is incalculable; no one will ever know how much human knowledge and achievement were obliterated. There were Christian bigots in Europe who rejoiced at the news and dreamed of converting the Mongols to Christianity, thus to bring the whole known world under the Christian faith. But to many Arabs and Muslims today, the sack and occupation of Baghdad is a turning point in their history, and comparable to the fall of Rome to barbarians or the fall of Constantinople to the Turks in western tradition.

Abbasid remains in Iraq are best known at Samarra. At Baghdad, the minaret of the Suq al-Ghazal dates to the early tenth century. The so-called Abbasid palace, dating to the thirteenth century, a structure with an *iwan*, may have been part of a school.

One contemporaneous Arab poet, Taqi al-Din Ismail, penned an ode in which he mourned the city and expressed his regret that he was destined to outlive it:

> *That crown of the caliphate,*
> *That abode wherefrom its offices drew such glory,*
> *Now lies desolate and ruined.*
> *Dawn rose over the marks the storm left*
> *On that abode in its hour of trial*
> *And over traces running tears left in its debris.*
> *O fire now burning in my heart, from the conflagration of the war*
> *That burst upon that abode, while the tempest laid it low!******

Bibliographical Note to Chapter 10

In addition to the works cited in in the Bibliographical Note to Chapter 9, see Shams C. Inati, "Baghdad in the Golden Age: A Historical Tour," in Shams C. Inati, ed., *Iraq, Its History, People, and Politics* (Amherst, NY: Humanity Books, 2003), 35–48. For the translation movement, Dimitri Gutas, *Greek Thought, Arabic Culture* (London and New York: Routledge, 1998) is strongly recommended; this is the basis for the brief remarks given in this chapter. There are numerous anthologies of Classical Arabic in English translation. In addition to the collection of Kritzeck (see Bibliographical Note to Chapter 9), see Robert Irwin, *Night & Horses & The Desert* (New York: Anchor Books, 2001) and, for pre-Islamic Arabic poetry, Michael Sells, *Desert Tracings: Six Classic Arabian Odes* (Middletown, Ct.: Wesleyan University Press, 1989). For the importance of the invention and spread of paper, see Jonathan M. Bloom, *Paper Before Print, The History and Impact of Paper in the Islamic World* (New Haven: Yale University Press, 2001), especially Chapter 2. For the Mongol attack on Baghdad, see Guy Le Strange, *Baghdad during the Abbasid Caliphate* (Oxford: Oxford University Press, 1900), 340–343. For the Seljuks, see Claude Cahen, *Pre-Ottoman Turkey* (New York: Taplinger, 1968) and Lapidus, *History* (see Bibliographical Note to Chapter 9).

Translated Excerpts

*Iliya al-Hawi, *Sharh Diwan Abi Nuwas* (Beirut: al-Madrasah 1983), 1:391–392.

**R. A. Nicholson, *A Literary History of the Arabs* (Cambridge: Cambridge University Press, 1907).

***After the Russian translation of A. K. Arends, *Rashid-ad-Din, Shornik Letopisej* (Moscow-Leningrad: Academy of Sciences, 1946), 3:44.

****Ibn al-Tiqtaqa (Muhammad ibn Ali ibn Taba'taba'i), *Al-Fakhri fi al-Adab al-Sultaniyyah wa al-Duwal al-Islamiyyah*, ed. Mamduh Hassan Muhammad (Cairo: Library of Religious Culture, 1999), 311.

*****Shams al-Din al-Dhahabi, *Tarikh al-Islam* (Beirut: Dar al-Kitab al-Arabi, 1987), 48:38. The ode was first edited by Joseph de Somogyi, "A Qasidah on the Destruction of Baghdād by the Mongols," *Bulletin of the School of Oriental and African Studies* 7 (1933/5), 41–48.

Chapter 11

Iraq in the Ottoman Empire

1. Iraq under Mongol Rule

We know little of Iraq following the Mongol conquest. Baghdad had been devastated and was now only a provincial town. Other cities in Iraq had been dealt with less harshly, but Iraq was now a poor province in a vast entity that ultimately owed allegiance to a great khan far away in China. The whole region was ruled from Tabriz in northwestern Iran, which soon took over much of Mosul's role as a regional center. Iraq went into a severe decline lasting for more than three centuries, with agricultural revenues declining as much as 90% from what they had been even in the last years of the caliphate. The local Mongol rulers, the Il khans, eventually converted to Islam by the early fourteenth century, but the caliphate was not revived. This was in part because the Fatimids, the rival Shi'ite caliphs still ruling in Egypt, were not recognized by many Muslims outside of Egypt. There were, of course, competing factions among the Mongol rulers. One of the most aggressive and successful of the Mongols from Central Asia, Tamerlane (Timur), invaded Iraq in 1393 and took Baghdad for his own state. His hold proved tenuous, however, so he returned in 1401, and the destruction brought upon the city again set back any gains it had made since the initial Mongol conquest.

An Arab poet, Safi al-Din al-Hilli, was born near Babylon in 1278, grew up during the Mongol rule of Iraq, and died at Baghdad about 1350. He cultivated a highly refined style, not esteemed by readers today, with elaborate conceits and figures of speech and demanding rhyme schemes. His verse gives little hint of the tumultuous times in which he lived. Poetry in this precious style became popular at the courts of local rulers, not only in Iraq, but in Iran and Central Asia as well. This excerpt is from a love poem, every line of which begins and ends with the letter K:

> *Enough of combat, let loose your captive's bond!*
> *Enough for you, the work your eyes have made of men.*
> *Your sidelong glance holds firm your victim slain,*
> *Who is there could best your valor, shedding lovers' heartblood?*
> *Enough, I say, what work you make of lovers,*
> *Had time dealt justly with them, some had been too strong for you.*
> *You limned a new ideal of beauty, omitting not a single stroke,*
> *Were only that, your beauty, conjoined with kinder heart!* *

2. Iraq under Turkish Rule

The main powers in Iraq in the fifteenth century were two large Turkoman (Turkish-speaking) federations, having their origins in eastern Anatolia, called the federation of the Black Sheep (Kara Koyunlu) and the federation of the White Sheep (Ak Koyunlu). The Kara Koyunlu ruled from Mosul to Erzurum, briefly holding Baghdad as well, whereas the Ak Koyunlu were established in the south. The situation in Iraq was further complicated by the emergence in the extreme south of the land by a militant group called the Musha'sha', a Shi'ite sect which proclaimed the coming of a new leader and promised a religious order in which the descendants of Ali would at last receive their due. This group overran the city of Basrah and began to expand to the north.

In the early sixteenth century, Iraq fell between two rival Muslim powers, the Safavids and the Ottomans, each with aspirations to universality. On the Iranian plateau, a dynasty known as the Safavids had created a state based on the allegiance of various tribal groups in Iran. The ruling family embraced a local form of Shi'ism. The Safavid royal family was considered the leaders of the order. In addition to these tribal and religious claims, the Safavid dynasty, to some extent, sought to revive the traditions of the Persian and Sassanian empires, adding the non-Muslim title of shah to the palette of their claims. The Safavids encountered the same problems that other Iranian powers had been obliged to overcome: definition of their legitimacy, the necessity of controlling unruly tribal groups dispersed widely on the plateau and on the steppes east of the Caspian, the difficulty of controlling a well-entrenched administration with its own independent traditions, and a certain fiscal weakness owing to the difficulty of maintaining regular revenues. But the early shahs of this dynasty were capable men, and in due course the Safavid capital at Isfahan would emerge as one of the most beautiful and lavishly built cities in the entire Middle East. The Safavids were thus an eastern, Iranian power in the same tradition as the Achaemenids and the Sassanians.

The Ottoman Turks, on the other hand, were heirs to the Mediterranean tradition of the Roman empire, with their capital in Europe at Constantinople. Under their greatest rulers, such as Suleiman the Magnificent, the Ottomans formed the most powerful nation in Europe and carried out an aggressive policy of expansion through the Balkans and on to Hungary and Austria, in the Mediterranean against such fortresses as Rhodes, in Arabia and Iraq, and in Egypt and North Africa. With the conquest of Egypt, the Ottoman sultans took the title caliph for themselves in 1517. The Ottomans were orthodox Sunni Muslims, so regarded the Safavids as heretics. The Ottomans had the advantage of a loyal administration, superior forces and military technology, including artillery, over the Persians, but the Persians sought to convert various Turkish groups living under Ottoman rule to Shi'ism, thus to undermine their enemy's tribal support. In the eyes of Europeans who felt immediately threatened by the menace of the aggressive Ottoman state, the Safavid state seemed an enlightened and promising ally as well as trading partner. Europeans living in Iran at the time had a different view, finding Persian ways sometimes difficult to understand, and fearing the suspicious nature and seemingly capricious decisions of the shahs.

Iraq was one of several areas where the competition between these two states came to open warfare. Iraq had no clearly defined border with Iran, so it was natural for the shahs to consider Iraq within their legitimate sphere of influence. This was the location of the holiest cities of Shi'ite Islam, Kufa, the burial place of Ali himself, and Karbala, burial place of his son Hussein. Many Persians settled around or in these cities as centers of Shi'ite faith and learning. So it was that in 1508 the shah moved against the Musha'sha' insurrection in southern Iraq, fearing its expansion north to the holy cities and also its rival claims to leadership of Shi'ite Islam. In the meantime, the Ottomans expanded into the Upper Tigris region and pushed south to Mosul, establishing a claim to that city which was to last until modern times. A major battle between the Ottomans and the Safavids was inevitable. This took place at Chaldiran in Anatolia in 1514, and was a resounding victory for the Ottoman sultan. The northern boundary between Iran and the Ottoman domains was drawn up along the present boundary line between Turkey and Iran, but further south there was still no established frontier for Iraq and indeed no concept that what is now Iraq was a single region. The Safavids held the south until 1533, when Suleiman the Magnificent invaded, seizing Baghdad in 1534 and pushing on for an outlet on the Gulf. Although the Safavids briefly reconquered Baghdad with the help of a local renegade in 1623 and held it until 1638, for most of its history until World War I, Iraq was to belong to the Ottoman Empire.

3. The Ottomans and Their Subjects

The three major cities of Mosul, Baghdad, and Basra were Ottoman administrative centers, with an additional rural administrative unit in charge of the Kurds in the north and northeast, and another in the Arabian desert region. Ottoman Turks were largely restricted to the principal cities. The plain and the marshes in the south were mostly Arabic-speaking. There was an Assyrian (that is, Eastern Syrian) Aramaic-speaking Christian community in Mosul, a Jewish community, especially in Baghdad, and smaller groups, such as Yezidis, a Gnostic sect alleging origins in Shi'ism, and Sabians, an ultimately pagan sect, in some regions. Half or more of the Arab and Kurdish population was nomadic. The Ottoman sultanate sought to impose direct rule on the region, sending out Ottoman administrators and at the same time cultivating local leaders, especially of tribal groups, to ensure their loyalty to the sultan. Certain Ottomans, especially the military class throughout the empire, were sustained by grants of land in return for their service. This mode of maintaining the government was begun in Iraq, but it was of importance mostly in the Mosul area.

Both the Ottoman sultans and the Safavids entered a period of relative weakness in the seventeenth century. Whereas the administrations and military were still effective, the leadership was not, often because future rulers were sequestered until their accession and so came to the task without practical experience and in some cases even of doubtful mental stability. The result was that in some provincial areas, such as Iraq, local administrators and notables could turn into more or less independent autocrats within their own sphere of influence. The term notables denotes community leaders of varying sources of authority, religious, tribal, or personal wealth or prestige, who assumed the role of leaders within their communities and as mediators, when necessary, with the Ottoman authorities, for example in the allocation and collection of taxes or in meeting service requirements. Notables were in consequence often in competition with other notables and the groups they represented for political and economic power and for social leadership and prestige on the local scene. In Iraq, the notables included sheikhs of tribes, important merchants with personal followers, and religious leaders. The religious leaders included scholars and teachers of Islamic law, judges, heads of Shi'ite groups, heads of mystical orders, and heads of families who were traditionally wardens of the major holy places. Certain prominent families in urban areas like Mosul and Baghdad often sought to dominate the politics and economy of their cities and surrounding regions. Within their own groups, notables had powers of patronage, decision-making, even command, so their cooperation was useful for the sprawling Ottoman government to reach out to its diverse subjects. Decline of the sultan's effective authority gave notables such authority the backing of the sultanate could bestow but left them free of much direction from the sultan's administration.

The border between what is now Iraq and Iran was initially sketched, essentially along the lines of the modern border, in 1639 and more formally in 1847, but there was still no concept of an Iraq — rather, it was the districts of Mosul, Basra, Baghdad, and outlying areas. Somewhere between a third and a half of the population was nomadic in subsistence and tribal in social structure. Agriculture had dwindled since the Mongol period to the area immediately north of Baghdad and around the Basra region. The religious composition of Iraq was among the most complex in the Ottoman Empire. It was the only part of the empire with a predominantly Shi'ite population, concentrated in the plain south of Baghdad, especially around the holy cities of Karbala and Najaf. Baghdad itself was divided into a Shi'ite quarter on the east bank, though the major Shi'ite shrine there, Qazimiyyah, was on the west bank where the Sunnite population lived. There was a large Jewish population in Baghdad, active in commerce but not in politics. The Shi'ite religious leadership largely kept away from politics. Since the Ottomans were Sunnite, it was natural that the Arabic-speaking Sunnite minority in Iraq would be the source of local administrators, as well as the much smaller Turkish-speaking population of the towns and cities.

European merchants and their governments, including the Portuguese, Dutch, Russians, and English, were working to establish trading stations and to win commercial concessions in various parts of the Ottoman Empire and Iran, beginning already in the sixteenth century. Catholic missions were also established in some areas. In Iraq itself, the English were the first to gain a substantial presence. The English, from their control of the sea, tended to be primary trading partners of the Basran merchants, for example. The British East India Company opened an office in Basra in 1763 and in 1798 posted its agent to Baghdad to look after British commercial and diplomatic interests, to represent the interests of British citizens in the area, and to report to British foreign ministry or to the government of India on local political and economic developments.

4. Mamluk Iraq

A distinctive aspect of Ottoman society was the creation of a professional military class formed of men who had been taken from their families, often in the Caucasus, as youths. They converted to Islam and were trained to be administrators and soldiers. They were in theory at least slaves of the Ottoman sultan, referred to as "Mamluks," in effect royal dependents who owed their livelihood to the sultan's discretion. They were in practice often highly capable individuals who moved to the upper ranks because of their abilities, valor, and intelligence, so gained status not from birth into an aristocratic family but through their own success and leadership in the ranks of the military or administration. Having no local ties, they could be posted anywhere and were deemed more reliable than local notables. A second military class was referred to as the "janissaries," youths taken from throughout the empire, including Greece and the Balkans, trained as elite soldiers, and maintained in their own barracks as a kind of palace guard. They were often difficult to control and took advantage of their status, as a kind of security service, to impose themselves on the local population.

One Mamluk administrator, Hasan Pasha, established himself as an effective manager in Baghdad in the early eighteenth century. He was careful to send regular payments to the Ottoman treasury, thus winning a reputation for reliability and loyalty, and at the same time he undertook to deal with the contentious rural tribes who both fought among themselves and regularly resisted Ottoman taxation and conscription, but whose leadership sought government support. All this was sufficient from the viewpoint of Constantinople, so the central government did not seek to monitor his internal policies. Hasan warded off invasion from Iran and expanded his control over much of what is now Kurdistan to the north and east, thus taking control of the northern trade routes that led to Mosul. He also pushed his authority south and took control of Basra, the key to trade with India and South Arabia. Hasan was able to pass his authority on to his son, Ahmet, who ruled from 1724 until 1747 as a loyal Ottoman subject but with nearly total discretion within his own realm.

Ahmet came to power at a critical time. The Safavid dynasty was defeated by Afghan princes in 1722 who expanded into the former Safavid domains. One of these Afghans, Nadir, took for himself the title of shah and invaded Iraq, unsuccessfully besieging Mosul and Baghdad in 1742. Forced to withdraw, he acquiesced to the previously established frontiers with Iran. This redounded to the advantage of Ahmet Pasha, who was now a defender of the Ottoman Empire against its hereditary foes in the east. Ahmet did not control Mosul, which had its own local rulers, but was certainly the most powerful person in Iraq in his time, because he had the Ottoman troops under his command and was not called upon to send them outside his province to support military actions not his own.

In this environment, the Mamluk administration in Baghdad grew into a powerful, cohesive unit that was beyond the ability of the Ottoman sultan to control, though the Mamluks presented themselves as his dutiful servants. The Mamluks proved effective in quelling local disturbances among the tribes, promoting commerce, and bringing a certain amount of law and order to the countryside. By 1822, they had broken the independent power of the janissaries and turned them into a garrison at Baghdad to help uphold their authority. However, after Ahmet's death, rival factions developed within the Mamluk community. Furthermore, there were always local groups resentful of Mamluk rule because it had reduced their own authority and opportunities.

This dissension presented an opportunity to an aggressive new ruler of Iran, Karim Khan Zand, who ruled from Shiraz as successor to Nadir shah. His forces wrested Basra from the Iraqi Mamluks, but after his death in 1779 the ousted governor of Basra, Suleiman, returned and was given the governorship of Baghdad, Basra, and the northeast by the sultan in Constantinople. Suleiman, then known as Suleiman Pasha or Suleiman the Great, ruled in Iraq from 1780 until 1802 as the most successful of its Mamluk rulers. He eliminated rival Mamluk factions, made sure the royal troops at his disposal were loyal to him, and sought to increase commerce in the region through Basra, the potential of which he well knew from his former residency there. He sought to suppress the nomadic tribes of northwestern Arabia. A strict and militant form of Islam was spreading in western Arabia in the eighteenth century, now known as Wahhabism. This was strongly orthodox, thus anti-Shi'ite, and its proponents even went to far as to attack the holy city of Karbala.

5. Ottoman Weakness and Reform

By the end of the eighteenth century, the weakness of the Ottoman Empire in the face of challenges from Christian Europe was becoming apparent. This was symbolized by the French invasion of Egypt, still nominally a province of the empire, under Napoleon in 1798, in which the French army rapidly defeated the Egyptian Mamluk forces there. The second aspect of this weakness was the determination of the European governments not to let any other government take advantage of this weakness; thus the French were driven from Egypt by the English. England's policy evolved in favor of supporting the integrity of the Ottoman Empire against other European powers, especially Russia, which England considered a threat to her prize possession, India, while at the same time seeking to gain as much advantage within the Ottoman Empire as possible. Thus the British Agency in Baghdad was an important indicator of this British determination.

To Christian European eyes, the Ottoman Empire seemed too decentralized. Though Ottoman governments had ruled for centuries a vastly larger area of the earth's surface than most other European states could command, and had passed authority through a longer continuous lineage than had, for example, France or England, the Ottoman system of government was seen by Europeans as archaic, capricious, inept, and promoting too much local initiative in the hands of such groups as the Baghdad Mamluks. The European governments lobbied Constantinople for reform and concessions, at the same time undermining any reforms that showed signs of making the Ottoman state too strong for them to influence. Pressures for reform came from within Ottoman society as well, especially from junior officers and administrators who were becoming impatient with the old ways and saw in change and progress opportunities for their own advancement. Nor was this example lost on the Mamluks. In Egypt, for example, Muhammad Ali, a soldier who had come to Egypt in English service, stayed on in the power vacuum created by the English withdrawal and created a new state powerful enough to invade Syria and to threaten the sultanate itself. Forced to withdraw to his own domains by the alarmed European powers, Muhammad Ali was allowed to create a hereditary dynasty in 1841, and embarked on an ambitious program of modernizing Egypt, reforming agriculture and land-holding, and building public works, much of it financed by European banks. So too the Mamluks in Baghdad, especially Da'ud Pasha (ruled 1816 to 1831), saw in European governments a source of loans, military training and equipment, and further commercial development, though they had nothing like the resources of Muhammad Ali at their disposal. Da'ud constructed a new market, one of the few major new Ottoman structures in Baghdad.

At the same time, the Ottoman sultan was concerned by the potential of local dynasties, such as the Mamluks, to act independently. So under sultan Mahmud II (1808–1839), the central government moved to rein in the Baghdad Mamluks and to replace them with a governor sent directly from Constantinople, thus reimplementing the centralization long ago favored by Suleiman the Magnificent. Da'ud's luck ran out. Flooding and a plague in the capital city in 1831 weakened his government. The Mamluks were dispersed, an Ottoman governor, Ali Reza, arrived from the capital, and the Ottoman army set out to subdue the principal cities of Iraq and to curtail the power of the local autocrats. The Ottomans were determined to remake the empire in a more modern European way. By the mid-nineteenth century, the Ottoman government had direct control of Mosul, Baghdad, and the areas around them, as well as the holy cities of Najaf and Karbala. The Arab and Kurdish tribes of the countryside were still difficult for them to control, so the Ottomans continued to rely on the sheikhs to implement their policies, mostly to collect taxes, while the sheikhs relied on the Ottomans to uphold their authority.

6. Iraq in the Late Nineteenth Century

The new Ottoman centralization brought many changes to Iraq. The foundations for a secular system of education were laid alongside the traditional Muslim religious schools and the schools and colleges operated by Christian missionaries and other religious groups. The new secular schools provided training for Ottoman government service, even if the top functionaries were still Turks sent from Constantinople. Communications improved: steamship service was begun on the rivers; a telegraph system was in place by the 1860s, and a postal service begun. Government too saw important reforms, on the basis of a new law of 1864. Henceforth lands like Iraq were to be formally organized as provinces (*wilayet*). The central government would now rule its subjects directly, rather than through a patchwork of local autocrats. The subjects would share in government through a series of municipal councils. The local military was thereafter increasingly composed of local conscripts, mainly Arabic-speaking, but with Turkish officers.

The activities of Midhat Pasha, an Ottoman official in Iraq and governor from 1869 to 1871, fairly represent this new Ottoman way at its most energetic. Within a few years, Midhat had embarked on numerous ambitious local projects. He built the first bridge across the Tigris at Baghdad, tore down the old city walls, laid streetcar tracks and water mains, paved and illuminated important roadways. Midhat Pasha also built Iraq's first oil refinery at Baqouba, north of Baghdad. He opened a city park, hospital, and bank. The port of Basra was modernized, the river system dredged, and municipal government organized. Through the new port of Basra, Iraq began large-scale export of wheat and especially dates. Midhat set up an official printing press from which came the first Iraqi newspaper in 1869. It was not long before Iraq developed a lively press, with more than fifty newspapers appearing for varying lengths of time before World War I, supporting a range of opinions and interests. The Iraqi poet al-Rusafi (1875–1945) wrote of newspapermen in 1918:

> *The Turks in Istanbul, I see, spend time in feeble-minded strife,*
> *They wound each other with vile words in which dishonor's rife.*
> *No lance worked such harm among them as the journalistic pen,*
> *You see them rolling up their sleeves to pick off each other's men.***

The large files of historical Iraqi newspapers in the National Library of Iraq were destroyed by arson and vandalism during the American invasion. The Ottoman archives of Mosul were destroyed by fire in 2003. The Ottoman archives of Baghdad were damaged by water in 2003 and there is little likelihood they can be preserved.

In 1858 the Ottoman government implemented a land law, the purpose of which was to guarantee secure title to private property and so systematize tax liability. Extensive lands in Iraq had no documented owners. Ottoman administrators tried to establish titles to these lands, many of which were considered owned by tribes, but individual tribesmen were reluctant to put their names on documents, owing to their suspicion of administration and unwillingness to be liable for taxation. Furthermore, the law forbade joint ownership. The result was that for many areas the heads of tribes were registered as owners and given title deeds. Because of this, tribal leaders of a sudden became major landowners in the new order, even as nomadism was declining, from a third or more to about 17% of the population in the early twentieth century and perhaps 7% or less in the years after World War I. The land law had created a new landed class that would emerge in the post-Ottoman period as a major social and economic force in the region, and guaranteed that a small percentage of the population would be legal owners of most of the rural land. Thousands of small cultivators found themselves legal tenants, sometimes of complete strangers, in place of whatever their traditional status had been.

7. Pressures of Modernity

Baghdad began to prosper as the leading administrative center of Iraq, as did Basra as the only practical gateway for both export and import, a role she was to keep as Iraq was destined to be without significant seacoast. The major mistake of the new Ottoman administration was failure to see the vast potential of Iraqi agriculture. This is not surprising, as the leading members of the Ottoman administration had backgrounds in civil service or the military, so had little understanding of or interest in agriculture. They tended to see commerce and industrial development as the road to prosperity and modernity. Agriculture in Iraq had been in eclipse so long that no one remembered how prosperous it had been under the Abbasid caliphate.

For many young men not interested in government service, the Ottoman military was an attractive career. Numerous graduates of the new secular schools and military academies became junior officers in the Ottoman armed forces, though the highest commands were still largely held by Turks from Constantinople. Iraqis eventually formed the largest Arabic-speaking cadre of officers in the Ottoman military. Though loyal Ottomans, these men were ambitious. They were in favor of modernization and of more opportunities for themselves in competition with the older Turkish command. They formed clubs and associations, discussed their interests and their futures.

In the meantime, Midhat Pasha had returned to Constantinople with a brilliant record as a provincial administrator. He was promoted to grand vizier, the highest administrative office, for a brief time and later served as minister of justice. He became increasingly involved in court politics, and in 1876 was a ringleader in a series of coups that saw three sultans reign in the space of a year. Midhat's final choice, Abdul Hamid II (reigned 1876 to 1909), was brought to power in the hope of continued modernization and the implementation of a constitution and a form of parliamentary government in the Ottoman state. But Abdul Hamid had other plans and in his hour of triumph, Midhat was exiled to Europe.

Abdul Hamid saw all too clearly how the new ways had undermined the authority of the sultanate. He preferred what he expressed as a return to the older, surer ways, so in areas like Iraq he sought to bypass the central administration, or at least check and balance its power, by building individual alliances with tribal leaders and notables. Within his government and his military, there were therefore many who became bitterly opposed to what they saw as regression to the old personal and unpredictable tyranny of the sultan, not to mention the administrative order in which officials sought to enrich themselves as quickly as possible and citizens could make headway mostly through bribery and patronage. These revolutionary spirits tended to be middle-echelon administrators and junior army officers. Some called themselves the Young Turks. By 1908 the Young Turks had gathered enough support and momentum to depose the sultan and to set up a Committee of Unity and Progress to run the government under a new, figurehead sultan. Members of this group tended to see themselves as secular patriots, even identifying Islam with backwardness in government, with a program of moderating arbitrary rule at home and dealing with the increasing challenges and defeats abroad. As a group they were not well educated and had little experience or even concept of how to run the empire. Furthermore, some of them stressed Turkism, an exaltation of Turkish values, tradition, and language at the expense of both Islam, the common denominator of the whole empire, and other nationalities, such as the Arabs.

So if in theory Iraqis could sympathize with the goals of the coup, they were not by and large supportive of the Young Turks. Rather, there were calls in Iraq and among the Iraqi officers for similar goals, but with a local accent: more local autonomy, use of Arabic rather than Turkish in schools and government bureaus. The more the Young Turks stressed Turkism, the more the Iraqi officers were drawn towards a distinctively Arab cause. Although still largely loyal Ottoman subjects, as no one in Iraq knew of any other form of government, Iraqis had many other claims upon their loyalties in their own land. The appeals for Arab nationalism and a new sense of Arab identity that had been raised, beginning in the mid-nineteenth century, especially in Syria, had less of an audience in Iraq because of local preoccupations. Some of the most vocal advocates of Arab consciousness were Christians, and, unlike Syria, Iraq had a fairly small Christian community which, outside of Mosul, tended not to be politically active. So too the lively intellectual ferment in Egypt and its concommitant new developments in Arabic literature (cultivation of new forms of expression, such as drama, the short story, and the novel, freer forms of poetry) were still remote from the Iraqi intellectual scene, as compared to Cairo, Beirut or Damascus. Thus the Arabist officers were a small group but they had ambitions for the future.

The work of a poet well known in Iraq in the nineteenth century, Muhammad Said al-Iskafi (1834–1901) shows his adeptness with classical styles and types. For example, he turned out traditional poetry of praise, as in these lines, comparing a patron's generosity to a flood from the Euphrates:

I bethink me when the Euphrates overflowed its banks,
Coursed over you, swelling up in flood,
Even if it sought to rival you in its splendid peak,
'Twould, unlike you, be followed by its ebb.

O my brother, generous and free, never one to neglect a care,
Upholding the bonds of brotherhood is the very mark of freedom.
Shall I neglect one faithful to every token of brotherhood,
Brotherhood for the turmoil of events, in time of need?
If you are not there for me when events crowd thick and fast,
Then who will be there for me in my hour of trial and need?
And if you are not there to help me in this my world,
Tell me, when may I call upon you to help, on judgment day? ***

All local developments in Iraq were co-opted by the convulsion of World War I, which brought, in a few years, more drastic changes to the land than it had seen since the thirteenth century.

Bibliographical Note to Chapter II

For a concise historical survey of the Mongol period, see Gavin Hambly, ed., *Central Asia* (New York: Delacorte, 1969). A good picture of the Seljuks is provided by Claude Cahen, *Pre-Ottoman Turkey* (New York: Taplinger, 1968). Information on early Ottoman Iraq can be drawn from historical studies of the Ottoman Empire, such as Stanford J. Shaw, *History of the Ottoman Empire and Modern Turkey* (Cambridge: Cambridge University Press, 1971). European attitudes towards the Ottomans are explored in Andrew Wheatcroft, *The Ottomans, Dissolving Images* (London: Penguin Books, 1993). For Iran, see David Morgan, *Medieval Persia, 1040– 1797* (New York: Longman, 1988), and for the Safavids in particular, Roger M. Savory, *Iran under the Safavids* (Cambridge: Cambridge University Press, 1980) For Iraq in the nineteenth century, see Charles Tripp, *A History of Iraq*, second edition (Cambridge: Cambridge University Press, 2002), Chapter 1; I have also used the sketches of key personalities, such as Midhat Pasha, in the *Encyclopedia of Islam*. An excellent and readable history of the nineteenth-century Middle East, including Iraq, is M. E. Yapp, *The Making of the Modern Middle East 1792–1923* (New York: Longman, 1987). For the temper of the transition from the nineteenth to the twentieth centuries in the Middle East, one may also recommend the stimulating essays of Elie Kedourie, *Politics in the Middle East* (Oxford: Oxford University Press, 1992), "The Legacy" and "The Modern World: Threat and Predicament."

Translated Excerpts

*Muhammad Huwar, ed., *Diwan Safi al-Din al-Hilli* (Beirut: Arab Foundation for Study and Publication: 2000), 3:1511.
**Mustafa Ali, *Sharh diwan al-Rusafi* (Baghdad: Cultural Affairs Press, 1986), 3:75.
***Ali al-Khaqani, *Shuara' al-Ghari* (Qom: Bahram, 1987), 9:94.

Chapter 12

Colonization and Monarchy

1. The First World War

The First World War made a mockery of the achievements of nineteenth-century European civilization. The first modern war fought with advanced industrial technology but still using traditional tactics, it caused an unprecedented slaughter of human beings. The Allies, including England, France, Russia, and the United States, together with the Central Powers, including Germany, Austria, and Turkey, mobilized more than forty million men in the war effort. Nearly eight million died in the war, and total casualties exceeded thirty-three million human beings. So great was the butchery that the total casualties of all conflicts in Europe between 1815 and 1915 did not total a single day's casualties in 1916. On 1 July 1916, for example, the British lost 60,000 men in one day. The Somme offensive cost 420,000 lives; 142,000 British troops died in the battle of Arras. Not long after the war, the great influenza epidemic claimed another twenty million lives worldwide, with modern science and medicine helpless before its ravages. In Western Europe an entire generation was decimated, and even the victorious powers had few territorial gains to boast of in Europe when the war was over.

The Ottoman Empire entered the war reluctantly on the side of the Central Powers, mostly because of well-founded fears of Russian designs on Ottoman territory. The Ottoman armed forces proved valorous and resilient, to the surprise of the Allies who had long dismissed Turkey as the sick man of Europe. Of all the belligerent states, however, the Ottoman Empire paid the highest price in territory, to punish a Muslim power that had attacked the Christian world. Some of its territories, like

Basra, had strategic and economic value; others, like inner Syria and Palestine, were largely of prestige or symbolic interest.

Not only a theater of war, invasion, and occupation by British forces, Iraq had been a subject of secret negotiations among the British, French, and Russians as early as 1915, the result of which was that Mosul was promised to the French after the war, and the British were planning to take Basra and Baghdad. The British government in particular deceived the United States government as long as it could on its post-war intentions. Thus the First World War brought change to Iraq with dizzying rapidity. The land would be the setting for a British colonialist effort at nation-building, along the lines of similar British efforts in India and Egypt, but with even less participation by the inhabitants.

The British authorities in India had long hoped for a strong presence in southern Iraq, which they considered a legitimate sphere of interest. So too, British authorities in Iran believed that control of the Basra region would help safeguard the oil fields of southwestern Iran, which were being exploited by a British-controlled oil company. In 1914, therefore, a British expeditionary force seized Basra. Greatly underestimating the difficulties, and with no obvious tactical goal in sight, British forces pushed north towards Baghdad but stopped, exhausted and reduced, at Ctesiphon, then retreated south with increasingly heavy losses. Trapped at Kut on the Tigris, the British force withstood a close siege of 146 days under terrible conditions before it finally surrendered. Charles Townsend, the British general commanding, by then mentally unbalanced, retired to house arrest, but his men were marched off into slavery where nearly all of them died. The campaign cost the lives of 10,000 soldiers of the original force and of 23,000 more sent in vain attempts to relieve them. The British invasion of Iraq had started with a straightforward protective maneuver but ended in catastrophe.

2. The Conquest of Iraq and Its Governance

A second British invasion, commanded by Major-General Stanley Maude, was launched in December 1916 and by March 1917 had taken Baghdad. To some British politicians, it seemed natural that southern Iraq should be assigned to the Indian government for administrative purposes. To others, that made little sense. They were thinking of setting up some sort of Arab kingdom under British auspices in the former Ottoman Arabic-speaking provinces. During the darkest days of the war, they had encouraged Hussein, sherif, or keeper of the holy places, of Mecca and warden of the Arabian holy cities of Islam, to believe that he might be such a king after the war and had urged him to revolt against Ottoman rule. As for Iraq, it had no recent history as a unified region. There were various local leaders and politicians, but many different tribes and religious groups who had no real basis for working together or common goals. There were few experienced administrators to draw on. A British proclamation trumpeted liberation, freedom and unity, but the British occupying authorities gave no signs of implementing these lofty goals, concentrating rather on creating a British administration. With the wisdom of hindsight, we can say that the British had no advance plans for management of the Ottoman territories they seized during the war and had little understanding of how complex governing them would be. Furthermore, there was insufficient coordination between the politicians of the government and the military in the region.

For Iraq, some English administrators favored direct rule by a British political officer backed up by British staff. The task of organizing the first administration was assigned to an experienced man, Sir Percy Cox. In 1920, for example, in the top echelons of the new administration, there were over 500 Englishmen but only 20 Arabs. The war had exacted a heavy toll on the region, so even basic public works had to proceed from the beginning. Many people, including the heads of prominent families and tribes and the large cadre of former Ottoman military officers of Iraqi origin, expected to move into positions of power following the collapse of the Ottoman government. Some of these initially supported British efforts, or at least cooperated with them, but were soon disappointed because the British favored land owners, tribal sheikhs, and urban notables, but not military men. These, then, began to identify with anti-colonial nationalism. The majority Shi'ite population and their religious leaders were largely sidelined by the British, who preferred to deal with the Sunnites, in part because of their local tradition of dominating in government and administration, and in part because of British reluctance to engage with Shi'ite religious leaders, who had no tradition of participating in government and who were suspicious of Sunnite cooperation with the Christian occupying power.

At the outset, there were major problems to solve. The Turks still claimed the Mosul region as part of Turkey, the French were demanding it in accordance with the secret wartime agreement that had promised it to them, while the British were occupying the city. Representatives of the Kurdish majority in the north pressed for self-determination, one of the goals of the war promoted by American president Woodrow Wilson. The exhausted Allies, who needed Wilson's support, had agreed to this in principle. But there were numerous rival Kurdish groups and leaders and the problem of what to do about the Kurds in Turkey and Iran.

In the summer of 1920, a violent revolution erupted in southern Iraq against the British occupiers, mostly in rural areas. Some saw this as a struggle between Sunnites and Shi'ites, others as a revolt of tribes against British control. In some cases the British could restore order only by deliberately flooding tribal lands. Over 400 English and 8000 Iraqis were killed before the revolt was fully suppressed, at a cost exceeding twenty million pounds sterling, perhaps as high as forty million. The British government and people, sick of war and its costs, were determined to reduce the British presence in Iraq as quickly as possible.

Winston Churchill, as foreign minister, convened a conference in Cairo in 1921 to which representatives of the different British administrations in the Middle East were invited to discuss the future of the region. Forty diplomats, military men, and representatives of the oil industry were invited. Iraq was represented by the first commissioner, Sir Percy Cox, and by a remarkable Englishwoman named Gertrude Bell. Two Iraqi politicians accompanied them but were not permitted to participate in the conference. One of Iraq's best-known and most ambitious politicians, Sayyid Talib, the most likely Iraqi ruler of any new state, was not asked to come at all.

Gertrude Bell, born in 1868, was an archaeologist, linguist, and a brilliant student of history. She had begun studying Arabic in 1897 and had gone to Arabia in 1914 on a political mission to Abdul Aziz ibn

Sa'ud, who was hoping to dominate Arabia at the cost of the sherif of Mecca, protégé of the Cairo office of the British government. She was a strong, indomitable personality; she was said, for example, to have survived fifty-three hours of an Alpine blizzard by hanging tenaciously to a rope. In 1914 she had helped form the Arab Bureau of the British Government, with T. E. Lawrence "of Arabia," and Sir Percy Cox had appointed her his "oriental secretary," responsible for all dealings with Arabs. Her command of spoken Arabic, her drive and intelligence, and her self-confidence won her a unique position in Iraq, and it was she, as an expert on the history and archaeology of the region, who sketched the original borders of the new country. She was convinced that the land should be a unity under an independent Arab ruler (though not an Iraqi one), whereas some were reluctant to cede power and others, like Churchill, felt that only Basra was worth keeping anyway. One of the main results of the Cairo Conference was the adoption of Bell and Cox's proposal for the creation of Iraq, to include the former Ottoman provinces of Mosul, Baghdad, and Basra. The problem of what to do with the Kurdish areas was set aside for the time being.

Hussein, the sherif of Mecca, who believed he had been promised the throne of an Arab kingdom after the war in return for his support of the British, had two sons ready for kingship, Abdullah, who was not particularly popular with the British, and Faisal, who had a good understanding of both Arabian and European politics, and who was also astute, charming, and intelligent. Bell and others believed he should be the king or prince of Iraq. Although a Sunnite, he could claim legitimacy even among Shi'ites as a descendant of the prophet and of the family that ruled the Arabian holy places. He had, of course, no power base or constituency in Iraq and was perceived of by many Iraqis as simply a tool of the British, even though he demanded a treaty with the British government as an independent sovereign. Some Iraqi officers saw support of Faisal as a stepping-stone to power for themselves, under British auspices, so they professed support for his candidacy. The British saw Faisal as reasonable and compliant, since they were giving him a throne and were paying both his father and his brother Abdullah large subsidies. A so-called "plebiscite" of selected Iraqis carried out by the

British announced overwhelming support for the new monarchy. Faisal arrived in Iraq, was crowned, and a constitution was finally implemented in 1924. While this constitution promulgated a legislative assembly, it left to the king the power to veto any law it passed without recourse. He also had the power to convene or dissolve the legislative assembly.

3. A New Monarchy

Faisal was ultimately in a weak position. His main support came from the army, largely run by former Ottoman officers, and from the British. He was a capable and experienced politician with a difficult game to play, above all, to create some sense of Iraqi national identity. Sir Percy Cox left in 1923. The new commissioner, Arnold Wilson, had been strongly opposed to an independent Iraq and harbored a personal antipathy to Gertrude Bell, so she was soon sidelined from politics. She therefore concentrated her energies and intelligence on the creation of an Iraq Museum, a government antiquities service, and cultural heritage laws and policies (see Chapter 15).

Meanwhile the new government turned to such fundamental matters as agricultural development and reform. A Department of Agriculture was organized, experimental farms created, and an extensive rural education program was begun. Settlement and development were encouraged and registration and ownership reviewed. Since only a small percentage of Iraq's land was actively cultivated, land and its development became important bases for patronage, as land could be distributed to influential supporters of the government.

One major technical problem was to overcome the tendency to cultivate land with wheat, barley, or maize, and simply to abandon areas that had grown too saline, so farmers needed training and encouragement to keep from wasting land resources. Cotton and tobacco were reintroduced, as well as fruit growing. Success was mixed, however. Cotton grew well in Iraq, but cultivators were slow to invest in it and the returns were low.

Irrigation was enhanced by the introduction of pumps to promote so-called "lift" irrigation, as opposed to "flow" irrigation that was based on tapping channels by opening sluices for water. Although pumps were easier to install than large irrigation works, they tended to increase the rate of salinization, as anyone could pump water whenever he wished. One major Ottoman irrigation project, the Hindiyyah Barrage on the lower Euphrates, had been completed before the war, and the kingdom began others, such as the Kut Barrage on the Tigris, opened finally in 1939, and the Table Mountain Dam on the Diyala, also opened in 1939. There seemed no limit to the agricultural potential of Iraq. Official documents often referred to the great productivity of the land in ancient and medieval times, suggesting there was no reason why this could not be attained again.

An ambitious program of road building was undertaken, and other services, such as a modern airport, were gradually provided. An Iraq Petroleum Company was organized to exploit the oil fields in the north, but it was dominated by British interests, with a large share of the company owned by the British government. An Armenian deal-maker named Gulbenkian owned 5% of the company.

Education was reformed to stress the rich historical tradition of Iraq itself, so was intended to be a means of promoting national feeling. But the narrative glorified the Abbasid caliphate, and so tended to exclude the Shi'ites, and the Kurds were not included in what was essentially an Arab story. In addition to intellectual training, schooling was intended to promote social development and personal health and well being. British officials were disturbed to notice a strongly anti-British and pro-German slant in history text books, the most important of which were written by Palestinians, rather than Iraqis. Primary schools taught religion as well as history, geography, civics, physical training, and health and agriculture. Secondary schools included general schools as well as technical, nursing, and agricultural schools. Education was designed to be universal, male and female. Colleges of Engineering, Medicine, Pharmacy, and Law were opened. In due course, schools would also begin to stress military training as well.

Although King Faisal had signed a treaty with the British government as a partner, the British High Commissioner in Iraq still effectively controlled the government. There were, moreover, important limitations on the power of both the British and the crown in trying to build a unified nation under their control. Many believed that universal military service, for example, would be a good way to create an Iraqi sense of identity, but to some groups this was anathema, recalling the old days of the Ottoman empire. Cabinets came and went rapidly, usually drawn from the same small circle of ambitious politicians. Iraqi society and government had several centers of gravity, for example, the royal family and its followers, with extensive powers of patronage and closely allied with British economic and political interests; the civilian politicians (some of whom had a military background), who built personal and party alliances of their own; the military, which soon emerged as a source of power the politicians could not ignore; landowners, religious and tribal leaders.

4. Aspects of Iraqi Culture under the Monarchy

Iraqi literature followed some of the trends of the time by stressing the glorious past of Iraq, the beauty and potential of its land and people, but at the same time expressing dissatisfaction with the current realities of Iraqi government and economy. According to some, Iraq's human and natural wealth were not being well exploited because of foreign domination and a corrupt, self-serving ruling elite. In an ode titled "Freedom's in Colonial Policy," published in a Baghdad newspaper in 1922, the Iraqi poet al-Rusafi railed bitterly at his fellow citizens' apathy:

> *Say nothing, people, God forbid you speak,*
> *Don't wake up now, the only one's who'll win stay fast asleep.*
> *Why not default on all you need to make a forward gain?*
> *Just cast aside your working mind, it's best you have no brain.*
> *Do persevere in knowing naught, lest you should have to learn,*
> *Politics? Jettison that, or you'll rue it in your turn.*
> *To its secret mumbo-jumbo there's a code you'd have to break,*
> *If your talk gets too revealing then you better obfuscate!* *

The distinguished Iraqi poet al-Jawahiri (1900–1997), for example, wrote in a highly individualized neo-classical style. He enjoyed the patronage of Faisal I but went into self-imposed exile and often criticized the monarchy and subsequent governments. In a long lullaby to the hungry he wrote:

Sleep to the lengthy addresses of potentates,
Sleep, while the livelihood they promised dwindles steadily
*   downward around you,*
Sleep to that pomp which bade no one who yearned for it to share.**

Likewise poets and novelists experimented with new forms and styles, and turned to new subjects, including social realism, away from what some saw as the hollow, tradition-bound, elitist, precious styles and genres of the Ottoman period. The lesser-known poet Hadi al-Khaffaji, for example, was born in Najaf in 1922 and grew up in Karbala, where his father had been an Ottoman police officer. His was a prominent family some of whom were active in the fighting against the British occupation of Iraq in the First World War. Some of his verse, written in classical style, shows an acute sensibility, such as a lament for a dead dog, for which a parallel can scarcely be found in Arabic poetry:

I'll never forget that dog,
Many times ere this day he was weak unto death.
He came to the city, exploring its narrowest alleys,
Striving to hold onto even a loathsome life there.
All he was hoping for, all he wanted for food
*   was garbage among the doorway sweepings.*
A gang of boys saw him, to them his misery was the butt of fun!***

Under the relative stability of the new kingdom, foreign archaeological expeditions began increasingly to carry out long-term scientific projects. Under Gertrude Bell's new Antiquities Law, foreign expeditions could no longer take whatever they wished, but had to abide by a division of the finds decided first by Bell, later by Iraqis. On the one hand, this encouraged foreign teams, who could more easily find financial support if they had something substantial to show in their home country for their efforts; on the other, Iraq's own collections developed rapidly. Some archaeologists had difficulty yielding their best treasures to a local museum, but Bell was both firm and fair. During the 1920s and early 1930s, sixteen expeditions from five foreign nations carried out archaeological research in Iraq, often maintaining long-standing projects, so this was a golden age of Middle Eastern archaeology. Undoubtedly the most famous of these were the excavations at Ur, where Woolley's discovery of the richly furnished tombs, with their evidence for extensive human sacrifice, made news around the world (see Chapters 2 and 15).

In 1932, Iraq finally achieved independence from many forms of British control and joined the League of Nations, the first state emerging from the European mandates in the Middle East to do so as a full-fledged, independent nation. There was still, however, a strong British military, economic, and political presence behind the scenes. The euphoria of this new beginning was undermined by growing economic depression and discontent in various parts of the country that sometimes broke out into violence.

5. Weakness and War

British colonial government, with its traditional emphasis on preservation of privilege for a fairly small elite within the population and on using that elite to govern the country, was, like it or not, the pattern for the monarchy in Iraq. Roads to power included owning extensive land, with which to reward supporters, and rising through the ranks of the rapidly expanding Iraqi army. Ultimately the new government was dependent on its military for survival, so the military sector grew and the old pattern of army officers exercising political power remained the norm. Faisal died in 1933 and was succeeded by his son Ghazi, a dashing figure with an English military education. Ghazi was a more charismatic personality than his father, but less effective as a politician and administrator, so some of the older, more experienced politicians of the period, such as an astute politician named Nuri Said, gained considerable power in the shadow of the monarchy.

The Shi'ite population of the south, including the religious and tribal leaders, were still not effective participants in the new government. More money seemed to go to the military than to public works projects in the south, where development was urgently needed and the population was growing rapidly. To the Sunnite ruling group, the tribal and religious leaders of the south seemed to be throwbacks to an earlier Iraq and hindrances to the development of a modern nation as they visualized it. Unrest grew in the countryside and there were episodes of violence. The monarchy was finding it increasingly difficult on the one side to control all its subjects, on the other to rein in the ambitions of the military officers whose harsh suppression of revolts and dissension had served to keep the monarchy in power. An instance of this was the case of the people who called themselves Assyrians, Turkish Christians who had settled in northern Iraq to avoid persecution in Turkey. Many Assyrian men served in the British army after World War I. This group was seen by militants in the Iraqi government as disloyal, so they were cruelly massacred in 1933, while the British government made no effort to intervene.

Ghazi was killed in a car crash in 1939, leaving a three-year-old son, Faisal II, for whom a young and inexperienced uncle, Abdallah, was chosen to act as regent, but the effective head of the government was the prime minister, Nuri Said. A small cadre of senior military officers also wielded considerable power behind the scenes, so no politician could act without their consent and support. With the outbreak of the Second World War, the British government expected Iraq to cut relations with the Axis powers and to provide support to the British military effort, in accordance with her treaty obligations. Nuri Said was compliant, and declared martial law, but there were important segments of both the military and the civilian politicians who strongly resented Britain's influence in Iraq and who hoped or expected the Axis powers would win the war. Some were motivated by Arab nationalism, hoping to achieve a larger Arab state from the countries that had emerged after the First World War; others were primarily interested in the future of Iraq. Many Iraqis felt that they should have a stake in the unfolding of events in Palestine, where, with British governmental support, large numbers of Russian and other European Jews were emigrating in the hope of starting a new Jewish society or state safe from the persecutions and anti-Semitism of Europe. Iraqi Arabs saw the Jewish settlement as simply another form of European colonialism in the Arab world.

A *coup d'état* in Iraq in 1941 was led by an army officer, Rashid Ali. It was focused on opposition to the monarchy and to British influence in Iraq, and was strongly pro-German. Because of the Palestine issue, the ancient Jewish community of Baghdad came under severe attack: Jews were killed and shops and homes looted and vandalized. The British military, however, moved rapidly, and the instigators of the coup soon had to flee. Nuri Said and the royal regent returned to power and the political aspirations of the Iraqi military were for the time being checked. However, it was clear that the monarchy and its supporters were vulnerable.

In the years after the Second World War, martial law was lifted, freer expression was possible, political parties could be formed, but many Iraqis had difficulty making ends meet because of the soaring costs of living. There were strikes, violence, and Kurdish unrest continued, to all of which the government tended to respond harshly. A new treaty, secretly negotiated with the British government, allowed the British access to Iraqi bases in time of war and tied Iraqi defense policy to Britain, including even the training of Iraqi officers. Therefore there were many issues to attract an increasingly vocal opposition that resorted to street demonstrations and public protests in 1947–1948.

The outbreak of war after the establishment of the State of Israel in 1948 aroused much public feeling as well. Iraqi troops were sent to Palestine, the largest contingent sent by any Arab state to that war. The failure of the Arab allies to prevail in the war with Israel provided more occasion for recrimination against those in power. More immediately, it provoked a new round of violence and persecution against the Jews of Iraq, many of whom sought ways to go to Israel. Between 1950 and 1952, the overwhelming majority of Iraqi Jews had emigrated to Israel.

The most important resource for the government of Iraq to bring under its control was oil. Nuri Said insisted that Iraq should have a larger percentage of the income from the oil being pumped there by the Iraq Petroleum Company. In the early 1950s, with the gradual decline in American oil production, Saudi Arabia, Iran, and Iraq began to realize enormous revenues from oil. In Iraq, this meant that the important politicians, still dominated by Nuri Said, had ready money at their disposal for development and as a means of building alliances and rewarding their supporters. At the same time, however, a new generation of junior military officers had grown up, trained in the Iraqi army, who were frustrated by their own lack of access to opportunity. To them, the monarchy was a survival of colonialism; why should they sustain a king and a small circle of politicians who kept so many of the spoils and trappings of power for themselves? The revolution in Egypt in 1952, in which a small circle of junior army officers toppled the government the British had created and inaugurated a new government in which military men held many of the posts, showed them that their dreams of power could be realized and that Britain might not be able to do anything effective to oppose them.

6. Archaeology in Iraq

Meanwhile, from its modest beginnings under Gertrude Bell, the Iraqi Directorate General of Antiquities had rapidly developed into a professional bureau with very high standards and an active research program. The Directorate sponsored various major excavations of its own, from prehistoric through the Islamic periods. Among ancient Mesopotamian sites Iraqi archaeologists explored were the ancient Sumerian sites of Uqair, where painted murals of the Uruk period were found, and Eridu in the south; the Old Babylonian cities of Der and Tell Harmal further north, and the Kassite city of Dur Kurigalzu, to the west of Baghdad. For the Islamic period, the Umayyad administrative capital at Wasit was investigated, and many others. The collections of the Iraq Museum, founded in 1923, grew proportionately, both with spectacular museum display objects, such as the Uruk vase (see Chapter 15) and with large study collections in the storerooms. The site of Hassuna, near Mosul, excavated by the Iraqis in 1943–1944, gave evidence for a farming village dating to the late seventh and early sixth millennia B.C.E., and was especially important for its pottery, which established a ceramic sequence for the late Neolithic period in northern Mesopotamia. The potsherds were not in themselves display pieces, but material of this kind, retained for further study, helped excavators at other sites to establish a relative chronology. This high-level scientific work was carried out despite the political turmoil of the period.

Iraq's leading archaeologist of this period was Fuad Safar (d. 1978). He was a native of Mosul with degrees from the American University of Beirut and the Oriental Institute of the University of Chicago. Safar excavated at Tell Uqair in 1940–1941, Wasit in 1942, Hassuna in 1943–1944, Eridu (1948 and thereafter), and Hatra (beginning in 1950). He was later active in the regional survey work carried out by Robert Adams and other American archaeologists in the Uruk and Diyala regions during the late 1950s and 1960s. The plan behind the choice of Hassuna, Uqair, and Eridu was, among other goals, to establish a sound chronology of development for the earliest phases of Mesopotamian culture. After Baghdad University was founded, Safar helped create its Faculty of Archaeology, and several generations of Iraqi archaeologists were his students. Rising through the ranks, Safar became Director-General of Excavations in Iraq and also Director-General of Antiquities. Safar worked closely with a British adviser, Seton Lloyd (d. 1996), during the war years. Lloyd was a seasoned field excavator, with experience in Egypt, Turkey, and Iraq. Theirs was a close and productive collaboration that showed that Iraqi archaeological projects could be carried out in full accordance with modern methods and their results promptly published in article and book form. Taha Baqir (d. 1984) was also active in excavations in Iraq, notably at Dur Kurigalzu (see Chapter 4) and at Tell Harmal, an ancient city threatened by the expansion of modern Baghdad. Among the noteworthy finds at Tell Harmal were numerous letters from the age of Hammurabi (see Chapter 3), and important literary works including manuscripts of the Epic of Gilgamesh. Baqir published an Arabic translation of the Epic in 1950, reprinted in 1970. Tell Harmal also yielded important mathematical tablets, which Baqir was the first to decipher and publish.

The Directorate began producing a scholarly periodical, called *Sumer*, in 1945. This was intended to promote historical research for all periods of the history of Iraq, so a typical issue included both pre-Islamic and

Islamic materials. Usually half the issue was in Arabic and the other half in European languages, especially English, which had been established as the primary foreign language taught in Iraqi state schools.

7. A Time of Revolution

Externally Iraq faced critical challenges in the Arab world during the Cold War period. First was the revolution in Egypt in 1952, followed by the rise of Nasser. Nasser championed revolution and Arab unity. The short-lived United Arab Republic, consisting of Egypt and Syria, brought Nasser's vision to the very frontiers of Iraq. The so-called Baghdad Pact, a defensive alliance that Iraq signed with Turkey and England, among others, seemed to Nasser a rebuff of his larger program for Arab unity, because, in his view, it united Iraq with the two powers that had done the most to oppress the Arabs throughout their history. Nasser was intent upon exporting revolution and became embroiled in a fruitless war in Yemen, hoping perhaps ultimately to destabilize the Saudi monarchy.

The Suez Crisis of 1956, in which England, France, and Israel conspired that Israel would attack Egypt and then England would move in as a peacekeeper and once again control the Suez canal, was a turning point for American interests in the Middle East. The United States government, despite its suspicion of Nasser, insisted that the British withdraw and forced them to do so with threats of economic reprisals. In Iraq, Nuri Said, however, saw no good coming from Nasser's proclaimed Arab unity; it was difficult enough to keep Iraq unified, and Arab unity would inevitably raise the question of the Kurds once again. But, as one of the most experienced politicians under the monarchy, Said was viewed by many Iraqis as an ally of British imperialism, whereas Nasser was seen as a hero.

To a close circle of military men in Iraq, the time was growing ripe for their own revolution on the Egyptian model. After Suez, England could never be the threat she had been, so her intervention was not to be feared. Soaring oil revenues had long since eclipsed agriculture as the basis for the Iraqi economy; control of oil revenues meant access to ready money, patronage, and resources unthinkable a few decades previous. A group calling itself the Free Officers plotted the next coup, with perhaps no grander visions than taking over the country and turning over its government to the military, though terming it a republic. None of these men had Nasser's charisma, but they saw their opportunity and took it on July 14, 1958. The entire royal family, as well as Nuri Said, were slaughtered, and a small group of army officers seized control of the country.

The Al-Zuhur Palace, seat of the monarchy in Baghdad, looted in 1958, was reorganized as a museum in the late 1970s. Saddam Hussein installed a communications center there. In 2003 the palace and its contents were destroyed by an American bombardment. Nothing was salvaged from the ruins but a collection of photographs of the royal family and some silverware.

Bibliographical Note to Chapter 12

For World War I in the Middle East and its aftermath, the best account is David Fromkin, *A Peace to End all Peace* (New York: Henry Holt and Company, 1989), from which I have drawn various ideas and statistics, including the casualties of World War I. For the colonial era, M. E. Yapp, *The Near East Since the First World War* (New York: Longman, 1996) gives a good survey, with attention to social and economic factors. For the kingdom of Iraq, an excellent account is Tripp, *History* (see Bibliographical Note to Chapter 11), from which I have taken numerous insights. I have drawn some data from *An Introduction to the Past and Present of the Kingdom of Iraq, by a Committee of Officials* (Baghdad, 1946). For Gertrude Bell, see Janet Wallach, *Desert Queen* (New York: Doubleday, 1996). This has a good account of the Cairo Conference from an Iraqi standpoint. There are various specialized studies on the period of the monarchy in Iraq, for example, Daniel Silverfarb, *Britain's Informal Empire in the Middle East: A Case Study of Iraq 1929–1941* (New York: Oxford University Press, 1986), with a good account of the modern Assyrians, chapter 4, and *The Twilight of British Ascendancy in the Middle East, A Case Study of Iraq 1941–1950* (New York: St. Martin's, 1994); Reeva Simon, *Iraq Between the Two World Wars, The Creation and Implementation of a National Ideology* (New York: Columbia University Press, 1986), which documents German influence in Iraq, and the authoritative survey of Peter Sluglett, *Britain in Iraq 1914–1932* (London: Ithaca Press, 1976); among other important topics, this devotes a special study to Shi'ite political interests in Iraq in this period.

Translated Excerpts

*Mustafa Ali, *Sharh diwan al-Rusafi* (Baghdad: Cultural Affairs Press, 1986), 3:122.

**Mustafa Badawi, *Mukhtarat min al-shi'r al-arabi al-hadithi* (Beirut: al-Nahar, 1969), 35.

***Ali al-Khaqani, *Shuara' al-ghari* (Qom: Bahram, 1987), 12:396–397.

Chapter 13

The Republic of Iraq

1. The Qasim Regime

The 1958 revolution brought to power a clique of military officers, headed by general Abd al-Karim Qasim and his close associate, Colonel Abd al-Salam Arif. As revolutionaries they wanted change; as military men, they were suspicious of anything but authoritarian rule. Qasim came from a poor family and was intent upon improving social conditions and raising the status of Iraq as an independent nation. Arif, on the other hand, saw the future of Iraq in broader, Arab terms. He was fascinated by the Egyptian revolution and Nasser's subsequent program of non-alignment in the Cold War and by the possibility of political unification of the Arabs. Qasim and Arif therefore soon had a falling out and Arif was jailed under sentence of death. Arif was backed by elements of a small but effective socialist political party, known as the Ba'th or Rebirth party. Some members of this party tended to favor political unity of the Arabs, but others wanted to put Iraq first. Although Qasim had few constituents outside his circle of followers, he did attract support from Iraq's even smaller Communist party. Thus the American government, which had planned to build a nuclear reactor in Iraq as part of its Atoms for Peace program in 1955, decided to build one in Iran instead and trained hundreds of Iranians in nuclear physics.

Qasim hoped to wrest greater control of the Iraqi oil industry from its foreign managers and owners. This was not practical, however, because Iraq had no personnel skilled in running an oil industry and no other country would train them for fear of reprisals from oil companies. Qasim therefore turned his attention to Kuwait, claiming that it belonged to Iraq since it had once been an extension of one of the Ottoman provinces that had gone into making up Iraq. The other Arab states, backed by Britain, moved quickly to protect Kuwait, so Qasim found himself with few friends on the international scene and increasingly unpopular at home, despite his ambitious public works. In late 1962 a student disturbance led to a successful revolution, organized by Ba'th party adherents in favor of Arif, whose sentence of death Qasim had never carried out, so Arif was returned to power and Qasim shot.

Arif purged the military, the civil administration, and university faculties of all he thought unsympathetic with his programs, laying the groundwork for one-party rule in Iraq. Before he could pursue his policies, he was killed in a helicopter accident and succeeded by his brother. Arif's Ba'th supporters, however, had been growing increasingly dissatisfied with his rule, as he seemed to them to be turning away from the socialist programs they had envisaged when he came to power. Another coup took place in 1968, led by Ahmad Hassan al-Bakr.

2. Iraqi Culture and Society

Iraq was changing rapidly during these critical years. Military men and party bureaucrats rapidly replaced the older elites in the government who had once been patronized by the monarchy. The population of Iraq was increasing exponentially, doubling between 1968 and 1978, for example. This meant that the majority of the population was young and in need of new opportunities. The overcrowded city seemed an alien yet promising place, as the contemporary Iraqi poet Abdul Wahab al-Bayati wrote:

> *It buzzes with people and flies.*
> *I was born there.*
> *I learned on its walls exile and wandering,*
> *And love and death and the loneliness of poverty*
> *In its nether reaches and at its gates.*
> *There my father taught me how to read*

Rivers and fire, clouds and mirage.
Rebellion and perseverance
He taught me, how to set sail and be sad,
How to visit reverently the abodes of saints,
Searching for the light, for the warmth
  of a springtime not yet come,
Hidden still in the depths of the earth, among the seashells,
Waiting to be called forth by some fortune teller.*

Qasim's regime had begun extensive social welfare programs in health, education, and housing, to gain support in the Iraqi cities, where most of the new population was gravitating. Large land holdings were confiscated and redistributed by the government, creating a large new agricultural class, even though agriculture held a rapidly declining share of the gross national product and was unable to keep up with population growth. Qasim began to create heavy industry in Iraq, such as steel, cement, and chemical plants, along with petroleum-related industries. Industry, with the infusion of oil wealth, soon outstripped agriculture in the Iraqi economy.

The Ba'th party, brought to power in the 1968 revolution, was determined to implement "Arab socialism." An important source of the party's growing strength was its own security forces and militia. This helped counterbalance the power of the regular army, the ranks of which were at the same time gradually staffed with Ba'thist officers. The party had an effective grass-roots organization through social and educational centers, unions, and organized party activities. Most upper-level government posts were held by party members. Al-Bakr was a native of the town of Tikrit on the Tigris river and brought various friends, relatives, and associates from that town with him into the government, among them Saddam Hussein, a party politician with no military background.

In 1969, a Soviet oil company broke the technological stranglehold foreign oil companies had imposed on Iraq to prevent the growth of a native Iraqi industry, preparing the way for full nationalization of the Iraq Petroleum Company by Saddam Hussein in 1972. The oil boom of the 1970s brought enormous wealth to the Iraqi government, which embarked on a highly visible program of economic development. The government felt strong enough to nationalize banks and industries and expanded its own payroll tenfold by the early 1970s. The free, comprehensive state education system expanded, for men and women, through the university level, and Iraq developed one of the highest rates of literacy in the Arab world. Women, advancing through the educational system, assumed important posts in government, industry, and education; the Iraqi military began to train women's corps.

Iraqi arts and letters had been turning in various new directions since the early 1960s. Some poets chafed under the old restrictions of the classical style. For example, Badr Shakir al-Sayyab (d. 1964), was experimenting with free verse in Arabic in the spirit of T. S. Eliot and Edith Sitwell, even as he criticized the new Iraq:

> *Rain*
> *Rain*
> *Rain*
> *Since we were children, the sky*
> *Was clouded in winter*
> *And the rain poured down.*
> *But every year — though the earth turns green — we starve!*
> *Not a year passes in Iraq without hunger.***

2. Saddam Hussein and War with Iran

Saddam Hussein had been placed in charge of security services for the Ba'th party and this left him in a good position to eliminate opponents. He moved quietly through the pathways of power, awaiting his opportunity. He made no overt move against his boss, al-Bakr, content rather to build a strong and effective party apparatus responsive to himself. His power grew so great that it was only a question of time before he took over as president; al-Bakr found it expedient to resign in 1979. Within a week, Saddam Hussein purged and shot numerous leaders of the party whose loyalty he doubted. In the months that followed, hundreds more members of the government went to their deaths; a reign of terror had begun.

In 1979, the American-supported government of the shah of Iran was toppled by an Islamic revolution. The new leader of that country was a religious teacher called the Ayatollah Khomeini. He insisted that only Islamic principles and law, as he and his followers interpreted them, could be the basis for rightful government. Even within Islam his was a radical position and his program could well be considered revolutionary, though some saw it as reactionary. Khomeini was intent upon building a new Islamic society and government in Iran and also exporting his ideas to other countries. He considered the greatest enemies of his envisioned new order to be the United States, Jews, and Baha'is. Americans were shocked by a well-orchestrated attack on the American embassy in Teheran and the subsequent holding of diplomatic staff hostage. At the same time, attacks began in Iraq on government officials. These the Iraqi government blamed on Iranian agents. Saddam Hussein soon abrogated an existing treaty with Iran and sent his armed forces across the Iranian border in the autumn of 1979. They made fast gains, but Hussein ordered them to halt in expectation of peace negotiations. Instead, the Iranians counterattacked and a costly war of attrition began, with prodigious loss of life and no significant gains of territory on either side.

Many nations, including the United States, backed Hussein in this war because of their fear of the revolutionary ideas of Khomeini and his followers. The Iraq-Iran war settled down to a destructive stalemate and so Hussein withdrew his troops in 1982. This was followed, however, by a devastating Iranian attack on Iraq itself. For six more years the war dragged on. The Iranian government refused to negotiate even as it grew weaker and its forces were exhausted and decimated. Iraq, in desperation, turned to air and missile bombardments of Iranian cities, from which thousands fled to the countryside. Finally in 1988 a ceasefire was agreed upon by both sides.

During the war, the Iranian government had promised independence to the Iraqi Kurds if they would join the Iranian side, even though no such independence was envisioned for the Kurdish population in Iran itself. Many Kurds joined, as they had experienced the harsh rule of

Saddam Hussein and hoped he would lose the war. Thus when Hussein had a free hand after the ceasefire, he turned his military to the massacre of thousands of Iraqi Kurds, destroying their villages and towns and encouraging Arabs to move into their territories. His agents even used such measures as dropping poisonous gas to wipe out entire communities of men, women, and children.

3. Archaeology in Iraq

Beginning in the mid-1970s, a new era in the archaeology of Iraq began. A Russian team dug at Yarim Tepe, west of Mosul; the Oriental Institute of the University of Chicago continued its long-term project at Nippur, so too the German expedition at Uruk. English teams dug at Abu Salabikh, near Nippur, and at the prehistoric site of Umm Dabaghiya. Another American team, from the Metropolitan Museum of Art and the New York Institute of Fine Arts, dug at al-Hiba, in the area of Lagash. A German team continued to work at Isin, a French team at Larsa. A Polish expedition worked at Nimrud, and joint Italian and Iraqi teams carried out extensive restoration at Hatra. Iraqi teams were in the field at Arpachiya, Tell es-Sawwan, Assur, and Sippar.

The influx of oil money meant that gigantic public works projects could be undertaken, such as dam projects on the major rivers. A consequence of these was the flooding of large numbers of important archaeological sites. Dam projects on the Euphrates and the Diyala rivers entailed the flooding of hundreds of archaeological sites, so Iraqi and foreign teams hastened to salvage as much as they could. In the Diyala region, Japanese, Danish, and Iraqi expeditions uncovered settlements of the latter half of the third millennium B.C.E., including an important settlement of the Sargonic period at Tell-es-Suleimeh, an extraordinary concentric oval structure at Tell Gubba, and a varied collection of Sumerian literary tablets at Me-Turan, including new manuscripts of the Sumerian Gilgamesh cycle. On the Euphrates, a ninth-century Assyrian provincial capital was found at Ana, and many other sites were briefly investigated. A dam project planned for the Tigris river threatened to cover the remains of Assur itself, but this was never built. Numerous excavations were undertaken in the Mosul region as well, by Iraqi, Italian, British, Japanese, and French expeditions. A new antiquities law, passed in 1974, required that all finds from these excavations remain in Iraq, even study materials, so they were transferred to the Iraq Museum and to various local museums. Although the new building of the Iraq Museum, opened in 1966, had been planned on a grand scale, the rapid influx of new materials meant that the storerooms became increasingly overcrowded, and housing the files, photos, and records of so many expeditions presented serious challenges.

4. The Ba'th Party

In the meantime, the network of patronage that had always characterized Iraqi society and government was at work in favoring the party elite, relatives, and close associates of Hussein. Although in theory the Directorate-General of Antiquities controlled every archaeological site in the country, in practice large domains were carved out in the countryside, especially in the Diyala region, for privileged people and closed to outside access, so sites within them were unprotected.

The Iraqi system of education, including the universities, became permeated by party officials and a network of spies and informers that stifled free discourse and association. Some of the ablest professionals in the antiquities service, museums, and university faculties, not to mention poets, scientists, and other professionals, found themselves uncomfortable in the new society, despite the real gains in social services and physical infrastructure that the government was making. During the early 1980s many left Iraq to live in often unhappy and embittered exile abroad; for them, employment was difficult to find even in the Arab world. The Ba'th party itself had long since been realigned to be solely the expression of Saddam Hussein's wishes. Administrators who remained in Iraq joined the party, molded their activities around its dictates, and used its rhetoric.

Under Saddam Hussein's direction, the party ideology increasingly embraced the ancient history of Iraq, to the extent that provinces were renamed with ancient or medieval names; thus al-Hilla province became

Babil province (Arabic for Babylon). Nebuchadnezzar II was even proclaimed an enemy of Zionism because of his attack on Jerusalem in 587 B.C.E.

5. The Invasion of Kuwait

The costs of the war with Iran had been staggering. At the same time, the price of oil dropped from what it had been during the boom of the 1970s, so the Iraqi government, which had become dependent on oil revenues for income, needed money. Oil had been its most important source of revenue; in 1980–1981 alone, because of the targeting of oil installations and tankers in the war and the decline in oil prices, government revenues had dropped more than 50%. By 1990, Iraq's Gross Domestic Product had dropped 50% over what it had been when the war had begun. Hussein claimed that Iraq had borne the brunt of defending its oil-rich neighbors, especially Kuwait and Saudi Arabia, from Iranian attack and revolution. In return, he demanded that these countries forgive their large loans to Iraq and that OPEC, the Organization of Oil-Exporting Countries, agree to allow the price of oil to rise on the world market by cutting production, thus allowing Iraq more profit from her own oil. Kuwait ignored these demands, so Hussein easily invaded and seized the country in 1990.

A worldwide coalition of nations, led by the United States, threatened military action if Hussein did not withdraw his troops by a fixed deadline. This he did not do, so in January 1991, the coalition attacked and in a few days the Iraqi forces in Kuwait were broken, surrendering or in retreat. Over a month of allied missile and bombing attacks on Baghdad and other targets, totaling over 90,000 tons of ordnance, exacted a heavy toll. There was extensive loss of life, soldiers and non-combatants, and severe shortages of necessities, no utilities such as electricity or running water, and not enough medicine and other supplies to treat the wounded. Gasoline, cooking oil, and other necessities of modern daily life were in short supply. Factories, hospitals, bridges, and communications were destroyed. Basra too was heavily bombed, with extensive destruction and loss of life.

In honor of that city one may quote a ninth-century A.D. Arab poet who mourned Basra's destruction, in his time because of an insurrection:

My gaze, transfixed by streaming tears, brooks no sweet sleep
for me,
Beholding Basra's ghastly fate, what sleep could e'er there be?
What sleep, indeed, when sacred closes of Islàm are smirchèd
shamelessly?
Events like this could scarce be seen when nightmares o'er us creep,
But now, awake, to us they seem the phantom scenes of sleep.
The betrayer marched towards Basra, Oh God! on such campaign,
He took the name of "leader" — Lord guide his course to
shame!***

6. The Embargo and Its Toll

The war brought about no change of government, but economic sanctions imposed by the United Nations in 1991 not only prevented reconstruction of the county, they ravaged the population further. In March 1991, a U.N. mission warned of "imminent catastrophe, which could include epidemic and famine ..."† By the end of 1991, food prices in Iraq had soared 1500 to 2000% and mean monthly earnings of the population had dropped below poverty level. The U.N. Security Council took no decisive action, though it proposed to allow Iraq to sell some oil. More than a third of the income, however, was earmarked for non-humanitarian purposes, and the Iraqi government rejected the proposal. A 1993 report of the U.N. Food and Agriculture Organization referred to "chronic hunger, endemic malnutrition, massive unemployment and widespread human suffering ... a vast majority of the Iraqi population is living under the most deplorable conditions and is simply engaged in a struggle for survival ... large numbers of Iraqis have food intakes lower than those of the populations in the disaster-stricken African countries ..."† In 1995 another Security Council resolution permitting the sale of Iraqi oil was rejected by the Iraqi government, resulting in near paralysis of the economy. The ruling elite, however, was not affected, but maintained their lavish lifestyle, largely because Iraq secretly sold oil to Jordan, Syria, Turkey, and Egypt, in violation of the embargo, but no move was made to prevent it by the governments charged with enforcing the embargo.

In January 1996, the Iraqi government finally accepted a so-called "oil-for-food" program, which began to bring some relief by the end of that year. Prices were staggering: basic food items were four to five thousand times more expensive compared to what they had been at the outbreak of the Iraq-Iran war, with no corresponding changes in wages. By this time, over 100,000 people a year were dying as a result of the sanctions, half or more of them children. Thus, as a U.N. report indicated,[†] an urban, mechanized society had been forced back into conditions of the pre-industrial age, with no relief in sight.

In these circumstances, the looting of archaeological sites began in earnest. At first, the Directorate carried out limited salvage operations at a few of the most heavily looted sites, such as Umma, Zabala, and Umm al-Aqarib, but these sites, and hundreds of other Sumerian settlements, were totally destroyed to depths of four to seven meters. Already in 1992, the Iraqi government had tried to persuade the Arab League to help cut down on antiquities smuggling, but without result. Members of the regime, who hitherto had been deterred by the severe penalties for stealing antiquities, became actively involved in the trade. Uday Hussein, son of Saddam Hussein, for example, sold clay vessels stolen from a Roman period site near Babylon. Objects disappeared from the local museums at Assur, Babylon, and Basra. By 1996, city-dwellers were selling their furniture, even the doors and fixtures of their homes, to buy food, in an economy where a month's salary of a mid-level civil administrator would buy three kilograms of flour. Even though the oil-for-food program began to make basic rations available, the economic plight of most people outside the ruling elite was desperate. The ruling elite profited handsomely from the program by demanding kickbacks from companies participating in the oil-for-food program, while leading European businessmen and politicians accepted large bribes from the Iraqi government.

Under these conditions, antiquities traffic moved freely across the borders of Iraq, into Iran, Saudi Arabia, Jordan, Syria, and Turkey, and onward to Europe, Japan, and the United States. This included statuary, reliefs, pottery, seals, jewelry, and cuneiform tablets, often in very large lots of more than a thousand in a group. Well-preserved tablets, for example, could be sold at their site of origin for $100 or more apiece, in foreign currency. Broken tablets were thrown away; since most tablets found in any excavation are broken, one can assume that the majority of cuneiform tablets were discarded or destroyed in the course of the illegal excavations. Most of the provincial museums in Iraq were broken into and looted of whatever antiquities they still contained.

6. The American Invasion of Iraq and the Destruction of Cultural Heritage

War with Iraq became an early priority of the presidency of George W. Bush, who took office in January 2001. This time, however, United Nations support was not forthcoming, and such key allies as France and Germany were firmly opposed. The United States and Britain claimed that they had certain evidence of Iraq's possession of weapons of mass destruction. The U.S. also linked the Iraqi government with the events of September 11, portraying Iraq as a haven for terrorists. By early 2003, it was plain that war was imminent. Nothing comparable to the section for safeguarding monuments, fine arts, libraries, and archives, such as the United States government had created during World War II, was organized (see Chapter 14). As the ground forces moved across Iraq, an orgy of looting began of every unguarded government building. The coalition forces did not have enough troops to control the countryside, so the major archaeological sites, especially in the plains south of Baghdad, were at the mercy of looters. In early April, with the taking of Baghdad, the Iraq Museum and many other cultural institutions were thoroughly looted (see Chapter 15). Looters of the principal libraries went to some pains to burn them using incendiary materials they brought with them for the purpose. Of all the looted collections in libraries and museums, only a group of documents concerning Iraq's former Jewish population, hidden in the cellar of the security ministry, was brought to the United States for possible restoration.

The looting of archaeological sites continued under American occupation. The United States agreed, for example, to buy the wheat and other crops from the south after the first harvest under occupation, since previously the crops had been bought by the Iraqi government and after its collapse the farmers had no other outlet for their produce. This policy was terminated, however, and local cultivators had no good market for their produce because of the disturbed conditions of the country and the poverty of its population. Therefore looting of sites in the south was, for them, their best and easiest source of income.

Although resolutions and temporary restrictions were imposed by some countries on importation of recently excavated materials from Iraq, this had very little effect on the trade, which was exporting thousands of cuneiform tablets alone every month. The Italian government took the lead in detecting and prosecuting dealers in Iraqi cultural property. UNESCO, an Austrian team, the U.S. Department of State, and the British Museum were most active in rapidly bringing expertise and funds to the rescue of the looted Iraq Museum, and other nations, including Italy, sent training teams. There was still, however, no effective supervision of archaeological sites in Iraq by the end of 2004. Indeed, the coalition forces were unable to control even major urban areas, much less ancient ruins scattered over the countryside. Thus the archaeological record of Iraq is being rapidly destroyed, and the percentage of recovered pieces is minuscule compared to what is moving quickly onto the antiquities market, thence to the private holdings of mostly secretive collectors.

Sumerian poets, who saw in their own times the destruction of their cities, found words to describe what they had experienced. A poet of Ur wrote of warfare and its aftermath:

Disorder befell this land, the like of which no one had ever known,
Nothing of its ilk had ever been seen, no name could be put to it,
it was beyond comprehension!
The lands were bewildered in their fear,

The very gods of this city turned away from it in anger,
its ruler disappeared,
The people could scarcely breathe for terror,
The tempest paralyzes them, the storm does not let them return,
There will be no return for them, the time of their captivity will
never pass.****

A poet of Isin portrayed the city's goddess, mourning her ruined sanctuary:

This is my house, where no happy husband lives with me,
My house, where no sweet child dwells with me,
My house, where I, its mistress, may never walk again with pride,
No, never walk again in pride, wherein I dwell no more!*****

Another poet of Ur described looting:

My silver! Indeed, those who knew nothing of silver have stuffed
their hands with it!
My gems! Indeed, those who knew nothing of gems have dangled
them around their necks!******

Bibliographical Note to Chapter 13

Of the many histories of modern Iraq, Tripp's *History* (see Bibliographical Note to Chapter 11) may be recommended, as well as Marion Farouk-Sluglett, Peter Sluglett, *Iraq Since 1958: From Revolution to Dictatorship* (New York: I. B. Tauris, 2001). The account of the embargo, including quotations (†) and data, is drawn from Abbas Alnasrawi, "Sanctions and the Iraqi Economy," in Inati, *Iraq* (see Bibliographical Note to Chapter 10), 215–231. For archaeology in Iraq, the development of the Iraq Museum, and the politicization of Iraqi archaeology, the fullest discussion is Frederick Mario Fales, *Saccheggio in Mesopotamia* (Udine: Editrice Universitaria Udinese, 2004), from which I have taken material used here. For accounts of the planning for war and the looting of the Iraq Museum, see Andrew Lawler, "Mayhem in Mesopotamia," *Science* 301, 1 August 2003, 582–589, and Benjamin R. Foster, "Missing in Action: The Iraq Museum and the Human Past," in Irwin Abrams and Wang Gungwu, eds., *The Iraq War and its Consequences, Thoughts of Nobel Peace Laureates and Eminent Scholars* (Singapore: World Scientific, 2003), 295–317. I have derived first-hand information on certain sites from Philippe Flandrin, *Le Pillage de l'Irak* (Paris: Editions Du Rocher, 2004) and from information presented at the international congress "A Future for Our Past," Istanbul, 24–26 June, 2004. The most comprehensive accounts of the destruction of Iraqi cultural heritage during and after the Iraq war are Khalid Nashef, *Tadmir al-turath al-hidari al-Iraqi, fusul al-karitha* (Beirut: Dar al-Mura'i, 2004) and Fales, *Saccheggio* (cited above), from both of which I have drawn various data; the latter has additional information about efforts to restore the Iraq Museum and other damaged sites. Four richly illustrated articles by Joanne Farchakh, "Irak, 10 ans d'archéologie sous embargo," *Archéologia* 374 (January, 2001), "Comment protéger l'archéologie en Irak juste avant la guerre?," *Archéologia* 397 (February, 2003), "Le massacre du patrimoine irakien," *Archéologia* 402 (July–August, 2003), and "Irak, témoignages d'une archéologie héroïque," *Archéologia* 411 (May, 2004), give remarkable first-hand reportage on the looting and efforts to curb it, with attention to its socio-economic background.

Translated Excerpts

*Adapted from the translation in *Abdul Wahab Al-Bayati, Love, Death and Exile. Poems Translated from the Arabic by Bassam K. Frangieh* (Washington DC: Georgetown University Press, 1990), 42–43 "Elegy to the Unborn City."

**Translated by Bassam K. Frangieh, "Song of Rain," *Banipal*, Summer 2003, 29–31.

***From Hussein Nassar, ed., *Diwan Ibn al-Rumi* (Cairo: Center for Guaranty of Heritage, 1981), 6:2377.

****Adapted from Piotr Michalowski, *The Lamentation over the Destruction of Sumer and Ur* (Winona Lake, Ind.: Eisenbrauns, 1989), 40–41 lines 65–71.

*****From *Cuneiform Texts from Babylonian Tablets in the British Museum* XXXVI (London: British Museum, 1921, reprinted 1977), plate 42 lines 3–6, adapted from Thorkild Jacobsen, *The Harps that Once ... Sumerian Poetry in Translation* (New Haven: Yale University Press, 1987), 476.

******From Samuel Noah Kramer, *Lamentation over the Destruction of Ur, Assyriological Studies* 12 (Chicago: Oriental Institute of the University of the Chicago, 1940), 50–51 lines 280–281.

Chapter 14

Archaeology Past and Present in Iraq

Western interest in the ancient sites and artifacts of the Middle East began in the first centuries of the Christian era, motivated largely by a desire to experience first-hand the topography and tangible relics of the lands so closely associated with the Bible. Pilgrims to the so-called Holy Land, followed by Crusaders, often returned to Europe bearing objects wrapped in Sassanian silks. While most of these souvenirs were of dubious authenticity, one Crusader presented a genuine Mesopotamian cylinder seal of about 2300 B.C.E. to the Capella Palatina in Palermo, probably the first such piece to reach Europe.

Medieval and later artists produced numerous renderings of Middle Eastern settings in manuscripts, engravings, stained glass, and other media to serve as suggestive backdrops for biblical narratives. Certain images, especially those of Babylon and the Tower of Babel, also conveyed a sense of fascinated disapproval of Mesopotamian places supposed to have been centers of immorality and pagan chaos.

With the rise in the early nineteenth century of archaeology as a field of endeavor, Europeans set forth to appropriate the buried remains of ancient Mesopotamia. Did not the storied cities of the Bible — Nineveh, Nimrud, Babylon, and Ur, among others — belong to the Western past rather than to the Arab, Islamic, and Ottoman present? And what more fitting ornament for the imperial capitals of London and Paris than monumental sculpture from the Assyrian seats of empire?

In the 1840s, the Frenchmen Paul Émile Botta and Victor Place and the Englishman Austen Henry Layard were the first to tunnel beneath the Assyrian palace mounds of northern Mesopotamia, sawing into more transportable pieces many of the stone reliefs that adorned the walls and extracting whole the colossal winged bulls guarding the doorways. When the slabs reached Europe, with a large number having come to grief in shipwreck en route, they were parceled out to museums and other institutions. Some of the sculptured panels traveled onward to American colleges and theological seminaries.

Eager viewers saw in these reliefs proof of the downfall of Assyria, exactly as Isaiah had foretold. If his prophecies were true, many reasoned, then assuredly the rest of the Bible was equally veracious. Those who sought truth in the Bible were further confirmed in their ideas in the wake of the definitive decipherment in 1857 of Akkadian, one of the principal languages of ancient Mesopotamia. The Flood story so familiar from the Book of Genesis, for instance, turned up in a strikingly similar version on tablets unearthed at Nineveh in the library of the Assyrian king Assurbanipal (ca. 640 B.C.E.). When Layard read the cuneiform label on one of the wall reliefs, to cite another example, he realized that the besieged town depicted was none other than the Lachish of the Bible, whose celebrated siege by Sennacherib in 701 B.C.E. had been vividly commemorated on his palace walls.

Spurred on by such successes, the pace of European archaeological investigation throughout Mesopotamia quickened. In the 1870s, the Ottoman authorities granted multiple permits to Hormuzd Rassam, whose goal was to claim as many new sites and tablets as possible for the British Museum before Russian influence in Constantinople swayed the Sublime Porte to suspend or curtail Western operations in the region, a groundless fear as it happened. Rassam's approach to excavation was almost entirely focused on the recovery of tablets. Whereas his predecessors had kept such scientific records as met the standards of the day, Rassam did not.

Several developments with bearing on the present situation in Iraq resulted from Rassam's activities. The Ottomans decided to restrict permits to one site per person and to require that major finds be sent henceforth to Constantinople. In the Western market, demand for Mesopotamian artifacts was, however, still high, and so the first large-scale illicit antiquities trade was organized. From Baghdad, agents fanned out to the sites Rassam had opened and left ill guarded, engaging scores of workmen to dig up salable objects, especially tablets. In 1888, the British Museum sent out Ernest Wallis Budge on three occasions to stop what it called "the leakage of tablets from our sites" and to secure those already on the market for the museum. This Budge did, managing to ship numerous consignments of tablets to London, in contravention of the prevailing Ottoman laws regarding material from Mesopotamia.

By the beginning of the twentieth century, archaeology had become a serious scientific discipline. With every passing decade, thanks to collaborative research ventures with other fields such as geophysics, ethnobotany, analytical chemistry, and genetics, new methodologies have augmented our ability to reconstruct the human past. The heart of archaeology is the conscientious retrieval and accurate recording of data from artifacts, features, and ecofacts, which, taken as a whole, shed light on behaviors and transformations specific to a site in time and space. This, in a word, is context.

It is crucial to keep in mind that unlike what may be done in other scientific areas, archaeological projects cannot be replicated. Archaeology is not an experiment that may be reproduced. Once a site is excavated, context is gone forever, preserved only in the documentary records of the project. And sites that are plundered lose irrevocably any hope of context.

Without context, an artifact floats in a void, a mute witness to its long-vanished world. Consider, for instance, a cuneiform tablet whose context is unknown, bought on the antiquities market. Specialists may read its text, discuss its grammar and vocabulary, date it more or less precisely, and so forth. But we will never know what tablets or other artifacts were associated with it, perhaps in a temple foundation deposit, an independent merchant's establishment, a schoolroom, or a royal library. We will never know if it had been stacked with other tablets in a basket, fallen with the rest from its wooden shelf in the palace archives, a key to the thought patterns that structured the storage of information some 4000 years ago. The tablet without context may speak to us, but only in whispers compared to the messages it might have proclaimed.

Archaeology also distinguishes between primary and secondary context, the former referring to a pristine state untouched since deposition and the latter reflecting subsequent human intervention or environmental disturbance. Take a lapis lazuli cylinder seal, for example. If it had been interred with its owner, we may learn much about it from its primary context of the burial and other grave goods. If, on the other hand, the seal had been saved over several generations as a valuable heirloom, the secondary context in which it was found is likewise of great significance. A seal without context can tell us nothing, save what we may see in its intaglio patterns.

Mesopotamian sites present extraordinary challenges to the archaeologist. The lack of readily available stone resources in the region meant that mud brick was the usual construction material. As settlements tended to occupy the same locations for several thousand years, successive levels of mud-brick structures, built and rebuilt dozens of times over the millennia, formed enormous mounds known as *tells*, or ruin-hills in Arabic. Consequently, the stratigraphy and chronological interrelationships of such sites are extremely complex, requiring careful clearance and recording by well-trained personnel. In addition, it is quite difficult for any but the most experienced eye to determine the plans of buildings, since degraded mud-brick walls are nearly indistinguishable from their matrix of soil and debris and only one or two courses may be preserved.

The excavations at Babylon, directed from 1899 on by Robert Koldewy under the auspices of the German Oriental Society, demonstrated for the first time that despite these challenges it was possible to carry out scrupulous archaeological work in Mesopotamia. The German architectural, epigraphic, and artifactual reports showed that a wealth of information could be obtained if archaeological methods of the highest order were applied.

Subsequent projects undertaken by German and other foreign teams soon followed this lead. At Ur, for example, the Englishman Sir Leonard Woolley, working on behalf of the British Museum and the University of Pennsylvania Museum of Archaeology and Anthropology, held off excavating the Royal Graves he found in 1922 for four years so he could train his workmen sufficiently in the necessary techniques of observation and recording.

Shortly after the creation of the nation of Iraq in 1921, the Englishwoman Gertrude Bell was named Honorary Director of Antiquities. With the support of King Faisal, himself an amateur archaeologist, Bell organized the Iraqi Antiquities Organization, a national museum in Baghdad, and a network of provincial museums. She wrote a new antiquities law, which reserved all exceptional finds for Iraq, as well as half of any other finds. Also, she recognized the importance of preparing Iraqi scholars for the vital tasks of directing and staffing the Antiquities Organization, of superintending foreign excavation projects, and of initiating an Iraqi program of field research.

The decades before and after World War II saw new directions in archaeology in Iraq. The search for biblical validation and prestige sites was replaced by a desire to understand more fully such matters as social and economic history, connections between core and peripheral areas, and the origins and growth of the world's earliest agriculture, writing, and urbanization. Several institutions, notably the University of Chicago, undertook ambitious survey projects, which entail the creation of detailed maps of ancient sites in a given region, based on analyses of surface finds and geomorphological features.

By the 1970s, the cultural heritage organization in Iraq was one of the best anywhere, with a new national museum in Baghdad, including a children's wing, as well as thirteen regional museums, numerous displays at archaeological sites, 1600 site guards, and a cadre of expert curators, conservators, and field archaeologists. In 1974, the antiquities laws in effect for half a century were amended to permit foreign excavators to take out of Iraq only scientific samples and study materials. Almost no Mesopotamian artifacts were being illegally exported or illicitly excavated, for punishment was swift and severe, including being shot on the spot (or on Iraqi television). Nine people were publicly hanged for having sliced a colossal head of a winged bull from Nineveh into marketable pieces.

The Gulf War and its aftermath dealt this situation a grievous blow. The U.N. sanctions forced severe cutbacks in the Antiquities Service, especially in its ability to support site guards and regional museum staff. In southern Iraq, the heartland of the Sumerians and Babylonians, there was for the first time formalized looting of regional museums and sites, motivated by the hard currency dealers and collectors, based mainly in the U.S., Switzerland, Great Britain, and Japan, were willing to pay for Mesopotamian art and tablets. Individuals highly placed in Saddam Hussein's government, as well as members of his immediate family, also participated. On very limited resources and to little avail, the Iraqi Antiquities Service struggled to counter this and to conduct salvage digs at looted sites.

With antiquities stolen from other parts of the world having been steadily and predictably available over the years, the black market embraced with enthusiasm the new trade emerging from Iraq. Buyers were also often seduced by the hardy notions of biblical substantiation, ever present in popular concepts of Mesopotamia. Most purchasers knew little of modern archaeology, cared nothing for context, and rationalized that there were ample sites to go around. Major museums, well aware of the issues, appear to have decided that the benefits of being able to exhibit new acquisitions in Mesopotamian art outweighed the scholarly and moral costs.

Unfortunately, some specialists in cuneiform studies have been happy to read, translate, and publish tablets and other inscribed objects of unknown or dubious provenance. While many professional journals refuse to accept articles treating material of this ilk obtained since 1970, as well as advertising from firms dealing in illicit antiquities, not all publishers share these principles. Scholarly attention and publication confer legitimacy on the artifact(s) involved and enhance the monetary value of the entire class of objects, which in turns drives up prices and demand.

During the Gulf War, military operations for the most part avoided ancient and Islamic sites, preferring to concentrate on desert areas in which there was maximum maneuverability. Damage inevitably occurred, notably to the ziggurat, or temple platform, at Ur (ca. 2100 B.C.E.), to the great brick vault over the Sassanian audience hall at Ctesiphon, and to the medieval university complex in Baghdad. Foreshadowing the events of 2003, nine of thirteen provincial museums were looted.

By January 2003, it was evident to many in the American archaeological community that the imminent war posed a far more serious threat to sites and artifacts in Iraq. A delegation of Mesopotamian specialists supplied the Pentagon and the State Department with background information, as well as a CD-ROM map of 5000 important sites. They also stressed the significance of the national and provincial museums and warned of the scientific and other risks if planners failed to safeguard cultural heritage in Iraq.

Government officials in Washington paid scant heed, instead meeting more regularly with a group called the American Council for Cultural Policy, composed mainly of museum curators and private collectors, whose treasurer, a lawyer who represents the National Association of Dealers in Ancient, Oriental, and Primitive Art, ominously characterized Iraq's current antiquities laws as excessively "retentionist." The group has been pressing for a "sensible post-Saddam cultural administration" that will amend Iraqi laws to allow selected antiquities to be exported, a self-serving scheme harking back to the situation in nineteenth- and early twentieth-century Iraq.

In late March, the Pentagon's Office of Reconstruction and Humanitarian Assistance sent a memo to the Coalition Forces Land Component command. This listed buildings to be secured immediately after the taking of Baghdad, in descending order of importance. At the top of the list were the Central Bank and the National Museum, which a military briefing foretold would "be a prime target for looters."

As American troops moved toward Baghdad, there is some indication that they did try to avoid archaeological sites in southern Iraq. Once they entered the city on 8 April, however, no effort was made to safeguard the museum, despite repeated entreaties to do so, even as the Oil Ministry, sixteenth on the Pentagon list, was fully protected from the start. Photographs, video footage, and eyewitness reports of the looting in the museum captured worldwide attention. The White House tried to trivialize the catastrophe. Secretary of Defense Donald Rumsfeld set the tone, asking, "How many vases could they have in that country, anyway?" National and international pressure finally forced the U.S. in late April to organize an investigative team to coordinate recovery, reconstruction, and conservation in the museum. The archaeological consequences of the failure to protect the museum and other cultural institutions are discussed at greater length in the next chapter.

Meanwhile, far greater damage was occurring to ancient archaeological sites and pre-Islamic monuments, especially in southern Iraq. For now, Islamic-era material appears not to be involved, probably for a combination of religious and economic reasons. From the moment the Iraq war began, there has been systematic looting, often with two or three hundred men journeying by coordinated taxi service daily back and forth to sites. Increasingly, they are armed with Kalashnikovs and grenade launchers. Many of them work at previously excavated mounds, deepening old trenches, while others dig in new locations. To continue during the summer heat and duststorms, looters have been tunneling beneath the surface, undermining the already fragile sites so they soon collapse.

Furnished with published archaeological survey maps identifying probable sites and their time frames of occupation, looters can target specific places to obtain antiquities of particular periods, enabling them to be highly responsive to market demands. Some enterprising former site guards and excavation workmen rent out small plots expected to be productive, thereby profiting several times over from their knowledge of certain areas.

For the men at the lowest level of the illicit antiquities trade, the financial rewards are great. A small tablet fetches $7 to $10, a more impressive one $100, a figurine $50 to $60, a cylinder seal $200, a plaque with the goddess Ishtar $500. The money is urgently needed by the extended families of the diggers for basic living expenses and medical supplies. Without it, the mortality rate, especially for infants and children, would climb even higher in Iraq.

For the numerous middlemen involved, the prices and profits rise with every step of the journey. The final buyer may pay $1000 for an interesting tablet, $50,000 for a group of related tablets, $12 million for a fragment of an Assyrian relief sledgehammered down to salable size.

Cylinder seals start at $5000; back in 2001, a seal sold at Christie's in New York for $424,000. Some experts estimate that the trade is worth $10 million to $20 million a year.

In Iraq today, few safe alternative sources of income exist for the majority of the population. Farmers have little or no markets for their products (see Chapter 13). As for site guards, after the Gulf War they saw their pay plummet to $5 a month, rising to $15–$20 during the oil-for-food program. In the first months after the fall of Saddam, they went unpaid. The U.S. now offers them $60 a month, but this salary is not very tempting, given the thus far inadequate arms and technical support they have received to defend against attacks from the well-equipped, determined looters. It is likewise dangerous to be policemen and other security personnel, who are targets of assassination, kidnapping, and death threats in reprisal for what is viewed as collaboration with the occupying forces. Finding and selling one Sumerian figurine a month remains a less hazardous way to earn the same money.

Looters, by contrast, enjoy the protection and support of their tribal leaders, who have always controlled the areas surrounding many sites. Since the nineteenth century, archaeologists have recognized the necessity of gaining the trust and good will of the district sheikhs. Indeed, during the late 1990s, tribal leaders began to work with Iraqi archaeologists to control the looting, with positive results. The sheikhs in the Uruk area have been steadfast in their protection of the site. Today it is largely income from the sale of antiquities that enables tribes to provide for their members, which they regard as an obligation of honor.

Iraqis from other walks of life and cultural milieus are being drawn into the antiquities trade. A jewelry shop owner in Baghdad, for example, found himself paying over $1300 for a group of cylinder seals he was offered so he could return them to the museum whence they had been stolen in April 2003. An undercover investigator spent months tracking down several of the more spectacular pieces taken from the museum, receiving no more tangible reward than the satisfaction of a job well done. One wonders how long it will be before social and economic pressures impel men such as these to yield to the temptation of buying and selling antiquities.

In their search for desirable objects, looters cast aside the unprofitable: potsherds, broken sculptures, tablet fragments, cracked cylinder seals, and the like. Archaeologists estimate that for every salable object, 2000 sherds and 1000 small finds are discarded onto vast rubbish heaps. Three hundred looters digging holes five meters deep will go through 450,000 cu m of a site in the course of a year. To put these figures into perspective, we may compare them with those of a standard two-month-long excavation season, during which 20,000 sherds are typically recovered from an area of approximately 2500 cu m.

Compounding the situation is the fact that archaeological sites are also at grave risk from their use by the military. The prime example is Babylon. In April 2003, American forces established Camp Alpha, headquarters of the Multinational Division Central-South, in a 150-ha compound in the heart of the ancient site. The camp quickly comprised helipads, living quarters for 2000 troops, parking areas, fuel depots, and numerous trench cuttings, among other installations. Command of the camp passed in September 2003 to Polish forces, who turned it over to the Iraqi Ministry of Culture on 15 January 2005. Not until June 2004 did the Coalition Provisional Authority issue a statement concerning the protection of Babylon.

While in the early days of the war, a military presence at Babylon may have prevented looting, the construction and full-scale operation of a major camp have caused irreparable damage to one of the world's most famous cities. Heavy vehicular and helicopter traffic crushed ancient pavements and affected underlying structures. Large areas were leveled and graveled for various purposes, thereby contaminating the site with building material brought in from elsewhere, as well as with spilled fuels and leaching chemical treatments. Further contamination has come from the many thousands of bags and wire mesh baskets stuffed with sand and earth similarly brought in from elsewhere, after repeated protests from archaeologists put a stop in November 2003 to the use of filler bulldozed from depths of up to two meters throughout the site, which contained quantities of potsherds, tablet fragments, and other artifacts. Everywhere there are signs of defacement and graffiti by soldiers. Outlying parts of the site are said to be mined, raising the probability of accidental or deliberate detonation causing additional destruction. As of this writing, comprehensive assessment reports are being compiled to update and augment the lengthy documents prepared by Polish and British archaeologists.

Some preliminary, ineffectual efforts have been made by the Coalition Provisional Authority to curtail the site looting. In May 2003, for example, U.S. Marines arrested a hundred looters at the site of Umma, but hundreds more have dug at the site daily since then. In the fall of 2003, a plan was formulated to train 1700 or more Iraqi Facilities Protection Service guards and to equip them with radios and watchtowers so they could notify Iraqi police of looting activity. The police would then arrive to arrest the looters. Even if this were not such a cumbersome, unrealistic plan, as of December 2004 these guards still lacked adequate equipment and vehicles. The handful of vehicles presently provided by the Ministry of Culture must patrol hundreds of sites in southern Iraq, a Sisyphean task. The Iraqi guards posted at oil assets, by contrast, have long had ample logistical backup.

There have been a number of international initiatives as well. In the fall of 2003, groups of Italian Carabinieri, well used to policing archaeological sites at home, began patrolling, but they have been defeated at nearly every turn by the looters' familiarity with the terrain, by their switch to night work (powered by car batteries), and by the support afforded by Iraqis fighting against the coalition troops. The U.N. Development Group has allocated $5.5 million for a three-year cultural program, including sending forty-five vehicles for site security (still being delivered). UNESCO member nations have earmarked funds for such projects as collections management systems (Switzerland), improvements in the Iraq Museum (Japan, Belgium), guard training (Italy), and installation of security lighting and fencing for the palace of Sennacherib at Nineveh (Switzerland).

In sum, the cultural heritage of Iraq is vanishing at a disastrous rate. Hundreds of sites have been utterly destroyed. While the looting of the Iraq Museum gained international press coverage and attention, there has been little public concern expressed for the larger issues discussed in this chapter. Why should this be so? In the first place, popular opinion still regards archaeology as a kind of glorified treasure hunting, with no conception of its rigorous methodology or research programs. Relatively few understand the consequences for human knowledge when artifacts are deprived of their context or when sites are destroyed. The great modern lesson of evolutionary biology — extinction is forever — applies equally to archaeology, but the connection is rarely made. Cultural heritage is not a renewable resource. What is happening in Iraq affects us all.

Bibliographical Note to Chapter 14

For the history of Mesopotamian archaeology, see Seton Lloyd, *Foundations in the Dust: The Story of Mesopotamian Exploration* (London: Thames and Hudson, 1980); Mogens Trolle Larsen, *The Conquest of Assyria* (London: Routledge, 1996); John Malcolm Russell, *From Nineveh to New York* (New Haven: Yale University Press, 1997). For the development of Mesopotamian archaeology in its wider context, see Glyn Daniel, *A Short History of Archaeology* (New York: Thames and Hudson, 1981). Good introductions to modern archaeological method and theory include Wendy Ashmore and Robert J. Sharer, *Discovering Our Past: A Brief Introduction to Archaeology* (Mountain View: Mayfield Press, 1988); Brian M. Fagan, *In the Beginning: An Introduction to Archaeology* (Glenview: Scott, Foreman, 1988). Recent treatments of the antiquities trade and archaeological ethics include Neil Brodie and Kathryn W. Tubb, eds., *Illicit Antiquities: The Theft of Culture and the Extinction of Archaeology* (London: Routledge, 2002); Karen D. Vitelli, ed., *Archaeological Ethics* (Walnut Creek: Altamira Press, 1996); Phyllis Messenger, ed., *The Ethics of Collecting Cultural Property* (Albuquerque: University of New Mexico Press, 1999); Neil Brodie, Jennifer Doole, Colin Renfrew, eds., *Trade in Illicit Antiquities: The Destruction of the World's Archaeological Heritage* (Cambridge: McDonald Institute for Archaeological Research, 2001). Among the many articles and reports on the present archaeological situation in Iraq, the following are particularly authoritative and useful: the special issue on "Art Loss in Iraq" in the *IFAR Journal* 6:1 (2003), 30–61; Andrew Lawler, "Iraq's Antiquities War," *National Geographic* 204:4 (2003), 58–75; Micah Garen, "The War Within," *Archaeology* (July/August 2004), 28–31; John Malcolm Russell, "Robbing the Archaeological Cradle," *Natural History* 110:1 (2002), 44–55; Joanne Farchakh, "Le massacre du patrimoine irakien," *Archéologia* 402 (July–August, 2003), 14–31 and "Irak, témoignages d'une archéologie héroïque," *Archéologia* 411 (May, 2004), 14–27. See also the sources noted in Chapters 13 and 16.

Chapter 15

The Iraq Museum and the Future of the Past

In 1923, Gertrude Bell created a National Museum in Baghdad, convinced that displays of ancient Mesopotamian achievements would bolster modern Iraqi confidence in the future of the new nation. Since all excavated objects had hitherto left the country for the museums of London, Paris, Constantinople, and elsewhere, Bell had to build the collections from scratch. Under her newly written antiquities laws, the Iraq Museum, as it is usually known, would henceforth receive all exceptional items and half the rest of the material recovered during an excavation season. Bell also began training Iraqis in the tasks of cataloguing, conserving, and curating. She set up temporary quarters in two rooms in the palace, where she worked tirelessly until her death in 1926 to impress upon the international community that the Iraq Museum was destined to be a locus of great nationalistic and archaeological importance.

The sum of 50,000 pounds that Bell bequeathed in her will to the Iraq Museum enabled it to continue in the directions she had envisioned. In the 1930s, the burgeoning collections moved from a quasi-Beaux Arts building on Ma'mun Street to a more fittingly designed museum whose façade was modeled on that of the Assyrian palaces. Frank Lloyd Wright was among the architects whom King Faisal II invited to submit plans. The present museum compound (incorporating the old building) was begun in 1958, opened in 1966, formally inaugurated in 1969, expanded in 1984, and reopened in 1986, only to close again in 1991. Prior to the Gulf War, certain objects, among them gold and ivory pieces from Nimrud and Ur, were removed for safekeeping to sealed boxes deep in the vaults of the Central Bank in Baghdad. On 18 April 2001, the museum reopened, but did not yet risk retrieving the boxes from the bank. Behind the scenes, the effects of the U.N. sanctions were keenly felt, especially in the lack of up-to-date preservation and conservation capabilities. Nevertheless, as Bell had hoped, the museum had become one of the world's major repositories for ancient artifacts, including cuneiform tablets, with a Heritage Section for material from more recent periods and thousands of Islamic, Christian, and Jewish manuscripts.

At the end of February 2003, the museum closed, and preparations for war began. A five-person team in great secret moved 8366 objects in 179 boxes to an ultra-secure bunker whose location is even now known only to a few. Museum staff members attempted to forestall any damage to the massive, immovable sculptures, such as those in the Assyrian galleries, by spreading a cushion of sandbags on the floor and by encasing them in sandbags and foam. They also moved nearly 40,000 medieval manuscripts and most of the reference library. New inner walls were built to strengthen existing barriers. Some provincial and site museums followed suit, having by 2003 already sent much material to Baghdad for safekeeping.

Despite numerous warnings from many constituencies of the crucial need to protect the Iraq Museum, as outlined in the previous chapter, and despite a joint pledge on 8 April by George W. Bush and Tony Blair to safeguard cultural heritage, no military order was issued regarding the museum. On that very day, only a handful of curators and other personnel remained in the building, intending to stay there until all was secure. But attacks apparently directed at the neighboring Ministry of Information and a television station, as well as the arrival of Iraqi militia in the museum compound, persuaded them to abandon the museum about midday. They planned to return in a few hours, but U.S. soldiers holding the bridges over the Tigris would not let them pass. Shortly after they left, a clash ensued between American troops and Iraqis who had taken up positions atop the museum. At some point, perhaps not that day, a sniper fired from an upper window in the building. Contrary to early reports, the museum had not been used previously by the Iraqi military.

On 9 April, Baghdad fell to U.S. forces. That whole day, the museum itself was quiet. The following morning, a crowd began gathering in front, clearly ready to enter and loot. A smaller group went to a back gate. An Iraqi living on the museum grounds (which also housed a police station) rushed outside to an American tank parked at a nearby intersection. Thanks to his having worked as an interpreter, he spoke English to the crew, begging them to swing the tank around to threaten the looters. After checking with their commander, the Americans told him that they could not do so without orders and these were not forthcoming.

In the interim, successive waves of looters were already inside, smashing or taking everything from office equipment and electrical wire to ancient and medieval artifacts. The looters comprised local residents intent on finding easily salable goods, opportunists who saw unexpected windfalls in the chaotic situation, and professional thieves well equipped with glasscutters, skeleton keys, and basic knowledge of gallery and storeroom contents. Reports of collusion by museum personnel are utterly without foundation. Some Iraqis, seeing what was happening, posed as looters, taking objects so they could return them later, which they did. The destruction continued for two days.

Staff members managed to reach the museum again on 12 April. They hung a handmade sign outside claiming falsely but effectively that U.S. forces were now protecting the premises. On 13 April, senior museum officials made their way to an American headquarters to renew their pleas for protection. They were stunned to be asked such questions as where the museum was. As news of the disaster spread around the world, U.S. Secretary of State Colin Powell said on 14 April that he had "issued instructions to all troops inside Iraq to protect museums and antiquities throughout Iraq." But "instructions" did not become orders. Another two days passed until an American tank platoon (four tanks, sixteen men, plus additional support) was finally sent to the museum, a full week after the city fell.

In mid-May 2003, two tanks were stationed in front of the museum, with a military guard and razor wire at the entrance and soldiers quartered in the library. As of December 2004, three-meter-high protective walls have been erected, which have not deterred snipers. Inside the museum, new defensive barriers and false doors have been built. Museum staff members courageously come to work, but they take different routes each day.

During that same week in April 2003, thieves tried to blast open the vaults of the Central Bank, causing them to flood, seriously damaging many of the fragile objects stored there. In addition, the Iraq National Library and Archives were looted and burned, as well as an important library of Korans. Other cultural institutions also suffered: the Museum of Fine Arts, university libraries, art galleries, the museum in Mosul, and so forth. Full discussion of this aspect of the destruction of Iraqi cultural heritage lies beyond the scope of the present book (see Appendix).

At first, there were conflicting stories about what had occurred and much discrepancy over the numbers of objects stolen from the museum. As tallies dropped from the 170,000 initially mentioned, defenders of U.S. policies in Iraq seized the occasion to decry the whole matter as a liberal ploy to inflame public opinion against the war. U.S. investigators, led by Colonel Matthew Bogdanos, arrived on 22 April to try to assess the situation more precisely and to coordinate recovery and conservation efforts.

From an archaeological point of view, however, the concentration on quantification, the main thrust of the media reports and counter-reports, has been quite misdirected. To its credit, the investigative team soon reached this conclusion, but general attention remained focused on what one periodical called "the scorecard" in an otherwise solid article. Each object is a unique window into the human past, not a mass-produced item in a modern warehouse inventory. The pieces kept in the study collections represented many seasons of painstaking excavation, yet to be fully catalogued, analyzed, and published. Lying now smashed and commingled on the storeroom floors, they are opportunities lost forever to glimpse moments of history, rather than an entry in a ledger of so many thousand objects. Damaged pieces returned through amnesty or detective work do not simply transfer from one side to another of a balance sheet, but are forever deprived of their former integrity. And how can the destruction of register books, excavation notes, file cards, and other documentation be quantified?

Above all, none of this need have happened had anyone in a decision-making position acted upon the warnings received months in advance of the start of the war on 19 March. On 9 April, it was still not too late to secure the Iraq Museum. U.S. planners let an entire week pass, in which irreparable harm was done, before military orders were issued at last.

The following pages present a small gallery of Iraq Museum pieces stolen, damaged, or still missing (IM designations refer to museum numbers). Our purpose is four-fold. First, since few accounts have discussed the objects beyond captions, brief mention of their cultural significance may be helpful to readers. Second, the art historical/ archaeological treatment outlined here aims to give an idea of the range of issues raised by this and similar material. Third, it is hoped that readers will note how greatly knowledge of archaeological context enriches the avenues of inquiry possible. And finally, by juxtaposing archival photographs of these pieces with views taken inside the museum in October 2003, readers may see more readily the extent of the damage.

Alabaster Vase from Uruk, ca. 3300–3000 B.C.E. (IM 19606)

The tall chalice known as the Uruk Vase (height 105 cm) depicts the earliest cult scene in Mesopotamian art, with priests bringing offerings to Inanna, the principal goddess of the Sumerian pantheon. The two lower bands, or registers, represent the fertility of fields and herds, over which Inanna presided. In the top register, a special attendant holds the end of a long scarf being given to Inanna, who stands further to the right, not visible in the photograph. To the left appear two vessels of the same type as the Uruk Vase, the first instance we have of a self-referenced object. The Uruk Vase is indeed one of a pair, the other having been too fragmentary to reassemble.

Above the goddess's head, a small section broke off and was repaired five thousand years ago. In carving the replacement piece, the sculptor matched well the rim molding, but did not reconstruct Inanna's headdress, so we do not know if at this period the goddess already wore

Overturned exhibit case with the Uruk vase base in the Iraq Museum, October 2003 (photo Catherine Sease).

Uruk vase fragments back in the Iraq Museum, October 2003 (photo Catherine Sease).

Alabaster vase from Uruk (after Eva Strommenger, *Fünf Jahrtausende Mesopotamien* [Munich: Hirmer, 1962], pl. 19).

the horned crown donned by deities in later Mesopotamian art. The fact of the repair, taken together with the vases' archaeological context, leads to the conclusion that the Uruk Vase and its mate were retained as heirlooms among the temple's furnishings, as valued in antiquity as today.

The Uruk Vase and its mate were found by the German Oriental Society in the Inanna temple precinct at Uruk (modern Warka, biblical Erech). Excavations begun in 1912 and renewed from 1928 on uncovered the remains of several sanctuaries built upon massive manmade platforms, or ziggurats, constructed towards the end of the fourth millennium B.C.E. Mesopotamian deities were thought to reside in their temples, at home in the mountainlike settings, high above the secular realm. The Uruk temples were embellished by cone mosaics, tens of thousands of red, black, and buff clay cones inserted into a plaster coating to form myriads of shimmering, geometric designs. As discussed in Chapter 1, it is at Uruk during this period that we see most clearly the development of the world's first great city, complete with monumental public and religious architecture.

In the Iraq Museum, the Uruk Vase occupied its own case. Curators debated the wisdom of moving it to safety in the winter of 2003, deciding that it was too fragile to transport. As seen in the photograph, the looters wrenched the vase off its pedestal foot, which remains attached to the overturned exhibit stand. The vase was returned during the amnesty; the second view shows it lying in pieces in a box. Preliminary assessments of its condition vary, but restoration seems possible, despite abrasions and chipping suffered by the tender alabaster.

Alabaster Head from Uruk, ca. 3300–3000 B.C.E. (IM 45434)

This unique sculpture of a female face (height 20 cm) was also found by the German Oriental Society in the Inanna temple precinct at Uruk. The rear of the Uruk Head, as it is often called, is flat, with drill holes to enable it to be attached, perhaps to a statue of wood or some other perishable material. The head originally had a very different appearance, for it was probably inlaid with highly stylized shell and lapis

Alabaster head from Uruk (after Eva Strommenger, *Fünf Jahrtausende Mesopotamien* [Munich: Hirmer, 1962], pl. 31).

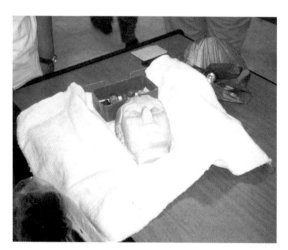

Uruk head returned to the Iraq Museum, October 2003 (photo Catherine Sease).

lazuli or obsidian eyes and lapis eyebrows. The hair was likely a sheet of gold or copper, chased with fine lines. The sculptured features, in great contrast, are a masterpiece of sensitive modeling, the earliest naturalistic rendering of mouth, chin, and cheeks, whether divine or human we know not.

Five months after the Uruk Head vanished from the Iraq Museum, it emerged, wrapped in rags, from a shallow pit in a suburban Baghdad garden. The asking price had been $25,000. The photograph shows it back in the museum, relatively unscathed. In his 29 September 2003 Op-Ed in *The New York Times*, William Safire termed the returned sculpture "a suitable symbol of the reborn nation." Is it rather an icon of the failure to protect cultural property?

Diorite Statue of Enmetena from Ur, ca. 2460 B.C.E. (IM 5)

During the Early Dynastic period, Sumerian temples continued to serve as the residences for the deities to whom they were dedicated. As access was probably increasingly limited to temple personnel, small votive, or worshipper, statues became popular. These stood on benches or tables in the temples, clasping their hands respectfully, conveying in perpetuity to the deity the good wishes of their donors. Both men and women could offer statues, which often bear short cuneiform texts giving their names and professions. Many of these figurines have been excavated buried beneath the temple floors, evidence that the Sumerians initiated a long tradition in the Middle East prohibiting the profane disposal of sacred items.

This votive statue (height 76 cm) represents Enmetena, ruler of the Sumerian city of Lagash, wearing the typical male dedicant's skirt of fleecelike material. While votives were generally carved of soft stones such as gypsum or alabaster, this is one of the earliest Mesopotamian statues of diorite, a hard black stone obtained via long-distance trade networks from Oman and Iran and often used in later periods for royal statuary (see Chapter 2). On his shoulders is a long inscription, unusual in that it includes the name of the statue, "Enmetena Whom [the god] Enlil Loves," as well as the record of a land transaction between the

233

Diorite statue of Enmetena from Ur (after Anton Moortgat, *The Art of Ancient Mesopotamia* [London: Phaidon, 1969], pl. 87).

king and the temple. This suggests that at least some dedicants expected a divine return for gifts rendered.

It is interesting that the statue was found at Ur, not Lagash. As discussed in Chapter 2, the Sumerian cities were often at odds with one another. It appears that this royal votive was taken from the Enlil temple at Lagash as booty during hostilities. Throughout Mesopotamian history, one frequently encounters examples of art objects seized as war trophies. Four millennia later, this statue again found itself plundered. As of this writing, Enmetena is still missing.

Inlaid Harp from Ur, ca. 2550–2400 B.C.E. (IM 8694)

Our most complete knowledge of Sumerian royalty comes from Ur, where in 1926–1930 Sir Leonard Woolley uncovered an extensive cemetery of the mid-third millennium B.C.E. His meticulous excavation and publication of the 1850 tombs, sixteen of which are known as the Royal Graves, shed considerable light on the burial practices, long-distance trade, and international contacts of the period. Though robbers had entered various tombs in antiquity, large quantities of grave goods of gold, lapis lazuli, carnelian, and other luxury materials remained.

Some of the burials reflected elaborate rituals, in which as many as seventy or eighty people died at the same time, accompanying the tomb's principal occupant into the underworld. Members of the court, soldiers, servants, and musicians descended the tomb's sloping passage, followed by men driving oxen or asses hitched to vehicles. When all were in place, they drank poison. The animals were killed, the bodies of beasts and people arranged, and the grave-shaft filled in with earth.

In recent years, there has been much discussion as to the nature of the ritual and identity of the principal occupants, with doubt cast upon whether or not they were members of the royal family of Ur. Taken as a whole, however, the epigraphic, archaeological, and textual evidence would seem to support Woolley's proposal that the ever more powerful kings of Ur introduced mass burial. One is reminded of the funeral rites staged for Gilgamesh, legendary king of Uruk, who, according to a Sumerian forerunner of the famous epic, was buried with his family,

Inlaid harp from Ur (after C. Leonard Woolley, *Ur Excavations: The Royal Cemetery* [Oxford: Oxford University Press, 1934], pl. 114).

Harp and other damaged pieces in the Iraq Museum, October 2003 (photo Catherine Sease).

courtiers, and retainers. And at Abydos in Egypt, members of the royal entourage were similarly interred with several Early Dynastic pharaohs in the early third millennium B.C.E.

Among the instruments recovered were nine or more harps, or lyres, carefully positioned near or atop the musicians' bodies after they died. Like the others, the harp in question here (height 120 cm) has been reconstructed based on impressions and hollows left by the wooden elements and strings that long since disintegrated. It comes from Grave 1237, dubbed the Great Death Pit, as it contained the richly adorned bodies of seventy-four men and women. The sound box and arms are decorated with shell, lapis, and red limestone inlays and sheet gold bands, with a gold bull's head on the front. The other harp protomes include gold-plated bull's heads with lapis beards, copper and silver cow's heads, copper-alloy stag's heads, and a copper-alloy head of a horned deity. On all the harps, the flat panel beneath the animal heads has shell inlays of human and animal scenes possibly derived from myths and rituals.

When the looters burst into one of the museum workrooms, they found the harp on a table, where it was being conserved. The gold bull's head had been taken to the Central Bank, where it was unharmed when the vaults flooded in the first days after the fall of Baghdad. As the photograph shows, the looters stripped the gold from the harp and did some damage to the fragile inlays.

Copper-Alloy Statue Made for Naram-Sin, ca. 2254–2218 B.C.E. (IM 77823)

Relatively few works of Akkadian sculpture exist, in part because the capital of Agade has not yet been identified, but those we have attest to a new artistic aesthetic designed to further the ambitions of the world's first empire. In 1975, during road construction in northern Iraq near the town of Bassetki, a massive hollow-cast copper-alloy statue was discovered. On a circular base (diameter 67 cm) sits a nude male whose upper half is not preserved. As his tasseled belt is typically worn by hero figures, it seems likely that he once held a standard that would have fitted into the socket between his legs. The piece is remarkable for

Copper-alloy statue made for Naram-Sin (after Joan Oates, *Babylon* [London: Thames and Hudson, 1979], 35).

Gouged stairs in the Iraq Museum, October 2003 (photo Catherine Sease).

its sophisticated treatment of the musculature, especially visible in the flexed tension of the feet and calves.

To the figure's left is a long cuneiform inscription telling us that the sculpture was made for the Akkadian king Naram-Sin, whose accomplishments are discussed in Chapter 2. The text further offers important documentary evidence for Naram-Sin's having become divine during his reign. According to the inscription, the people of Agade built a temple for the worship of their ruler, henceforth divine, "king of the four quarters of the world."

In the Iraq Museum, the piece was displayed on the upper floor. Its tremendous weight (more than 200 kg) discouraged museum staff from moving it in the weeks before the war. As the gouged marble steps in the photograph show, the looters simply pushed it roughly down the stairs. They disposed of it quickly for $300 in a flea market. The purchaser, who bought other pieces at the same time, put a price tag of $100,000 on it, coated it with protective grease, and dropped it down a cesspool for animal excrement. There it was recovered in November 2003, with some damage, mainly to the toes.

Ivory Furniture Panel from Nimrud, ca. 745–727 B.C.E. (IM 61898)

Within the first days of excavating at the Assyrian capital of Nimrud (biblical Calah) in 1847, Sir Austen Henry Layard came upon carved ivory inlays from palace furniture, but despite his best efforts, many of the fragile pieces disintegrated, as he lacked the proper techniques and tools for removing and conserving them. In 1854, William K. Loftus fared better with the inlays he found in a Nimrud palace burned by the Medes and Babylonians in 612 B.C.E., for the fire had served to harden the ivories. A century later, Sir Max Mallowan resumed excavations at Nimrud, recovering over successive seasons the largest corpus known of ancient ivories. Chronologically, they span the reigns of several kings of the ninth and eighth centuries B.C.E.; stylistically, they fall into three main groups — Assyrian, Phoenician, and Syrian — reflecting the internationalism characteristic of the period.

Ivory furniture panel from Nimrud (after Paolo Matthiae, *La storia dell'arte dell'Oriente Antico: I primi imperi e i principati del ferro* [Milan: Electa, 1997], 181, Photoservice Electa, Milan).

Damaged ivories in the Iraq Museum, October 2003 (photo Catherine Sease).

The panel illustrated here (width 55 cm) is one of a group of similar thronebacks, or bedheads. When the Medes and Babylonians sacked Nimrud, they stripped the gold sheets from these and other pieces of palace furniture, abandoning the unwieldy ivory panels. Afterwards, survivors tried to salvage the most precious items. They placed the thronebacks in orderly rows in a small palace room to await reconstruction. This was not to be, as the invaders soon attacked Nimrud a second time, putting a decisive end to Assyrian domination. In the course of Mallowan's 1957 excavations, he found the ivories still neatly stacked.

The decoration seen here is typical of the Syrian style, with its barefoot hunter/warriors and winged "genius" figures carrying enigmatic buckets and cones, as often seen in Assyrian wall reliefs, flanking an enthroned woman holding up a bowl. The carving is vigorous and lively, balancing linear detail with bold forms.

Many of the Nimrud ivories were kept in a basement storage room in the Iraq Museum, where prior to the war they were damaged by flooding. The conservation lab, seriously affected by shortages of equipment, was unable to treat them much beyond putting them in wooden trays to dry. When the looters came upon them, they overturned the trays and scattered their contents, pulverizing a large number of ivories in the process. In the foreground of the photograph may be seen the panel discussed here, surrounded by other damaged ivories. Important pieces are still missing as of this writing, notably an openwork winged sphinx, a tribute-bearer, and a cloisonné chryselephantine plaque of a lioness mauling an African.

Cylinder Seals from Kish and Girsu, ca. 2420–2220 B.C.E. (From top, IM 2780, 13239, 9709, 10958)

In the mid-fourth millennium B.C.E., people in Mesopotamia began carving designs on small cylinders and rolling them across the surface of hollow clay balls to serve as personal identifiers for the transactions signified by the balls' contents and exterior markings. The use of seals to signify ownership arose together with the world's earliest writing system (see Chapter 1).

Cylinder seals from Kish and Girsu (after Eva Strommenger, *Der Garten in Eden* [Berlin: Museum für Vor- und Frühgeschichte der Staatlichen Museen Preussischer Kulturbesitz, 1978], 103).

Storage cabinets in the Iraq Museum, October 2003 (photo Catherine Sease).

242

Over the next four thousand years, countless cylinder seals were made, each one unique, 3–4 cm high on average, which offer an unparalleled opportunity to study the development of Mesopotamian art. In miniature, seals encompass a full range of themes and subjects, from scenes of daily life to religious ceremonies to vignettes taken from myths and epics. Seals can also include cuneiform inscriptions integrated to a greater or lesser degree into the figural designs.

The four seals illustrated here with their modern impressions are representative of the genre. In the top one appear hero/bull-man and lion/stag combats. The second has a lion attacking a bovine in a wooded landscape, while a man tries to intervene. In the next, an eagle displays an impressive wingspan as it claws two gazelles. The bottom seal depicts three lesser gods approaching an enthroned deity whose radiating aura identifies him as Shamash, the sun god. All four exhibit the hallmarks of glyptic art in the Akkadian period (ca. 2420–2220 B.C.E.), especially a more sculptural treatment of the figures and a more deliberate use of negative space.

A considerable number of cylinder seals was housed in brown cabinets (see photograph) and in temporary boxes in the basement magazines in the Iraq Museum, along with an outstanding collection of Greek, Roman, and Islamic gold and silver coins. The looters went down a remote stairwell and broke through a steel door and a stone wall to reach the storage room where the seals and coins were kept. Somehow the thieves had located the duplicate set of keys to the cabinets, hidden in the museum in case the master set in the director's office was compromised. Once in the storage room, pitch black since the museum's power was cut, they lit packing material and cleared 103 plastic boxes of 4795 cylinder seals, in addition to a like quantity of jewelry, bronze weapons, and pottery, leaving untouched a nearby pile of cardboard boxes, which were empty. Then their luck ran out, for they dropped the cabinet keys in the litter of boxes on the floor. They lit more foam padding to search frantically and fruitlessly for the keys before the noxious fumes forced them to leave. When U.S. investigators finally found the keys buried in the debris, they opened the cabinets and confirmed that not a single item was missing. The director's master keys have not been seen since April.

The stolen seals, all acquired before 1991 from known archaeological contexts, had been moved several times for security reasons and were awaiting permanent storage in the cabinets. The four cylinder seals discussed above are among those taken. In June 2003, some of the items surfaced in the U.S. and Europe; three seals, bought in Baghdad for $200, were confiscated in New York and are now back in Iraq. The same group of thieves may also have planned to take the cuneiform tablets that had long been in this storage area. But some years previously, the tablets had been transferred to a less damp storeroom, a move of which the thieves were evidently unaware. These tablets, at least, are safe.

Bibliographical Note to Chapter 15

For a lively biography of Gertrude Bell, see Janet Wallach, *Desert Queen* (New York: Doubleday, 1996). On the events in the Iraq Museum, see especially McGuire Gibson, "Cultural Tragedy in Iraq: A Report on the Looting of Museums, Archives, and Sites," *IFAR Journal* 6:1 (2003), 30–37; Joanne Farchakh, "The Specter of War, " *Archaeology* (May/June 2003), 14–15; Andrew Lawler, "Mayhem in Mesopotamia," *Science* (1 August 2003), 582–589. On Mesopotamian art and culture, the reader may find the following particularly accessible and well illustrated: Dominique Collon, *Ancient Near Eastern Art* (Berkeley: University of California Press, 1995) and *First Impressions: Cylinder Seals in the Ancient Near East* (Chicago: University of Chicago Press, 1987); Joan Aruz, ed., *Art of the First Cities* (New Haven: Yale University Press, 2003); John E. Curtis and Julian Reade, eds., *Art and Empire* (New York: Metropolitan Museum of Art, 1995); Sir Max Mallowan, *The Nimrud Ivories* (London: British Museum Press, 1978); Henrietta McCall, *Mesopotamian Myths* (London: British Museum Press, 1990); C. B. F. Walker, *Cuneiform* (Berkeley: University of California Press, 1987).

Chapter 16

International and National Legal Regimes for the Protection of Archaeological Heritage

1. Introduction

Destruction of archaeological heritage is a significant problem throughout the world. While recent events in Iraq and Afghanistan have highlighted the problems of looting of archaeological sites as well as thefts from museums, this is a worldwide phenomenon. Archaeological heritage is under threat from many different forces, ranging from intentional looting to routine agricultural activities to construction and development projects on both large and small scale, such as the Three River Gorges project in China. Even natural forces such as erosion cause damage. However, the intentional looting of sites to obtain antiquities for sale on the international market is the most pernicious form of destruction. Such looting became increasingly prevalent in the decades following World War II and thrives particularly in regions where there is political instability, lack of centralized government authority, and poor economic conditions. The last threat to archaeological heritage comes from war itself. This was particularly evident during the wars of the 1990s in the Balkans where cultural, religious and historic sites were intentionally destroyed as a part of ethnic cleansing.

Both international and various national legal systems aim to discourage these types of destructive activities. In terms of the international art market, the legal system imposes adverse consequences on those who engage in its illegal aspects. These consequences range from loss of the financial investment in the archaeological object itself to criminal prosecution in appropriate circumstances. If one accepts the principles of market supply and demand, then the imposition of such consequences on those who acquire looted or stolen antiquities should discourage the acquisition of such objects. If demand is reduced, then the supply should be similarly depressed and the looting of sites to obtain such objects should decrease, even if it is not entirely eliminated.

International conventions similarly aim to protect cultural and archaeological heritage during time of war. Particularly the 1954 Hague Convention on the Protection of Cultural Property in the Event of Armed Conflict embodies aspects of the law of warfare that are intended to prevent the destruction of this heritage during military actions and occupation. The efficacy of this Convention has been at issue during both the Balkan wars and the Gulf wars. Although international conventions do not generally address the effects of construction and development projects on archaeological heritage, many individual nations have developed principles of cultural resource management that aim to minimize, even if not eliminate, these types of adverse consequences.

2. The International Legal Regime

A. *History of the international conventions*

The modern history of the appropriation of cultural objects began with Napoleon's wars of the late eighteenth and early nineteenth centuries. In the course of his conquests, Napoleon appropriated art works from throughout Europe, particularly Italy, in his desire to establish Paris as the new Rome and, in so doing, he planted the seeds for restitution claims for the next two centuries. The failure of France to restore many of these art works, despite the dictates of the 1815 Treaty of Vienna, provided part of Hitler's justifications for his thefts of art works during World War II, particularly from France.

Napoleon was not alone in cultural looting at the beginning of the nineteenth century. Napoleon's attempt to re-create the new Rome in Paris was answered by the British desire to re-create London as the new Athens. Thus, the taking of the Parthenon sculptures by Lord Elgin and their later acquisition by Parliament for the British Museum fit into the political reality of the military rivalry between France and Britain. The presence of the Parthenon sculptures in the British Museum has endured as the pre-eminent symbol of cultural heritage dispossession even until today, although Lord Elgin engaged the narrative of rescue, claiming that he was motivated by a desire to rescue the sculptures while also incidentally benefiting the English nation

Yet the looting of art works has a much older history, going back to Roman times and even earlier into Egyptian pharaonic and Mesopotamian periods. In addition to the rescue narrative, some Roman authors developed the notion that cultural objects should remain in their original context. The Roman historian Polybius of the second century B.C.E. questioned the Romans' excessive plundering during the siege of Syracuse. Cicero elaborated on this theme in the prosecution in 70 B.C.E. of Gaius Verres, the governor of Sicily, for corruption, including pillage of both private and publicly dedicated religious works of art. The actions of the Duke of Wellington following his victory over Napoleon fit into the tradition of Cicero, whose works were known in late eighteenth century England. At the end of the Napoleonic wars, not only were the French required by the Treaty of Vienna to return art works taken from throughout Europe, but the Duke declined the opportunity to take some portion of those works back to England as war booty. The end of the Napoleonic Wars thus gives us both the first large-scale repatriation of art works and the principle that art works are not legitimate war booty.

The ideas of Cicero can perhaps be traced through the acts of the Duke of Wellington to the founding of the modern principles of warfare as applied to cultural objects. A young Prussian soldier, present at the Battle of Waterloo, later studied the classics, moved to the United States and became a law professor at Columbia University. In 1863, President Lincoln asked Francis Lieber to draft a code of military conduct for the United States Army during the Civil War. The Lieber Code distinguished "public property" from other types of movable property and stated that public property could not be used as normal war booty. This principle was picked up in the 1899 and 1907 Hague Conventions on the conduct of warfare. These Conventions were the relevant legal instruments for the regulation of conduct during both World Wars and were used as a basis for some of the war crimes prosecutions of the Nazi leadership at Nuremberg. In response to the cultural devastations of World War II, the 1954 Hague Convention for the Protection of Cultural Property in the Event of Armed Conflict was written — the first international convention specifically to address cultural property and the basic instrument that governs the conduct of warfare as applied to cultural property today.

At the same time as these developments in the law of war were occurring, the science of archaeology was in its early phases (see also Chapter 14). In controlled, scientific excavation of archaeological sites, each layer (or stratum) is understood to represent a particular time period. If all the material cultural remains found in each layer are excavated in association with each other and with contemporaneous architectural features, then it should be possible to reconstruct each time period of a site and thereby gain a more complete reconstruction of past human cultures and societies. As field excavation evolved into a science, archaeological context became crucial to our ability to understand the past through stratigraphic excavation and it became clear that looting of sites destroys this context, making it impossible to achieve such reconstruction.

Also in the late nineteenth century, nations began to protect their heritage from foreigners. The desire to maintain cultural objects within a particular modern nation-state coalesced with the desire to protect archaeological sites from looting that destroyed context — and this eventually found expression in the legal system, often through laws that limit the export of cultural objects and through laws that vest ownership of undiscovered archaeological objects in the nation. So, for example,

Greece began to devise legal protections for its heritage and to demand that England return the Parthenon sculptures almost as soon as it was freed of the Ottoman yoke. Around the turn of the twentieth century, Turkey and Italy enacted national ownership laws and many other countries, including the United States, instituted legal measures that would protect their archaeological and indigenous heritages, at least to some extent, from removal to other countries. While such laws had their origins in nineteenth-century nationalism, today their primary purpose is to deny title to a looter of artifacts. Since the looter cannot convey title to a buyer, the buyer runs the risk of losing the artifact to the true owner. These laws are thus intended to serve as a disincentive to the sale and acquisition of the object.

After the cultural devastations in Europe during World War II and the economic recoveries that followed in the 1950s and 1960s, yet one more element was added to the mix — the international art market. Although the market had existed for more than two hundred years, it took on a significant role in the movement of art works and antiquities at this time. In terms of archaeological artifacts, the looting of sites to supply the art market has plagued every country in the world, including the United States, and raises particular problems. This looting destroys the fragile, non-renewable context and information that these sites contain and from which we are able to reconstruct the full story of ancient life. In 1969, Professor Clemency Coggins documented the destruction of Maya stele in Central America and the role of the international art market in fostering this destruction. Her findings played a significant role in the adoption of the second international convention that deals with cultural heritage — the 1970 UNESCO Convention on the Means of Prohibiting and Preventing the Illicit Import, Export and Transfer of Ownership of Cultural Property.

While the Hague Convention and the UNESCO Convention will be considered below in greater detail, there are several other conventions that address the protection of cultural and archaeological heritage. Perhaps the most significant of these is the 1972 Convention concerning the Protection of the World Cultural and Natural Heritage. This Convention provides a mechanism by which nations can voluntarily nominate sites of natural, cultural or mixed significance for listing on the World Heritage List. There is, in addition, a List of World Heritage in Danger, which brings attention to sites that are endangered from war, looting, development, tourism, or the environment. While the listing of such sites carries no legal or other consequences, listing does attract public attention, often both public and private financial investment, and tourism. However, there is a significant imbalance in the parts of the world represented on the World Heritage lists in that a disproportionate number of sites are located in Europe and thus the list has not had as significant a world-wide influence as it might.

In 1995, the Unidroit Convention on Cultural Property was promulgated. This convention, like the 1970 UNESCO Convention, also aims to control and inhibit the illegal market in cultural objects. However, it does so by focusing on the enactment of national laws that affect private conduct, rather than on requiring actions by the nations that are party to the convention. For example, the Unidroit Convention establishes a blueprint for national legislation that would address the ability of individuals, acting as private litigants, to bring claims in the courts of other nations that are party to the convention. It has specific provisions for statutes of limitation (which establish a time limit within which a legal claim must be brought) and the payment of compensation to those who acquire stolen or illegally exported cultural objects in good faith. Of particular relevance for preservation of archaeological heritage is its provision in Article 3(2) that states that "a cultural object which has been unlawfully excavated or lawfully excavated but unlawfully retained shall be considered stolen, when consistent with the law of the State where the excavation took place." While this provision goes to the heart of the problem of looting of archaeological sites and would therefore be of significant potential benefit, this Convention has not been adopted by any of the major Western market nations and their attention has turned back to the 1970 UNESCO Convention.

UNESCO has formulated two additional conventions in recent years. One is the 2001 Convention on the Protection of the Underwater Cultural Heritage. While this convention is particularly useful for establishing in its Annex scientific standards for the excavation and exploration of underwater heritage, this convention has not yet been widely adopted and many of the maritime nations have objected to several of the provisions, particularly those concerning maritime jurisdiction and related issues. Finally, in 2003 UNESCO adopted its Convention on the Intangible Cultural Heritage. This convention addresses intangible heritage, such as folklore and indigenous knowledge, and intersects with intellectual property law. This convention falls outside the scope of this chapter and is not likely to receive wide acceptance among the Western nations that have highly developed intellectual property legal regimes.

Finally, it is worth mentioning UNESCO's Declaration concerning the Intentional Destruction of Cultural Heritage adopted in 2003 in response to the intentional destruction of the Bamiyan Buddhas and other ancient art with figural representations by the Taliban in Afghanistan in March 2001. The Declaration reiterates many of the legal principles and norms associated with preservation of cultural heritage found in these earlier conventions and calls on all nations to respect these principles. However, the destruction of the Buddhas illustrates the shortcomings of international law and the difficulty of enforcing these principles against nations.

B. The 1954 Hague Convention

As was previously mentioned, the 1954 Hague Convention was written in the wake of the cultural devastations of World War II and builds on the earlier law of the conduct of war, particularly the Lieber Code and the 1899 and 1907 Hague Conventions. The 1954 Convention consists of three parts: the main convention and its two protocols, the first of which was also written in 1954 and the second of which was written in 1999 in response to the experiences of the Balkan wars. Article 1 of the convention defines "cultural property" as:

movable or immovable property of great importance to the cultural heritage of every people, such as monuments of architecture, art or history, whether religious or secular; archaeological sites; groups of buildings which, as a whole, are of historical or artistic interest;

works of art; manuscripts, books and other objects of artistic, historical or archaeological interest; as well as scientific collections and important collections of books or archives ...; buildings whose main and effective purpose is to preserve or exhibit the movable cultural property ... such as museums, large libraries and depositories of archives, and refuges intended to shelter, in the event of armed conflict, the movable cultural property ... .

The main convention addresses the conduct of warfare during active hostilities and the conduct of an occupying power with respect to cultural heritage located in occupied territory. The first obligation of parties to the convention is to "prepare in time of peace for the safeguarding of cultural property situated within their own territory" by taking whatever steps they consider appropriate to protect their cultural property from the effects of warfare (Article 3). During warfare, parties to the convention "undertake to respect cultural property situated within their own territory as well as within the territory" of other parties to the convention (Article 4). This means that during hostilities, nations must refrain from using cultural property and the area near any cultural property for strategic or military purposes if this would expose the property to harm during warfare. In addition, parties to the convention must refrain "from any act of hostility directed against such property ... [and] from any act directed by way of reprisals against cultural property." Thus nations that are engaged in military conflict must not target cultural sites and monuments. However, this same article contains a significant exception to this obligation "in cases where military necessity imperatively requires such a waiver." This means that if attacking a cultural site or monument is necessary in order to achieve an imperative military goal, then the military necessity supersedes and the protections of this article are lost. Unfortunately, the concept of military necessity is not specifically defined in the convention and some nations have expressed concern that a fairly low level of necessity would result in destruction or injury to cultural sites and monuments.

Article 4 also imposes an obligation on a party to the convention to "further undertake to prohibit, prevent and, if necessary, put a stop to any form of theft, pillage or misappropriation of, and any acts of vandalism directed against, cultural property ... ." This provision is highly significant in light of the experiences of the widespread looting that took place in Iraq during and after the cessation of hostilities. However, it is unclear whether this obligation applies only to prevent one's own military from engaging in this obligation or if the convention imposes an obligation to prevent the local population from engaging in looting and vandalism. Given the context of this article, it seems most likely that the obligation applies only to the conduct of the military forces of the nation and not to controlling the conduct of the individuals of the opposing nation. Although there may be basis in other international legal instruments to conclude that such an obligation does exist, the lack of an explicit obligation in the 1954 Hague Convention illustrates another of the problems in this convention which need clarification and updating. The military necessity exception does not apply to the obligation to prevent looting and vandalism.

Article 5 turns to the conduct of an occupying power and imposes several obligations. This provision clearly contemplates that the occupying power will work with the national authorities of the occupied country, to the fullest extent possible, in preserving the occupied nation's cultural property. The primary obligation placed on the occupying power is to "take the most necessary measures" to preserve cultural property that was damaged by military operations and only if the national authorities are not able to do so. Major drawbacks to this provision became evident during the second Gulf War and its aftermath. Probably the most significant is that the obligation to preserve cultural property is limited to the cultural sites, monuments and objects that were damaged during hostilities. This means that there is no obligation to carry out preservation or conservation measures for cultural property that is damaged by some other means, such as through looting and vandalism. The Hague Convention seems most concerned with preventing an occupying power from interfering with the cultural, historical and religious record of occupied territory and therefore requires preservation, which could become interference, under only these narrow circumstances. However, these limitations can produce a result that is inconsistent with the overall goals of the convention.

The First Protocol was also written in 1954, at the same time as the main convention. It is concerned primarily with the status of movable cultural objects and imposes essentially four obligations. First, an occupying power is obligated to prevent the export from occupied territory of any movable cultural property. Second, any nation that is a party to the convention must take into its custody any illegally exported cultural property that is imported either directly from the occupied territory or indirectly through another nation. Third, at the close of hostilities, any nation that is party to the convention must return cultural property to the competent authorities of the formerly occupied nation if the export from the occupied territory was in violation of the convention. Finally, any cultural property taken into custody during hostilities for the purpose of protecting it must also be returned at the end of hostilities.

During the Balkan Wars of the 1990s, several parties to the conflict violated provisions of the Hague Convention. These violations form part of the indictment of former military leaders for war crimes before the Tribunal for the Former Yugoslavia. As a result of these experiences, UNESCO recognized that there was a need to improve on some of the provisions of the original convention and so promulgated the Second Protocol in 1999. The Second Protocol clarifies that the convention applies to conflicts that may not be entirely of an international character and narrows the circumstances in which military necessity can be used as a justification for the targeting of cultural sites and monuments.

Article 9 of the Second Protocol clarifies the treatment of cultural property in occupied territory by prohibiting any illicit export or other removal or transfer of ownership of cultural property. It further prohibits the carrying out of any archaeological excavation, "save where this is strictly required to safeguard, record or preserve cultural property," and prohibits "any alteration to, or change of use of, cultural property which is intended to conceal or destroy cultural, historical or scientific evidence." Any excavation of or alteration to cultural property must be done to the fullest extent possible in cooperation with the national authorities of the occupied territory.

Article 9 broadens the circumstances in which archaeological excavation may be conducted in comparison to what Article 5 of the main convention provides in that it permits such activity in situations other than where the cultural property was damaged during hostilities. Thus, it would be consistent with the convention for an occupying power to carry out survey and salvage excavations if necessary to preserve the archaeological record during construction activities during occupation. However, a major failing of both the main convention and the Second Protocol is their failure to incorporate modern understandings of cultural resource management techniques. In many nations, before construction and development projects can be carried out, assessment of damage to cultural resources must be conducted and efforts taken to mitigate any negative effects. In part because the convention was written in 1954 before cultural resource management had become engrained in the laws of many nations and in part because the convention is largely a reflection of the way in which World War II was conducted, it is understandable that these principles are not incorporated into the Hague Convention. However, this is an aspect of the convention that should be clarified and remedied.

In addition to the problems previously noted that severely limit the efficacy of the Hague Convention and its Protocols, probably the greatest difficulty is that several of the major military powers, including the United States and the United Kingdom, have not ratified the convention. The United States signed the main convention (although not the First Protocol) almost immediately, signifying its intention to ratify it. However, Cold War tensions intervened and even after the United States' military withdrew its objections to ratification after the fall of the Soviet Union and after President Clinton transmitted the convention to the Senate in 1999, no action toward ratification has been taken.

The United States has not viewed ratification of the convention as a high priority, in part because the United States accepts and purports to follow many of the principles of the convention as part of customary international law. However, this situation is far from satisfactory. It leaves considerable doubt as to precisely which parts the United States accepts and which it does not. If the United States were to violate a provision of the convention, the United States can simply state that it does not view this particular provision as part of customary international law and it is therefore not binding. Even though President Clinton transmitted the First Protocol to the Senate along with the main convention, the status of the First Protocol under customary international law is not clear. The United States has also not signed the Second Protocol. While the United States is a party to the two earlier conventions of 1899 and 1907, their provisions are even less suitable for dealing with the nature of modern warfare and, in particular, our contemporary understanding of the mandate to preserve and protect cultural property during hostilities and occupation.

C. *The 1970 UNESCO Convention*

The 1970 UNESCO Convention was written in response to the growth of the international art market in the years of prosperity following World War II and the market's contribution to the theft and illegal export of cultural property, the looting of archaeological sites, and the dismemberment of other cultural monuments. While several of its principles can apply during wartime, its focus is on the operation and problems of the market. At this time over one hundred nations are party to the UNESCO Convention. The United States was one of the first market nations to ratify it, but today most of the significant market nations are party to the convention.

There are two main provisions of the convention that affect the international trade in illegally-obtained cultural objects. The first of these, Article 7(b)(i), calls on those nations that are party to the convention "to prohibit the import of cultural property stolen from a museum or a religious or secular public monument or similar institution in another State Party ..., provided that such property is documented as appertaining to the inventory of that institution." The second main provision is Article 9, which states:

Any State Party to this Convention whose cultural patrimony is in jeopardy from pillage of archaeological or ethnological materials may call upon other States Parties who are affected. The States Parties to this Convention undertake, in these circumstances, to participate in a concerted international effort to determine and to carry out the necessary concrete measures, including the control of exports and imports and international commerce in the specific materials concerned. Pending agreement each State concerned shall take provisional measures to the extent feasible to prevent irremediable injury to the cultural heritage of the requesting State.

Unlike Article 7(b)(i), which applies to all types of cultural objects, Article 9 applies only to archaeological and ethnological objects, although these terms are not defined in the convention. Because of this limitation, Article 9 has a much narrower scope of application.

Article 9 has two components. The first is that nations should provide a mechanism by which other nations that are party to the convention can seek assistance to prevent jeopardy to their cultural patrimony through pillage of archaeological and ethnological objects. While the steps that a nation should take under these circumstances may vary, most nations that are party to the convention have interpreted this provision to require the application of some type of trade, particularly import, restrictions to prevent the importation of illegally exported archaeological and ethnological objects. This provision also contemplates that this type of action will be taken within a multilateral context. The last sentence of Article 9, however, requires nations to take at least temporary measures, even in the absence of multilateral agreement, in emergency situations.

One other provision of the UNESCO Convention is worth noting. Article 10 requires parties to the convention to regulate their internal art market "as appropriate for each country". The convention specifies that nations should establish regulation of the art market through requiring dealers to maintain records of the origins of the cultural objects and art works that they sell, including the name of the supplier, and to inform purchasers of legal provisions to which the objects may be subject.

Although the United States Senate voted in 1972 to ratify the UNESCO Convention, it required that the U.S. enact domestic implementing legislation before the convention would be effective in the U.S. This legislation, known as the Convention on Cultural Property Implementation Act or CPIA was not passed until 1982, and it implements only the two main sections of the convention, Article 7(b)(i) and Article 9.

Implementation of Article 7(b)(i) was not particularly controversial as any property stolen abroad is still stolen property after it enters the United States. However, the CPIA changed the legal mechanisms by which such property could be seized and forfeited to the U.S. government for return to the country of origin. The CPIA permits the Bureau of Immigration and Customs Enforcement (formerly U.S. Customs) to seize at the border any stolen cultural property that had been documented as part of the inventory of a museum or other public institution located in another nation that is a party to the convention. All the U.S. government must demonstrate is that the property was stolen after both that country and the United States had become a party to the convention. This changed the burden of proof and the elements that the U.S. government must establish in order to seize the property, but it did not change the underlying legal principles.

The CPIA's implementation of Article 9 of the convention, however, introduced a new underlying legal principle. It is generally accepted that if property or goods are illegally exported from one country, the property is not illegal in another country absent some other form of illegal conduct. The CPIA, however, allows other nations that are party to the convention to request that the United States impose import restrictions on illegally exported archaeological or ethnological objects. The U.S. President can impose such restrictions on designated categories of archaeological and ethnological objects pursuant to either a bilateral agreement, which is negotiated between the U.S. and the other country, or an emergency action, in cases of crisis threats to the other country's cultural patrimony.

For the United States to enter into a bilateral agreement, four criteria must be demonstrated: first, that the other country's cultural patrimony is in jeopardy from pillage of archaeological or ethnological objects; second, that the other country has taken internal steps consistent with the convention (that is, the other country has undertaken education and law enforcement efforts to reduce pillage); third, that the U.S.'s action will be taken as part of a concerted or multilateral effort; fourth, that imposing import restrictions would further the public interest in international exchange of cultural materials for scientific and educational purposes. There is also an exception to the third criterion (the multilateral requirement) if the U.S.'s imposition of import controls would be of substantial benefit to preventing pillage even if other countries with a significant import trade in the same materials do not undertake similar import controls.

The emergency provisions of the CPIA permit the U.S. president to impose import restrictions unilaterally. The criteria here are different and focus only on whether there is a crisis situation in the requesting nation that threatens its cultural patrimony. However, the other nation cannot bring a request for emergency action; rather, it must first request a bilateral agreement and the same, lengthy process to determine whether the criteria for both a bilateral agreement and emergency action are satisfied is required.

The CPIA process imposes an additional burden on nations that have already joined the UNESCO Convention and, until Switzerland enacted its implementing legislation in 2003, the United States was the only nation that required this additional process for other States Parties to gain the protections that are part of the convention itself. The length of time that it takes to complete the CPIA process, from the time a country makes a request to the time that the import restrictions are imposed, means that importers have months, sometimes years, in which to bring such materials to the United States before their import is prohibited. In addition, the CPIA requires archaeological materials that are protected by import restrictions to be at least 250 years old. This limits the effectiveness of the CPIA particularly with respect to countries that have a rich archaeological heritage of historic time periods. Perhaps the most severe limitation of the CPIA is that the import restrictions endure for only limited amounts of time. The emergency actions can last up to five years and can then be renewed for only three years, for a maximum of eight years. The bilateral agreements can last for up to five years but can be renewed an indefinite number of times. While this can provide long-term protection (and the import restrictions on cultural materials from some Central American nations are now approaching twenty years), the fact that the agreements must be renewed for relatively short periods of time means that the incentive to loot archaeological artifacts is not effectively removed. Looters, middlemen and dealers may be willing to hold looted materials for five years, in the hope or expectation that the bilateral agreement at some point will not be renewed and these objects will then become salable in the United States.

With the exception of the United States, most nations that ratified the UNESCO Convention applied import controls across the board — that is, they prohibited the import into their country of any cultural objects that had been illegally exported or stolen from their country of origin. Canada is an example of this in that while Canada has an elaborate mechanism for licensing the export of Canadian cultural objects, its statutory provision simply prohibits the import of illegally exported cultural objects from other States Parties to the convention. Australia goes a step further in that it prohibits the import of all illegally exported cultural objects, including objects whose country of origin is not even a party to the convention.

In 2002 and 2003, particularly in the aftermath of the war in Iraq, several new market nations ratified the UNESCO Convention. These states include the United Kingdom, Japan, Denmark, and Switzerland. As part of its ratification, the British Parliament enacted a new Dealing in Cultural Objects (Offences) Act 2003, while Switzerland also enacted new legislation to take effect in 2005.

The British legislation creates a new criminal offense for dealing in "tainted cultural objects." One commits this offense if he or she "dishonestly deals in a cultural object that is tainted, knowing or believing that the object is tainted." The statute defines a "tainted object" under the following circumstances: "A cultural object is tainted if, after the commencement of this Act (a) a person removes the object in a case falling within subsection (4) or he excavates the object, and (b) the removal or excavation constitutes an offence." Subsection 4 refers to objects removed from "a building or structure of historical, architectural or archaeological interest" or from an excavation. For purposes of the statute, it does not matter whether the excavation or removal takes place in the United Kingdom or in another country or whether the law violated is a domestic or foreign law.

The new Swiss legislation, the Federal Act on the International Transfer of Cultural Property, implements the UNESCO Convention in a manner that is closer to the United States' model of implementation, through expansion of import restrictions, rather than following the British model of expanding on the criminal law. The new Swiss legislation permits the Swiss Federal Council to enter into agreements with other nations that are party to the UNESCO Convention to protect "cultural and foreign affairs interests and to secure cultural heritage". The Federal Council can also take additional measures when a "state's cultural heritage [is] jeopardized by exceptional events".

The other significant change in the Swiss legislation is its definition of "due diligence." Article 16 sets forth the following definition:

> *In the art trade and auctioning business, cultural property may only be transferred when the person transferring the property may assume, under the circumstances, that the cultural property:*
>   *a. was not stolen, not lost against the will of the owner, and not illegally excavated;*
>   *b. not illicitly imported.*

A clear definition of due diligence under Swiss law is significant because of the Swiss good faith purchaser doctrine, which permits the transfer of good title even of stolen goods to a good faith purchaser. The phrase "under the circumstances" would seem to require that one who wishes to claim to have acted in good faith must have considered all the circumstances of the transaction, including the high prevalence of stolen art objects and particularly of looted archaeological objects in the art market. Article 16 also imposes additional obligations on those who are active in the art trade to maintain written records concerning their acquisition of cultural property, to acquire a written declaration from sellers concerning their right to dispose of the object, and to inform customers of existing import and export regulations of other nations that are UNESCO Convention parties.

3. United States Domestic Law and the International Art Market

In addition to the international conventions and their adoption into domestic law of the market nations, it is also necessary to consider facets of the domestic law of market nations that have an impact on the operation of the international art market. The domestic laws of the United States will be used to illustrate this. There are three aspects: recovery of property stolen from collections (public or private), "archaeological theft", and illegal import into the United States.

A. Recovery of stolen property

The past 50 years have been notable for large-scale spectacular thefts of art works, such as the thefts from the Isabella Stewart Gardner Museum in Boston in 1990 and the more recent theft of Munch's *The Scream*, as well as an uncounted number of thefts of less well-known objects of lower value. Such less well-known objects are more difficult to trace and are therefore more easily sold on the market. In countries that follow the common law of property (the United States, England, Canada, Australia and New Zealand), a thief can never convey good title to stolen property even if the property is sold to a good faith purchaser. This contrasts with the rule of many civil law nations (such as the European continental nations) in which a thief can transfer title to a good faith purchaser under certain circumstances.

Although in common law countries a thief cannot transfer title to stolen property, the original owner may be barred from recovering the property by a statute of limitation. Statutes of limitation provide time periods within which a legal claim must be brought. If the claim is not brought within that time period, then the plaintiff loses the ability to bring suit. The purpose of statutes of limitations is to provide security of title and to avoid filing of stale claims, particularly after evidence may be lost and witnesses may be unavailable or their memories faded. While the barring of the original owner's claim does not technically transfer title to the current possessor, it has a similar effect in that possession is an indication of ownership and there is no other accepted mechanism for establishing title to art works and other forms of personal property.

Statutes of limitation, which in the United States are a product of state rather than national law, generally provide fairly short time periods for the recovery of stolen personal property, including art works and cultural objects. Most statutory time periods range from two to six years. This short time period would make it relatively easy for a thief or current possessor to hide the art works until the statutory period expires and then, in theory, the owner is barred from recovery. The statutory time period begins to run from the time the owner's cause of action accrues, although the statutes do not define what is meant by "accrual." Because art works are easily hidden and transported to other jurisdictions and it is difficult for the true owner to locate the work or learn the identity of the current possessor, most courts have interpreted the accrual of the cause of action for recovery of stolen art works in such a way as to give the original owner a realistic opportunity to bring suit.

For example, in New York, the heart of the art market in the United States, the courts have consistently interpreted the accrual of the cause of action to occur when the original owner makes a demand for return of the property on the current possessor and the possessor refuses. Use of this "demand and refusal" rule means that the statutory time period will not elapse before the original owner knows the identity of the possessor. In other jurisdictions, the courts apply the "discovery rule." According to this approach, the owner's cause of action does not accrue until the owner discovers or with reasonable diligence should have discovered the location of the stolen art work. While this rule places a burden on the original owner to search for the stolen property, it again protects the owner by assuring a reasonable opportunity to find the property before the statutory time period begins to run. California is unusual in that it has a specific statute of limitations that applies to "any article of historical, interpretive, scientific, or artistic significance". The statutory time period does not begin until the owner has discovered the whereabouts of the stolen article. Finally, some jurisdictions, particularly New York, may bar the claim under the equitable defense of laches, even if the statutory time period has not elapsed. Laches is an affirmative defense in which the defendant establishes that the plaintiff's unreasonable delay in bringing the claim caused the defendant to suffer prejudice (some type of legal detriment).

As previously mentioned, most civil law nations, such as those on the European continent, accept some variant of the good faith purchaser doctrine by which even a thief can transfer title if the goods are sold to a good faith purchaser. This means that if stolen property is transferred in a civil law nation, then the title can be "laundered" so that when the property is taken to a common law country, the current possessor can claim to rely on having acquired title in the civil law nation. Several cases have occurred in the United States where the defendant has relied on such a claim.

This scenario is exemplified by the well-known case involving the Pre-Iconoclastic Byzantine mosaics stolen from the Kanakaria Church in northern Cyprus in the late 1970s following its occupation by Turkish forces in 1974. An art dealer from Indianapolis, Peg Goldberg, purchased the mosaics in 1988 in the Geneva free transit zone and brought them back to the United States. When the Church of Cyprus learned the location of the mosaics, it sued for their recovery. Goldberg tried to rely on the Swiss good faith purchaser doctrine, claiming that she had acquired the mosaics in Switzerland in good faith. While the court's analysis was extended, it held, following lengthy consideration of the choice of law rules, that the law of Indiana should apply. According to Indiana law, Goldberg could not acquire good title from a thief. Furthermore, because the Church of Cyprus had utilized due diligence in attempting to locate the stolen mosaics, the statute of limitations did not bar the claim. The court held that the mosaics should be returned to Cyprus. In the alternative, the court analyzed the outcome of the case under Swiss law. The court held that even under Swiss law, Goldberg did not acquire title to the mosaics because she had not acted in good faith. Her failure to conduct meaningful research into the background of the mosaics and the obviously suspicious circumstances of the transaction negated her claim that she had acted in good faith. It is interesting to note that the changes in Swiss law, as part of Switzerland's ratification of the 1970 UNESCO Convention, increase the standard of good faith required before a purchaser can gain good title to stolen property. These changes further reflect a desire to eliminate Switzerland as a transit point and place for laundering of title to stolen art works.

B. Archaeological theft

In addition to ordinary theft and the problems posed by legal doctrines that may bar the original owner's claim to recover stolen property, there is a particular form of theft that applies exclusively to archaeological objects that are looted directly from the ground rather than stolen from a museum or private collection. Such objects may be particularly appealing to the international art market because their existence is undocumented and there is no record of their theft. It is therefore extremely difficult to trace such objects through normal law enforcement methods and to establish their true origin.

To combat this form of theft, many nations have enacted laws that vest ownership of undiscovered archaeological objects in the nation. These ownership laws apply to any objects discovered or excavated after the effective date of the statute. If an object is excavated (or looted) after this date and removed from the country without permission, then the object is stolen property and it retains this characterization even after it is brought to the United States. Anyone who knowingly transports, possesses or transfers stolen property in interstate or international commerce, or intends to do so, violates the National Stolen Property Act. Depending on the factual circumstances and the proof available to the government, the stolen property may be seized and forfeited and the individual may be subject to criminal prosecution. Furthermore, such objects are subject to seizure and forfeiture under the lower civil standard because their import would violate U.S. Customs statutes.

This doctrine was tested in the 2001 prosecution of the prominent New York antiquities dealer, Frederick Schultz. Until shortly before his indictment, Schultz was president of the National Association of Dealers in Ancient, Oriental and Primitive Art. Schultz was indicted on one count of conspiring to deal in antiquities stolen from Egypt in violation of Egypt's national ownership Law 117, which was enacted in 1983. Schultz's co-conspirator, the British restorer Jonathan Tokeley-Parry, would plaster over ancient Egyptian sculptures, including a head of the Egyptian pharaoh Amenhotep III, to make them look like cheap tourist souvenirs and export them to England. There, Tokeley-Parry would restore the sculptures to their original appearance and he and Schultz would attempt to sell them in the United States and England. To this end, the two of them fabricated a fake "old" collection, attributed to a relative of Tokeley-Parry who had traveled in Egypt in the 1920s. Schultz and Tokeley-Parry reportedly soaked labels in tea and microwaved them to make them appear old. Nonetheless, Tokeley-Parry was eventually discovered by Scotland Yard and convicted in England for handling stolen property. Schultz's prosecution followed not long after.

The legal basis of Schultz's prosecution relied on an earlier case, United States v. McClain, in which several dealers were convicted for conspiring to deal in antiquities stolen from Mexico, which also has a national ownership law. Schultz tried to argue that the Egyptian law was not a true ownership law and, further, that the *McClain* decision should no longer be accepted, in part because it was superseded by enactment of the Cultural Property Implementation Act. The court examined the Egyptian law and held that it was a true ownership law, both because it plainly stated that it was and because it was internally enforced within Egypt. The court also held that the *McClain* decision was valid law and that the CPIA and this application of the National Stolen Property Act (NSPA) could co-exist. While recognizing that there might be circumstances in which both the CPIA and the National Stolen Property Act would apply to the same conduct, the court held that this did not pose an inherent conflict because of differences in their nature (the CPIA being civil in nature and the National Stolen Property Act being criminal) and in the elements of proof required for a violation. The court concluded by stating:

Although we recognize the concerns raised by Schultz and the amici about the risks that this holding poses to dealers in foreign antiquities, we cannot imagine that it "creates an insurmountable barrier to the lawful importation of cultural property into the United States." Our holding does assuredly create a barrier to the importation of cultural property owned by a foreign government. We see no reason that property stolen from a foreign sovereign should be treated any differently from property stolen from a foreign museum or private home. The mens rea requirement of the NSPA will protect innocent art dealers who unwittingly receive stolen goods, while our appropriately broad reading of the NSPA will protect the property of sovereign nations.

C. Illegal import/smuggling

The third aspect of illegal conduct is illegal import or smuggling. While goods that have been illegally exported from one country are not generally regarded as contraband once they enter another country (absent an additional agreement, such as a bilateral agreement under the CPIA, or the status of the property as stolen), illegal import renders the goods subject to seizure and forfeiture under the Customs laws. The U.S. Customs statute prohibits the entry into the United States of goods imported contrary to law. Application of this provision is based on a variety of laws, ranging from the National Stolen Property Act (in the case of stolen property) to statutes that require declaration of the country of origin and value of the goods to be imported.

Illegal import therefore often results from improper declaration of the goods upon entry into the United States. This is illustrated by the 1999 decision, United States v. An Antique Platter of Gold, which involved a late fourth-century B.C.E. phiale (or open bowl) that was imported into the United States for purchase by the New York collector, Michael Steinhardt. The dealer had seen the bowl in Sicily where it had been found. The dealer received the bowl at the Swiss-Italian border, carried it through Switzerland and, from there, brought it to the United States. The Customs declaration forms, however, stated that the country of origin of the bowl was Switzerland (rather than Italy) and misstated the value of the bowl by close to $1 million.

Both the trial and appellate courts held that, because of these misstatements, the bowl was contraband property. Steinhardt disputed both the materiality of the misstatements and the correct standard for determining materiality. However, both courts held that the misstatements were material if they tended to influence the decision of the Customs official in determining whether to allow the import of the goods. In this case, because Italy is known to have a national ownership law, a truthful declaration that the bowl was from Italy would have influenced the Customs official's determination because the bowl might have been stolen property. The courts did not consider as extensively the misstatement of value, probably because all art works more than one hundred years in age can be imported into the United States without payment of duty. The court thus allowed the forfeiture of the bowl because it was imported into the United States by means of false declarations. The court's decision also implicitly held that the country of origin of archaeological objects is the place where they are found or excavated in modern times.

4. Problems in Controlling the International Art Market: The Paradigm of Iraq

These principles of international and domestic law can be illustrated by applying them to the problems of protecting the archaeological heritage of Iraq particularly since the time of the second Gulf War in March 2003. The paradigm of Iraq demonstrates both the difficulties of applying these rules so as to prevent looting of museums and sites and the uniqueness of the situation in Iraq because of the significant public attention that it has attracted. What is most unusual about the situation in Iraq is that U.N.-mandated sanctions on the import of goods from Iraq had been in place since August 1990. In the United States, these sanctions were implemented through a Presidential Executive Order and were administered through the Treasury Department's Office of Foreign Asset Controls (OFAC). Archaeological and other cultural objects that were exported from Iraq after August 1990 were therefore already prohibited entry into the United States even before the second Gulf War began. Nonetheless, we can examine the full set of applicable legal principles to see which apply and the obstacles they each raise.

The Iraq Museum in Baghdad, the largest repository of artifacts from ancient Mesopotamia, and several other museums and archives were looted in the days immediately following the fall of Baghdad in mid-April 2003 (see also Chapter 15). As can best be estimated, approximately 15,000 objects were looted from the museum. While some of these objects were voluntarily returned and others were intercepted by law enforcement in Iraq and in other countries, approximately 12,000 are still missing. The exact number will never be known, however, because the museum records were ransacked and vandalized during the looting. About thirty objects of those still missing are considered to be well-known, museum display quality works and are presumably not salable on the international market. Nearly five thousand of the remaining missing objects are cylinder seals.

Any of these objects clearly constitute stolen property and as such implicate numerous legal doctrines previously discussed. However, because of the state of the documentation of the museum holdings, it is not clear how many of these objects can be clearly documented as part of the inventory of the museum. If they are so documented, then their import into the United States is prohibited under the Cultural Property Implementation Act and under the National Stolen Property Act, if their value exceeds (or the value of a shipment exceeds) $5000. Anyone who knowingly receives, transports or deals in any of these objects is liable to criminal prosecution under the National Stolen Property Act, the Customs statute and the general OFAC sanctions. This is illustrated by the indictment in 2003 of the author Joseph Braude who tried to bring three cylinder seals, still marked with their Iraq Museum numbers, into the United States. Braude ultimately pled guilty to a felony but was given a sentence of only probation.

A much more difficult problem is raised by the looting of archaeological sites (see also Chapter 14). To the extent that it has been possible to obtain first-hand information, it seems that the sites of particularly southern Iraq, primarily of the Sumerian cultures of the fourth and third millennia B.C.E., have been looted on a massive scale. It has been reported that two to three hundred looters have been working at one time at such sites as Isin, Mashkan Shapur, and Umm al-Aqarib. It is estimated that hundreds of thousands of objects, including cuneiform tablets and cylinder seals, have been looted and even more discarded if they are not considered salable. The contexts of these sites are completely destroyed and the information contained in the sites is irretrievably lost. This is admittedly but one aspect of the dire security situation in Iraq, but it is of great significance for our understanding of the Mesopotamian past.

Before the second Gulf War, the United States government recovered from an auction house in New York one foundation cone of the mid-third millennium B.C.E., which had been excavated at the site of al-Hiba and stolen from a regional museum following the first Gulf War. While the precise legal theory used for this recovery is not known, the stolen property provision of the CPIA would have applied because both the U.S. and Iraq are parties to the 1970 UNESCO Convention, regardless of the lack of diplomatic relations between the two nations. However, during the time of the Saddam Hussein regime, Iraq could not bring a CPIA request to the United States because the two countries did not have diplomatic relations. Therefore, it has not been possible to impose import restrictions under either a bilateral agreement or emergency action pursuant to the Cultural Property Implementation Act that would prohibit the import of illegally exported archaeological materials that belong to designated categories. On the other hand, Iraq has had a national ownership law in effect since 1936 and so any archaeological objects removed without permission after this date are stolen property. The knowing import of such materials would violate the National Stolen Property Act. However, the burden of proof and the elements required under the National Stolen Property Act are more difficult for the government to establish than under CPIA import restrictions.

The considerable media attention that focused on the looting of Iraq, particularly the looting and vandalism at the museums, libraries and archives in Baghdad, led to the enactment of several provisions unique to the Iraq situation. In anticipation of the lifting of the general trade sanctions, on 22 May 2003 the United Nations Security Council passed a resolution (UNSCR 1483) that included a specific provision (paragraph 7) for dealing with the cultural materials of Iraq. This provision states that the Security Council

Decides that all Member States shall take appropriate steps to facilitate the safe return to Iraqi institutions of Iraqi cultural property and other items of archaeological, historical, cultural, rare scientific, and religious importance illegally removed from the Iraq National Museum, the National Library, and other locations in Iraq since the adoption of resolution 661 (1990) of 6 August 1990, including by establishing a prohibition on trade in or transfer of such items and items with respect to which reasonable suspicion exists that they have been illegally removed, and calls upon the United Nations Educational, Scientific, and Cultural Organization, Interpol, and other international organizations, as appropriate, to assist in the implementation of this paragraph.

Several of the market nations undertook particular legislative or administrative actions to implement this Security Council Resolution, as they are required to do under the United Nations Charter. For example, the United Kingdom enacted Statutory Instrument 2003 No. 1519, which prohibits the import or export of any illegally removed Iraqi cultural property. The dealing in any such items constitutes a criminal offense unless the individual "proves that he did not know and had no reason to suppose that the item in question was illegally removed Iraqi cultural property." The Swiss Federal Council enacted an Ordinance on Economic Measures on 28 May 2003, which imposed a ban that "covers importation, exportation and transit, as well as selling, marketing, dealing in, acquiring or otherwise transferring Iraqi cultural assets stolen in Iraq since 2 August 1990, removed against the will of the owner, or taken out of Iraq illegally. It includes cultural assets acquired through illegal excavations. Such assets are presumed to have been exported illegally if they can be proved to have been in the Republic of Iraq after 2 August 1990."

While the United States issued a general license on 23 May 2003, thereby lifting the sanctions on import of goods from Iraq, it included a "carve-out" so that the prohibition on import of or other transactions involving Iraqi cultural materials as described in the United Nations Security Council Resolution continued without any hiatus. In addition, on 3 December 2004, the Emergency Protection for Iraqi Cultural Antiquities Act was signed into law. This legislation allows the president to exercise his authority under the Cultural Property Implementation Act to impose import restrictions on any cultural materials, again as defined in the United Nations Security Council Resolution (which is broader than the definition of archaeological and ethnological materials contained in the CPIA), illegally removed from Iraq after August 1990. The goal of this legislation is to ensure that there are no gaps in the import restrictions protecting Iraq's cultural heritage by eliminating the need for Iraq to bring a formal request for import restrictions to the United States and eliminating review of the request by the Cultural Property Advisory Committee. While many of these legal provisions in both the United States and other nations are unique to the situation in Iraq, the rapid and relatively widespread implementation of these provisions demonstrates that the legal system can respond when there is sufficient public attention brought to the issue of archaeological looting.

5. Conclusion

Through this discussion we can see that both the international and national domestic legal regimes of many countries have developed to assist in deterring the looting of archaeological sites. However, many weaknesses remain. At the international level, the outdated approach of the Hague Convention to such issues as the conduct of modern warfare and cultural resource management and the failure of many major military powers, such as the United States, to ratify the Convention remain impediments to its effectiveness. Most significantly, the relative lack of effective enforcement of its provisions except in a few cases means that even nations that are party to the Convention rarely need to fear any consequence for violating it.

Ratification and implementation of the 1970 UNESCO Convention have met with greater success in recent years. Yet the limited adoption of the Convention's primary provisions into domestic law of the major market nations again remains an obstacle to its full implementation. In the long-term, both legal advances and changes in the method of collecting by both private collectors and museums depend on public education through both the media and the efforts of scholars. However, basic societal change requires a long period of time and this may not be available as the looting of sites goes on at a rapid pace, particularly in countries such as Iraq and Afghanistan. Legal consequences provide a short-term disincentive to engage in conduct that injures archaeological heritage, while education efforts in both the market nations and the archaeologically rich nations begin the long-term process of changing societal outlook and norms. With public outreach efforts, collecting of undocumented archaeological objects should no longer be considered an acceptable activity. This remains the fundamental challenge to both the legal system and public education efforts in achieving the goal of preserving archaeological heritage.

Bibliographical Note to Chapter 16

Roger Atwood, *Stealing History: Tomb Raiders, Smugglers, and the Looting of the Ancient World* (New York: St. Martin's Press, 2004); Neil Brodie, Jennifer Doole and Colin Renfrew, eds., *Trade in Illicit Antiquities: The Destruction of the World's Archaeological Heritage* (Cambridge, UK: McDonald Institute for Archaeological Research, 2001); Patrick J. O'Keefe, *Commentary on the UNESCO 1970 Convention on Illicit Traffic* (Leicester: Institute of Art and Law, 2000); Patrick J. O'Keefe, *Trade in Antiquities: Reducing Destruction and Theft* (London: Archetype Publications, Paris: UNESCO Publishing, 1997); Lyndel V. Prott, *Commentary on the Unidroit Convention* (Leicester: Institute of Art and Law, 1997); Jiří Toman, *The Protection of Cultural Property in the Event of Armed Conflict* (Aldershot: Dartmouth Publishing Co., 1996); Kathryn W. Tubb, ed., *Antiquities Trade or Betrayed: Legal, Ethical & Conservation Issues* (London: Archetype Publications, 1995).

Iraqi Libraries, Research Centers, and Centers for the Arts

The National Archives and Library was founded in 1920. After 1970 it was attached to the Ministry of Culture, and so was designated to receive multiple copies of all publications printed in Iraq or of publications about Iraq appearing elsewhere, as well as publications by Iraqis living abroad. By the 1990s, its collections were estimated at about 1,200,000 items. The library was looted and burned in April 2003. Employees were able to save some books by moving them to nearby mosques. Some manuscripts had previously been moved to the Saddam Manuscripts Library, but an important group of documents from the Hashemite period remained, and pieces of this collection were found scattered in the courtyard after the fire. The reference collections, catalogs, and a large microfilm and newspaper collection were destroyed. Losses to the main collection have not yet been determined, as the books were hidden in various locations.

The Library of Awqaf was founded in 1922 for the purpose of uniting in one collection the books and manuscripts scattered among the various mosques and religious schools of Baghdad. It formally opened in 1928 and moved to its present quarters in 1966. By the 1990s it held over 6300 manuscripts (some sources give a higher figure), mostly in Arabic but some in Turkish and Kurdish, and over 110,000 printed books, including many rarities. It too was looted and burned in April 2003, with an estimated loss of 40% of its manuscripts and 90% of its printed books.

University and Research Libraries, such as the library of Mustansiriyyah University, the Mosul University Library, the Baghdad University Library, and the Basra Central Library were looted and vandalized and in some cases burned. Important individual research collections of various university faculties, such as the Library of Ancient Languages, belonging to the Antiquities Service, housed at the University of Baghdad, were totally destroyed. The library of the Iraqi Academy, containing about 50,000 Arabic and about 10,000 Kurdish and Syriac books, was looted and vandalized. The library of the Iraq Museum, formerly that of the Baghdad School of the American Schools for Oriental Research, was spared except for the theft of a few rarities.

The Saddam Manuscript Library in Baghdad was the main repository for rare manuscripts. Prior to the invasion, the staff of this library packed the most important items in this library in 337 large packing cases, which were moved to a secure location and guarded zealously. This part of the collection is still safe.

The Library of the Imam Ali Mosque in Najaf, with rich manuscript collections, was looted by Iraqi government troops in 1991; the fate of its collections is unknown.

The Palace of Culture and the Arts in Baghdad, a center for publishing books and periodicals on politics, economics, law, and philosophy, was looted and vandalized, its library and printing equipment destroyed.

The Saddam Center for the Arts was the main collection of contemporary Iraqi art in all media, including painting and sculpture. This was looted and burned, though a few paintings and other pieces were saved. Others have been recovered from dealers in stolen goods.

Iraq House, a historic structure restored and furnished in the late Ottoman style, with a distinguished collection of woodwork, glass, ceramics, textiles, and other historic items, was looted and various pieces from its collection were seen in the antiques market in Amman, Jordan.

Of twenty **museums** looted, vandalized, bombed, or burned, only the small museum at Babylon, repaired by the occupying forces, was reopened in September 2003. The antiquities museum at al-Nasiriyyah, which was spared major damage during the invasion, was later totally destroyed by partisan forces.